Keep On Dancing

Keep On Dancing

AN AUTOBIOGRAPHY

Sarah Churchill

Edited by Paul Medlicott

Weidenfeld and Nicolson
London

First published in Great Britain by
George Weidenfeld & Nicolson Limited
91 Clapham High Street, London SW4 7TA
1981

ISBN 0 297 77906 0

Printed in Great Britain by
Butler & Tanner Limited
Frome and London

Contents

Illustrations

Comparing notes with Fred Astaire (*Author*)

A special backstage visitor: President Truman (*Author*)

(*Between pages 150 and 151*)

On vacation with J.C. Hall of Hallmark at Grand Lake, Colorado (*Author*)

Ophelia to Maurice Evans's Hamlet in the *Hallmark Hall of Fame* television series (*Author*)

The King and I, Sacramento, 1956 (*Author*)

My painting, *Malibu Day* (*Author*)

A well-staged photograph in the Los Angeles Hall of Justice (*Popperfoto*)

Malibu Night, also by me (*Author*)

On the way into court in Malibu (*Camera Press*)

With my family between shows of *Peter Pan*: Julia Lockwood (Wendy), Arabella Churchill, my father, me and my mother, with Emma and Jeremy Soames (*Keystone*)

Mending Pan's pipes, closely observed by Julia Lockwood (*Houston Rogers*)

Henry and I just before our wedding (*Ken Walker*)

Mary with Emma and Jeremy Soames and some of my greyhounds (*Keystone*)

With David Hemmings in the play *Fata Morgana* (*Author*)

With Lobo and his dog in Rome (*Farabola*)

With my father at the Guildhall; the statue is by Oscar Nemon (*Central Press Photos*)

A Matter of Choice with Idris Evans (*Author*)

Keep on dancing (*Author*)

Preface

I was born in World War I to mature in World War II. Growing up through that and getting to know myself have been quite an experience.

So what can I tell you? Why have I decided to write this book? I have always found ways to express myself in some form or other – music, dancing, acting, writing – but the last form that ever occurred to me was an *auto*biography. As children, we were never encouraged to divulge our private lives to the public, but now that the years are rolling on and so many of us passing with them, I feel free to write about myself, and increasingly free to tell my story as I have seen it and lived it.

Having been written up, written down and always written about, it seemed to me useless until now to add further to the accumulating published facts about my life, a life so closely knit with those of my family. I shall offer no excuses, nor seek them, nor try to juggle the facts. This is the same person you have heard of or read about in the press. The story, though, is told from a different angle, with a different perspective and emphasis; and for those who have not heard of me, this is simply the story of a woman who happened to be a daughter of one of the 'greats' of history, who found that skies are not always so blue. . . .

My thanks are due to Juliet Clark, who did a magnificent job of correlating the press cuttings and innumerable letters into a workable filing cabinet. I also had many temporary secretaries, all helpful but too numerous to mention. I would like especially to thank Ruth Harrison, who has stayed the course for over a year and who has tied together the bits and pieces left by the 'temps'. Inevitably, of course, I feel great gratitude to my mother, who carefully kept all my letters to her, which were passed to me on her death and which revived the past for me vividly. My thanks also to my sister Mary, who has kept a check on the family details of the book, which contains much laughter, some tears and not a little toil!

I could not have completed this book without the help of my friends Delphine Clues, Lorraine Merritt and Jewel Baxter, who have been my efficient personal assistants, and have jogged my memory about incidents that I would otherwise have forgotten. I would also like to thank my steady friend through many years Colin Watson, the fine sculptor who gave me my first two exhibitions in New York. My special thanks also to a close friend Michael Maher, who has had to suffer through the prolonged birth pangs of the book with an attentive ear and a dignified silence.

I was in London celebrating the ninetieth birthday (on 1 April 1975) of my mother, Lady Spencer-Churchill, when I heard the news that Charles Hamblett, who was to have been my biographer and subsequent editor, had collapsed and died. He was a good friend of many years and a fine poet: 'Poets need poets'. His death was a great blow to me, but I thought I would, for better or worse, go it alone. Fortunately, however, a *chevalier galant* appeared in the wings: a skilled writer and producer, Paul Medlicott, who stepped on to the stage to help me. His patience with my alternate exuberance and despondency was steadying in the 'living autopsy' which has become this story.

This book is solemnly and devotedly dedicated to myself....

But seriously, of course, it is dedicated to my nephews and nieces, whom I have not had the privilege to know as well as I would like. Perhaps this will give them a glimpse into their Aunt 'Sasa'.

Finally, this book is most lovingly dedicated to my sister Mary.

SARAH CHURCHILL

Family Album

I was conceived, presumably, during a lull in the conversation – we are, after all, a rather talkative family.

I was born on 7 October 1914 – I believe it was a Wednesday – and the war with Germany had been on for two months. My father was then First Lord of the Admiralty and the event took place in Admiralty House. He was not present at this auspicious occasion. Always one to try to avoid an impending disaster, he had gone to Antwerp to show his faith in that beleaguered city and that small nation, Belgium.

Posters showed the brave Belgians barring the way to the Hun hordes. 'They Shall Not Pass.' People and posters were mown down then, as they were to be again some twenty-five years later. My father returned from Antwerp forlorn. He had not been able to stem the tide.

He was greeted by the fact that his 'Darling Clementine' had delivered him another child. They (there is always a 'they') told him, 'She is the living spit of you.' David Lloyd George, in the House of Commons, said to my father, 'I hear the baby looks like you, but then *all* babies look like you.' They named me Sarah Millicent Hermione. I was not consulted on this, but through the years have skilfully lost Millicent and Hermione and stuck with Sarah.

I was wrapped, cuddled and cosseted and remained with my sister Diana and my brother Randolph at the Admiralty, until my father resigned after the defeat of both naval and land forces, but not his judgement, in the Dardanelles. This remains to this day one of the most controversial of British military decisions. It was to haunt him to the end of his life.

We moved to some temporary house. I remember, or think I remember, being carried downstairs during a Zeppelin raid to the wine cellar, the racks of which were converted into bunks. I was far too young to be scared and the impression left on me and, I believe, on Diana and Randolph was of a wonderful midnight party.

As the war intensified, my father and his brother – our very dearest Uncle Jack – agreed that all wives and brats should be out of harm's way. They chose Lullenden, a small country farmhouse in Sussex, where we remained while my father joined Uncle Jack in the war in France. Uncle Jack's wife, Aunt Goonie (our version of Gwendeline), joined us with her sons, John Spencer Churchill, later to become an artist, and Peregrine Spencer Churchill, in later life an inventor. Later, my mother's sister, 'Nellie' Romilly, joined us on the farm with her two 'angelic' boys, Giles and Esmond. So my early life began as part of a large family community.

The children's quarters were separate from the big house where the grown-ups lived. It seemed to me that the ceiling of our house was immensely high. Round our tall studio-like room ran a gallery from which our bedrooms could be reached. There were large French windows that led to a wild and overgrown garden full of stinging nettles; there was no outside help to curb their growth. The garden seemed full of mystery and imagined dangers for children.

Diana, Randolph and Cousin Johnny teamed up as they were the older ones (between six and nine), so Peregrine and I, only eighteen months apart and younger than the others, were naturally thrown together – leaving, I'm sorry to say, the Romilly boys somewhere in between and isolated. Perhaps because they came later, like newcomers to a railway carriage, we Churchills had a definite antipathy towards them, and this was to grow through the years until we were all properly grown up and affection was restored. The early antipathy was made stronger by the fact that their mother would insist on calling them, right into their teens, 'My darling angelic boys, Gy-gy and Ese-wee', when they both had respectable names like Giles and Esmond – and a very fair share of brains.

One day, I enticed them both to the French windows which gave on to the wild lawn, apparently to show them something in the garden. The moment they were outside, I slammed the door on them; maybe I thought the railway carriage was too crowded.

There were four beautiful Angus cows. They were black and white, with belly bands. Peregrine and I would lie concealed in the long grass by their field and contemplate these dinosaur-sized creatures. The milk which they so graciously supplied was to bring about the first of my many childhood illnesses. It was before the day of pasteurization and I was at the milk-drinking age and caught tubercular fever from this milk. Overnight, as they say, I changed from a bonny baby with a mop of springy red hair (my nickname then was Bumblebee) and became a listless 'little old lady'. The baby plumpness went and I began to show, too early, the sharp bone structure of my face. I withdrew into a protective shell and for the next eight years or so my health was not good. I had the usual measles, scarlet fever and whooping cough (twice – which is not 'done', since the doctors say you can only have it once). But worse was to come.

I do not think the doctors recognized how far my glands had been invaded by tuberculosis. They decided that my tonsils and adenoids should be removed. For this operation the bathroom at Lullenden was converted into an operating theatre. I am not quite certain why this was done. Perhaps the local hospital was full, possibly with wounded soldiers from the war. There must have been a sound reason. I was summarily plonked onto a table and the anaesthetic mask was held firmly over my nose. There were none of the pleasant anaesthetics of today. I was terrified of the sickly odour, the black vertical lines that danced before my eyes against a yellow background, losing consciousness into sulphurous dreams, and the continuing pressure of being held down. In an instant, I was fighting like a little animal. Strong arms pinned me down. The mask pressed harder and I was out.

Experiences in childhood such as this have, perhaps, made it distasteful to me, even now, to be arbitrarily touched or grasped. I put up an instinctive resistance. Two or three years later – I was still a sickly child – my neck became very swollen. We were now back in London. This time the operation was to be in a nursing home. My mother took me there herself. I knew something was up – no Nanny, therefore special treatment.

The nursing home would at any time have struck me as a dismal place; observing my mother's face, I knew she thought so too. I noticed her turn down the sheets. One look and she summoned the nurse:

'Get me Mr Churchill on the telephone and ask him to come here immediately.'

While we waited for him to come from the House of Commons a fire broke out across the street. I was thrilled. Fire engines, bells, ladders. It took my mind off the certainty that I was in for it again. By the time my father arrived, the excitement of the fire engines was over and I waited for what was to come next. My mother and father held a rapid and

3

low-toned conversation. 'The sheets are dirty,' I heard my mother say.

My father inspected them and then did something that surprised my mother, as she later told me. He ran his fingers along the mantelpiece and across the top of the chest of drawers – and looked at the dust on his fingers: 'Take her home, I'll talk to the doctor.'

He strode out of the room with rumbling reverberations issuing from him. My mother and I followed in dignified silence. I was in the middle of a drama; I was reprieved. That night I slept in my mother's bed; I was a star. But, alas, the performance began again the next day when I was rushed off to a hospital. The doctor insisted there must be no further delay. Once more I was placed on a table. I was told to be very good, to take three deep breaths and it would be over very soon. 'Not bloody likely' as Eliza Doolittle would say. Once again – stronger now – I leapt off the operating table. Wriggling, terrified children are slippery as eels. But once again defeat. The sweetly sulphurous chloroform had its way. An incision was made from just below the ear to the level of my Adam's apple and the offending glands removed.

Waking up from chloroform and ether is almost as bad as going under. The nausea and retching and soreness and thirst are horrible. Yet I am told I am very lucky, for my scar is hardly noticeable. Make-up men have often failed to notice it until the end of a film, when they exclaim, 'Heavens, how could I have missed it?' Many people who at that time had this operation were not so lucky. It can pucker, even draw the face down. Of course nowadays it would all be cleared up with antibiotics.

There was to be one last operation and from the age of twelve I was to suffer no more poor health. For years, though, my parents watched me carefully; had they not done so, my story might have ended there.

I was sent to a school in Broadstairs. The south-easterly winds prevailing in those coastal parts were to blow away the recurring bouts of incipient tuberculosis, which my parents still feared. During my third operation, which was for acute appendicitis, tubercular glands were found, though they were dead.

At Broadstairs, I was carefully guarded from over-strenuous exercise. At cricket, for instance, a sport in which I eventually became a team captain with colours, I used to field at square leg and batted third. If I did not make any runs, it was hard to get me out. Hockey was out since that meant bending; lacrosse, however, was in, since it was an upstanding sport. Swimming I was good at. In the gymnasium I would have to

4

hang from the ribstalls to lengthen my spine as I was told I appeared to be smaller than other children of my age. All these constraints, rather insignificant in retrospect, were clearly successful since I reached five foot, five-and-a-half inches without shoes – in heels I can comfortably make five foot, seven inches and so look tall, especially on stage.

Most young children want to be conformist. One year at Speech Day, my mother was invited to participate; she was to distribute prizes to the studious, attentive and successful students. The schoolmistresses tried hard to find me a prize to win, even going so far as to invent a bed-making competition, which I failed as well. We were each given a small plot of land in the school garden, but I cannot remember ever succeeding in growing anything of note in mine. I am very impatient and the only thing I recall cultivating successfully – on a damp piece of face flannel – was mustard and cress, which obligingly appeared to grow overnight. The school finally decided to give up. When my mother came to the speech day she looked so beautiful I was almost ashamed of her. She was not 'mum-shaped', and she made what was referred to as a rather racy speech.

Apart from my latent cricketing talent, I had two other distinctions: first I could learn more poetry than my contemporaries and recite it with a certain assurance; and secondly I was asked to play Alice in *Alice in Wonderland*. Whether this was proof of a talent or the gift of privilege I don't know, but it was spoiled for me by my school friend Diana Witherby, three inches taller than me, saying: 'They've chosen you just because you're easier to direct.' Furthermore, she had distinct signs of a bosom, whereas I was – as I remain – as flat as the proverbial pancake.

The school was not devoid of other forms of cultural activity. For example, there was Ben Greet, a Shakespearian actor who would turn up with a troupe of dancing girls to dance outdoors while we gazed with admiring eyes at their frolics in the bushes. We would sit in rows on the grass, though preferably not the front row, as he had a tendency to spit; so adopting an appropriately demure expression, we would humbly seek position out of range. In the regular curriculum, an interesting aspect was eurythmics – the Greek-inspired method of co-ordinating the body; a sort of 'pat your head and rub your tummy' routine, more correctly described perhaps as the ability to beat 3/4 time with one arm while beating 4/4 with the other. I was intrigued and attentive, and rather good at it.

I must admit that I took every advantage of those schooldays; enjoying even the rest periods forced upon us as punishments for unpunctuality which gave time for more thought. In those days, the English educational system did not encourage 'young ladies', as we were termed, to do anything but accept the inevitable; so it was fortunate after certain rebellious instincts developed in me and I was nearly expelled, that my mother came to the rescue. After consultations with the doctors, it was decided that the childhood threat of tuberculosis had been cleared.

But what was to be done with me? My father was not keen to send me to Germany, although it was fashionable in 1931 and my young Mitford cousins were there. I was already equipped with more than a fair knowledge of French, as my mother had taken the opportunity when I was being rebellious or bored at school to remove me from the French classes taught by a sad Englishwoman with an appalling French accent. Recognizing a different fault in her child, my mother said briskly to the headmistress: 'It's not much use her learning a foreign language if she can't even write English. Let her spend her time improving her handwriting.' And then my mother promptly introduced a stream of French governesses to Chartwell during holidays and was able to arrange, naturally in co-operation with my father, for us to spend our family holidays in France where we learned the musical cadences of French.

My father, who, despite his abiding love for France, remained the firm Anglo-American that he was born, thought some of it was going too far. 'After all,' he said, 'one can communicate in many ways.' Then, speaking in an atrocious accent, he said, *'Parler français? C'est l'argent pour confiture* – 'money for jam'. At any rate, it was to France that I was sent to be finished at the age of seventeen.

I was sent to Paris, where I was to meet some of the most important influences in my life – people on an intellectual par with those I had met in my father's house. Our teachers were all professors from the Sorbonne, and our lessons were conducted in French. My subjects were history, literature and philosophy – thank goodness, no mathematics and no gymnastics. The school was run by the sisters Ozanne, three Protestants from Brittany. This may have influenced my parents' choice of the school, since religion had never been pressed on us except for disciplined childhood Sundays, and there were no compulsory visits to church in Paris. Mlle Alice was head of the school. Mlle Marie was our 'mother', encouraging us to be young ladies looking to the future, for frankly she was bored with the past. The third, Mlle Lydie, had taken to her bed early in life, consumed with melancholy thoughts which, we were told, were *politique*. Who knows that she wasn't right? But she certainly didn't mingle with the rumbustious, healthy English girls who were learning to '*parler le français très bien*'. We hardly ever saw Lydie, but I did catch a glimpse of her once: she was really rather beautiful – a Mona Lisa figure, reclusive, rather sallow and sad. I do not recall anyone ever having a conversation with her, though I often referred to her ailments in letters to my mother.

The principals of the school, therefore, were Mlles Alice and Marie. They were extremely correct in their appearance and never seen unless immaculately dressed. They both wore wigs, which they exchanged for rose-coloured caps at night, so they were never caught *en déshabillé*. The wigs showed a well-tuned commercial sense, because they looked the same age to every generation. Mlle Alice was the sterner figure; she was very much the head of the school, and we were all a bit frightened of her. She did not share all Marie's ideas, but obviously realized that there was a balance to be found in the training of these sturdy hockey-field girls to become feminine figures. Before we returned home, it was Mlle Marie who took us out for our free hair-do and cosmetic session. This gave her the opportunity to offer her philosophy: one must never lose one's sense of vanity. Considering the social balancing act young ladies were expected to undertake in the rest of their lives this was no frivolous piece of advice. She would also subtly encourage our interest in men – not that some of the young ladies needed encouragement. But you had to be *comme il faut* – so we learned how to flirt discreetly from across a room.

A letter to my mother soon after I arrived in Paris gives an impression of what it meant to be finished in the thirties:

Mlle Alice took Daphne Binny and me out to tea yesterday. First we went and saw a modern picture gallery, where a young Englishman was showing some pictures. They were rather nice – though very hard colours. I think they were done with a spatula and then varnished. Then we went to Patou and saw some lovely clothes, and then we went and had tea at the same teashop where Cousin Sylvia took us. Mlle Marie told us how she loved spoiling '*la jeunesse*' though nowadays of course she had to be so careful. I think she gets rather bossed about by Alice and ignored by Lydie – poor Mlle Marie, she is so sweet and has promised to take us out again. At Patou's there were nothing but large fat ladies and pekineses and how they ever hoped to look nice in some of the lovely things the mannequins wore, I do not know. It was all the wrong way round – the old fat ladies should look after the shop and the really (some of them) lovely mannequins should buy the frocks which they look so nice in.

On the academic side, the most important of the professors in my life was M. Clarac, professor of literature at the Sorbonne, and later to become head of it. I recall him as rosy-cheeked, capable of blushing, and continually taking out his handkerchief to mop up his brow. Perhaps he was terrified of the well-brought-up young English ladies he was meant to instruct. He was the first person who ever paid me a compliment in my life and so I promptly fell in love with him. He gave me encouragement to take an interest in writing, even though it was in a foreign language, Not so foreign, perhaps, since my mother, who was fluent in both French and German and had lived much of her childhood in France, was determined that her children should have command of two other languages.

Soon after my first term began, I was doodling at my desk when I heard my name called 'Sarah Chu-chill'. It took me a moment to realize that *I* was being called as M. Clarac, with Gallic politeness, said: 'I welcome you all, but after this first *exposé* I wish to congratulate Mlle Sarah and hope she will continue in literature.' I still didn't believe it and sat down blushing, out-doing my red hair; and M. Clarac mopped his brow. Somehow, although I had been loved and cherished, I had never been particularly encouraged in any artistic pursuits. From that day, although I didn't know it, the school sent my compositions home, where they were read and treasured by both my parents.

Before leaving the Ozanne School, I composed this awful poem in English for M. Clarac:

> Why was I silent
> When my heart was rent
> By words I might have said –
> But now their moment o'er
> Like dead or dying ghosts
> Some, still unborn –
> They float through space
> Forever gone.

When he returned our *cahiers* with a book he gave to all departing students, mine contained a reply, in French, which said: 'There are some silences more profound than words.' Two years later, I made a visit to Paris and naturally went to see the Ozanne sisters. Marie, with her romantically intriguing mind, whispered in my ear, 'M. Clarac is here.' We tiptoed up the stairs and stood at the back of the classroom; for a moment he didn't notice us. Then, when he looked up, our eyes met over the heads of the class and I had the pleasurable thrill of seeing him stop dead in his tracks. Maybe my memory leads me astray, but I'm sure he didn't blush – it seemed to me that he went pale, and after a few seconds of awkward silence, he continued with his lecture. Afterwards he came to talk to me; we shook hands formally, and then he *did* blush. We said goodbye and he went on his way.

Another very interesting teacher was called M. Bidault, a dapper man and our professor of history. We got on very well, though naturally not as well as with M. Clarac. With my own somewhat politically tinted ideas and English background, I was not always convinced that M. Bidault's views on, say, the Napoleonic wars were entirely accurate. He later became French Foreign Minister and my mother told me what he said when he sat next to her at a reception.

'Did you know that I had the pleasure of meeting your daughter when she was in the Ozanne school? I happened to be from the Sorbonne and we were asked to instruct well-brought-up young ladies in the elements of history.'

My mother inquired how I had done.

'Unfortunately, I was asked to leave owing to an encounter with a young lady in a dark corridor.'

'Not Sarah, I hope?'

'*Non, hélas!*' M. Bidault replied with Gallic charm.

'Thank goodness for that,' said my mother, 'and now that you can take your mind off history, you will be able to concentrate on current affairs.'

I do not know how the rest of the dinner went, but my mother told me she thought him very attractive.

My third professor was of philosophy, M. Meningen. He would look as lugubriously at us as I think most philosophers do at students and the world. He was stocky, formidable, with a white beard which covered most of his face, but his eyes were piercing. He did not rivet me; which I regret since there are many truths to be found in the diverse philosophies of the world. In the later years of my father's life, when he had decided to write no more, I wanted him to do a book for me on the philosophies of the world. Short and to the point, it would have been an illuminating guide, perhaps in the style of his *Young Contemporaries*. I am sure it would have been of immense value to students of all ages, and I almost got him to do it. But in the end he waved it away with a tired brush of his hand.

M. Meningen did drum into our heads some idea of basic philosophy.

9

Of his own philosophy I remember his concept of the 'middle course'. Every virtue, he maintained, has extremes which are to be avoided: caution can become cowardice, bravery can become foolhardiness. The middle course is the rare and sane course of action to adopt. How much M. Meningen practised his own philosophy I can't tell; but I spotted him one day with M. Clarac on the spiral staircase in the school. They were hitting each other with damp umbrellas. I never discovered what they were fighting about – I slipped away into the shadows.

I must confess that I remember little of friends at this school in Paris. I think I began to realize that I was to be a loner – though my subsequent adventures into the world would seem to be in strict contrast to that statement. I do, however, remember Eleanor Keating – she was Eleanor Escort then – who played the violin beautifully. She became a close friend of those days, only to be lost later, not in memory but because our lives were so different. We were not allowed to speak English in the classrooms or the social rooms, but as soon as class was over and we were in our own rooms things became different. I shared a room with Eleanor. I would gaze out of our window at the nearby rail terminal in the Avenue Octave Géard and wonder where I was going, while she would pick up her violin and to her muted and expert chords we would wander in our own worlds.

We went on many outings from the school, to the opera and to the theatre, on trips down the Seine to Sèvres where the famous porcelain comes from. We would go in small groups, always strictly chaperoned. A most important lady in this was Mlle Cabrol, a blonde and forlorn lady of 'at least forty', obviously underpaid and generally disregarded. A rather superior governess figure, she did most of the actual work with the girls, dragging us around on the outings. She also had the unenviable task of teaching us grammar. French without tears? Not for Mlle Cabrol. The Ozanne sisters would have been lost without her. I feel that she, too, was perhaps overawed by her charges. She would read our essays or *exposés* and put in grammatical corrections before the professors saw them. Professors from the Sorbonne were more interested in literary construction than grammar. I remember one occasion when Mlle Cabrol tried to alter a point of syntax in one of my compositions. I stubbornly refused to have it altered – for once perhaps encouraged by M. Clarac's approval of my style. She couldn't really find anything specific to fault, it just wasn't textbook French with or without tears. Was there a moistness in her eye as she let the essay go by?

We had two lessons a week with Mlle Cabrol: the only formal school-room lessons in the curriculum. She was also responsible for the 'dramatics'. She once organized us into a rather polite revue; on another occasion we performed the children's classic, *Poil de Carrotte* – in which, with or without prejudice and really only because I had red hair, I was chosen for the lead. This was not, however, the beginning of my theatrical ambitions – just something which had to be done. My principal preoccupations in Paris were M. Clarac, my writing and the beginnings of wanting to look pretty.

At the end of my time with the Ozannes, a trip was arranged for the pupils who had, in my case enjoyably, survived the finishing of their education. The journey was to take us to see the chateaux of the Loire and my mother had to pay for it out of her pin money. The school fees, by the way, were £125 a term for board, lodging, tuition – and chaperonage. The journey to the Loire was a bonus I had not dreamed of and an experience I shall never forget. Either M. Meningen's philosophy or M. Clarac's literary creativity must have had some effect on me as I wrote in the journal of the trip which I kept for my mother:

Going away is always a puzzling feeling. First there is the exhilarating, wild feeling of just going – which means that suddenly you break all monotony, all routine, all tying ropes. I think it is rather like the launching of some ship – for it seems with the grinding and groaning of the car, the first slow movement forward, the people left behind waving, one slips like a ship into deep cool water – 'freedom'. So for a while one allows oneself to be lulled by the motion. But then there are the people left behind, already one has forgotten the expression of their faces as they said 'Good-bye'. One would like to recall it. But the ever-changing scenery will not allow one's mind to settle – nor to probe into what is now the past. And so it was today as we left the Avenue Octave Géard, and so it will be I suppose whenever I go on a journey. The threads of ordinary life are broken. Let us forget them.

I worked hard at my journal guide book:

Loches stands grim and medieval – almost sinister after the pleasant, welcoming atmosphere of Chaumont and Amboise. It is mostly in ruins, only cachots, oubliettes – and instruments of torture – remain as a memorial to that grim époque. . . . Some of the walls of the cachots are painted and sculptured – by prisoners – some who remained ten years in almost complete darkness and smelly dampness.

M. Meningen's grim philosophy that human nature really doesn't change came to mind. Are we born to torture? My father once said to me that we had to a large extent succeeded in the civilized world in erasing the lion and the tiger from the human soul. But that we had not succeeded in removing the donkey. At Rouen, seeing the statues of the Maid of Orleans, I recalled my father's remark that there were two great stories in life's history: Jesus Christ and Joan of Arc. Perhaps he always sensed the mystery of hearing 'voices' from the past – saintly or otherwise. Martin Gilbert, now his distinguished biographer, has told me that my father described Joan of Arc as 'the winner of the whole of French history'.

2

A Step Forward

The Paris episode ended with that lovely journey. I left that enlightened world and returned to the more solemn duties of being a debutante, and preparing for presentation at court. Among the escorts who livened up the deb dances were Harry Llewellyn and Dick Sheepshanks. They were wildly contrasted: Harry, fair and sturdy, born and bred to horses; Dick, dark, svelte and lithe, a real deb's delight, a fact he knew well but which he treated with contempt. He became a distinguished foreign correspondent for Reuters and was killed by flying shrapnel with three other colleagues in an open jeep observing and reporting the Spanish Civil War. I was dazzled and devoted to them both.

Another gentle creature drifted through my deb life, William Sidney, known affectionately as 'Sweet William'. He was to win the VC on Anzio beaches showing a steel and bravura totally absent from his personal life and social behaviour. He is now Lord de l'Isle. Dudley Cuthbert, another friend of that time, was shy and devoted and possessed of a gleaming innocence. He was to die in the successful onslaught at Alamein. And there were many others who proved that the so-called lissom young men enticed by would-be matchmaking mothers were not so lissom after all.

When I met Dick Sheepshanks, he was suffering from heartbreak over the end of an affair with Sidney Cuthbert's sister. Most of my time with him was spent sitting on the edge of a cricket green chewing daisy stalks and watching him play. Considerably older than my other escorts, he was forever teasing me and gently trying to make me laugh. At the age of fourteen, my younger sister Mary fell violently in love with him and practically went into mourning for him when he died.

Harry and Dick were frequent visitors to Chartwell and both, in the end, were much loved by my family. At the first encounter my father turned a cold and critical eye on each of them from which neither flinched. The

13

somewhat sceptical glance he bestowed on Dick became a ferocious glare. Dick, who was of a socialistic turn of mind, refused to dress for dinner. This was ignored the first time but the insistence did not go unremarked by my father.

'Young man,' he said to Dick. 'What do you do?'

'I'm at Reuters, sir.'

The glare softened. 'Good. What department are you in?'

'Obituaries, sir,' he replied, and the family contorted themselves not to laugh.

After a moment's silence, my father said, 'Have you got a lot on me?'

Dick replied, 'Pages and pages, sir.' They became firm friends.

I was to spend many happy weekends at Harry Llewellyn's home in Wales. Although we had been taught to ride with comparative skill on my father's polo ponies, Harry tried to strengthen my will and stamina by taking me hunting, which I loathed and which frankly scared me stiff, although I kept this strictly to myself. He made me change horses at the end of the day and ride home on a different one: 'Any real horseman or woman,' he said, 'must get used to riding any mount.' He was already interested in showjumping and I used to watch him training a horse called Silver Step for hours, making her take off on a cigarette packet which Harry would place at different lengths from the jump. The rest, of course, is well-known. Harry and Foxhunter became inextricably linked and were a bright gleam in the drear post-war years and for many years after.

One curious thing about the weekends spent at Harry's home was that although I was to meet all the rest of his delightful and warm-hearted family, his father, Sir David, never appeared. One day I asked Harry, 'Where is your father?' Harry looked a bit embarrassed and said, 'He's not very social.' On one of Harry's visits to my family at Chartwell, we were perusing the visitors' book for 1926 and came across Sir David's name. It was the year of the General Strike. Sir David never forgave my father for his part in breaking it and categorically refused to meet any Churchill.

There were many individual dinner parties in the London season, but should you be going on to a dance, the two gentlemen next to you at the table would mark your card for four dances at least, and it was a great coup to be asked for two or three dances by an admirer and be able to say that some of them were already filled. It was not considered correct to dance more than three dances with the same young man. At the dinner table, I learned to follow the hostess: to know by the turn of her head when to turn to speak to the man on the right or left of me. Great emphasis was placed on the 'correct' way – in the end the simpler way – of doing things, and much of our time was spent in absorbing this.

The deb dances were rather sad affairs. The mothers would chaperone the girls, sitting chatting among themselves along the walls. You were never left alone, and if a girl was seen without a partner, fathers would be nudged and sent to fetch one of the lissom boys from the bar to do his duty. I was not exactly bored by it all, but in the speech of today it was just not my 'scene' or 'thing'. I was told much later by Peter Cazalet, the Queen's horse trainer for many years, that I had appeared beautiful and I told him, 'It's a bit late to tell me now.'

He reiterated the compliment and said, 'But you appeared to be formidable, unapproachable and far-removed.'

I had just been shy in those days and inarticulate.

My mother was beautiful and elegant. I felt clumsy and awkward and wanted very much to be pretty. I loved the dresses and clothes, and my mother chivvied the dressmakers, insisting that dresses be made to flatter me – sleeves to be lengthened to hide large hands, chiffon bows to be placed where a bosom should have been. On one occasion Diana came with us to one of these fittings. I remember the dress – it was bronze and cream satin. The excited dressmaker said, 'Bronze for your hair, cream for your skin,' while my mother and Diana stared out of the window to control their hysterics. It was an extremely pretty dress, rather sophisticated, without frills. My mother, very pleased about the way the dress was taking shape, said in a conversational tone to Diana, 'Sarah is so easy to dress.' She couldn't know that this was a near mortal blow to Diana. Diana was the tiny one of the family. She was like a little fairy, tiny hands, tiny feet, slim ankles, but not very tall and given to a certain plumpness. It certainly never occurred to my mother that she had said anything wounding, because Diana was extremely pretty and was known in her childhood as 'the gold and cream kitten'.

My mother once recalled to my father a day when she was taking Diana to one of her debutante dances. As they were walking up a marble staircase, Lady Cunard met them. My mother introduced her: 'This is my eldest daughter, Diana.'

Lady Cunard looked Diana up from toe to head and back to toe again. 'My,' she said, 'but you are pretty.'

Diana took this rather brash appraisal in her stride and said, 'Aren't I meant to be?'

Total collapse of Lady Cunard as Diana and my mother swept on. This confidence was suddenly to leave Diana, and as she was not married by the time I came out (a terrible tragedy in those days), she felt embarrassed and *de trop* which was to lead her into a hasty, ill-advised and short-lived marriage.

On the way out from the dressmaker's, as my mother led her two kittens down the stairs, Diana lagged behind and looked very unhappy. I had heard the remark and knew exactly what she was feeling. I squeezed her hand and said, 'Mama didn't mean it unkindly. She was trying to bolster *me* up.' From that day onwards we sealed our friendship. Whatever Diana's lack of confidence may have been, I had my own, which accounted for my stony, perhaps even sulky appearance, and I was still envious of the beauties – the Glorias and Bettinas – as they swirled around the dance floor. I wanted to bite my fingernails, but couldn't because of the inevitable white gloves. My wardrobe was not extensive but carefully chosen to cover the wide range of occasions: a register was kept of what I had worn at every event. I would return from the hairdresser's to find the clothes I was to wear for the evening laid out on my bed – and I would be expected to be dressed and ready before my mother, and to present myself in her room before we went downstairs.

Throughout all these London occasions, dances and dinners, Dick, Harry and I all felt the same – we couldn't wait until they were over, to get away to our various pursuits: Harry to his horses, Dick to his journalism, and me to my dream world.

The country house weekends, however, were a delight, carefully arranged by parents who acted as catalysts bringing together not only those for whom there was a prospect of suitable marriage but also, with affection, those who seemed naturally to like each other. And again, the rule of manners – we had already been instructed in behaviour – was drummed into me. You tipped the ladies' maid, but not the butler – that was done by the young men. If you wrote a letter, you must leave it on the table in the front hall with the appropriate pennies for the stamp. You must arrive on the train suggested by your host or hostess. If you were invited to a distant house, say in Scotland, it was never considered offensive to receive your return ticket enclosed with your invitation. Pocket money was calculated by my parents and given to me in a purse before each visit. I had no idea how much it was, but knew it must cover everything I might need, and that on no account would my pride allow me to ask for more before my return.

There was only one country house weekend that I remember not enjoying. After a long day of dancing and a long drive (I now had the use of a car and was allowed out on my own), I fell asleep in an armchair during a game of intellectual musical consequences, and was awoken by my erudite host saying, 'Of course, you must have much more interesting conversations in your father's house.' As soon as I could, I contrived to visit the local post office in great secrecy, and sent myself a telegram supposedly requesting my return home. The scheme was successful, but it meant that I arrived two days early at the next house to which I was invited, the Heathcoat Amory's. There was a lovely atmosphere there, and I was welcomed naturally when I explained my early arrival. The younger Heathcoat Amory boy had a private plane in which he would arrive home, landing in a field at the back of the house, but in which he was later, tragically, to kill himself.

The debutante world, however, was not enough for me. There was something lacking from the programme, and I did what many adolescents do – I mooched around the house. This consisted in dancing to a hand-wound gramophone, handed down to me by my sister Diana. Her favourite record was 'Auf Wiedersehen' – she was in love with a handsome sailor. One of our duties at Chartwell was to arrange the flowers, and while we were abstractedly fulfilling this task we started the sister/confidante relationship. She told me about her beau. I listened with envy hoping for my turn. But her handsome sailor was going away for prolonged sea duties and she sighed as she put droopy tulips into a vase.

'What am I going to do without him? How shall I fill in the time?'

'I know what I'd do,' I replied. 'I'd go on the stage.'

'What a wonderful idea,' she exclaimed, and without more ado enrolled herself in the Royal Academy of Dramatic Art.

Her stay there was brief and hilarious. She was very much an individualist and took to direction rather dimly, her mind I suspect being otherwise occupied. But she did meet a student called Diana Churchill: no relation, it was her own name and she was later to become an excellent and dedicated actress. When I finally arrived on the stage some years later, there was always confusion about this Diana Churchill being my sister. I used to grin at her and say, 'Do you mind?' and she would say, 'Not in the least if you don't.' We found it too boring to go into lengthy explanations that we weren't related, and as our theatrical paths alas did not cross, they did not seem necessary.

On my parents' twenty-fifth wedding anniversary, a group of friends commissioned the distinguished painter William Nicholson to paint a picture of them. Incongruously, they were seated at the big round table in the dining room having breakfast. The picture with its delicate and fragile skill is filled with a kind of mystic mist marred only for the children by the fact that never once did they see their parents having breakfast together. My father in later life said that one of the secrets of a happy marriage is never to speak to or see the loved one before noon.

Nicholson became a great friend of the family and a sort of fairy god-father to me. He went to my parents one day and said, 'Sarah is looking for something.' He had noticed my mooching and dancing to Diana's gramophone which later became known as 'Sarah's Solace'. 'Why don't you let her go with my grand-daughter Jenny to the De Vos School of Dancing?' My parents were persuaded this was a splendid idea as throughout my childhood I was round-shouldered and clumsy. I fell off a fifteen-foot wall and landed on my back while playing Blind Man's Buff at Chartwell; I cut the back of my head dramatically on a barbed wire fence while trying to keep up with my brother Randolph; and later there was a calamity with a scooter. Whenever there was a loud crash in our house, they would all look at each other and exclaim, 'That's Sarah.' So one day I clattered up the stone stairs of the dancing school and one more window of life was open to me.

The De Vos School of Dancing was run by two sisters, Kathleen and Audrey. Audrey was to become one of my first 'spiritual' teachers. She taught all ages and already well-known dancers would come to her for private and specific training if they had some difficulty with a particular movement or limb for which they could not hold up ballet rehearsals. With enormous sensitivity she immediately spotted my gaucheness, my rigid although now strong body, my large awkward hands and the pain-ful awareness that I had of these defects. She insisted to my mother that I should have private lessons. Inch by inch, Audrey de Vos loosened the knots, and for hours on end I did special hand exercises and foot exercises. She said to me one day, 'You have double-jointed hands and a near double-jointed spine!' Perhaps this was because of the summer holidays which I spent with my cousin Peregrine Churchill – up a tree. Or the long minutes in Broadstairs spent hanging from the ribstalls?

Audrey de Vos was most upset when I was later persuaded by C.B.

Cochran to take to the legitimate stage. But I treasure her remark, 'I could never have made you a good classical dancer, but I could have made you a good modern dancer.' Her style of dancing was the beginning of a new style of teaching. Instead of the hidebound bar practice, which left you musclebound, she interspersed it with shaking each arm and leg for up to half an hour until your body was loose and each limb in command of itself. Then subtle, graceful movements in a sort of waltz time, and then tap dancing, and then the rigours of Spanish dancing, for which both sisters had been famous before they took to teaching.

William Nicholson's grand-daughter, Jenny, was a delightful girl. She was tall as a giraffe with a short body and beautiful legs, and was a very accomplished dancer. The length of her legs – the envy of every dancer – placed an additional strain on the pelvis, spine and muscles. The squarer, more equally proportioned figure may be easier, but nature demands a compensation and the 'square' fellows need additional effort to achieve the same effect of length.

In the Diaghilev Exhibition, which I went to at about this time, there was a little bronze of Pavlova that she sculpted herself and I would stare at it for hours. It is in the final position of the dying swan. She never finished the fingertips or toes. (If it ever crossed my mind to steal anything, it was this!) The importance of dancing was expressed in this figure – the reaching for the limit. You cannot dance when you are slumped, and this is why dancing is so beneficial. When you reach your limits physically, the stretch and spiritual life follow inevitably. It is the purity and dedication in a dancer's face that moved me profoundly and, as I have said, was to form a step forward in my life, if away from my conventional upbringing.

In January 1935 the routine of dancing classes was interrupted by a Parliamentary by-election. My brother Randolph decided to stand as an independent Conservative candidate in the Wavertree division of Liverpool. He was not, needless to say, looking for a safe seat, but he took the candidacy with alacrity as a challenge. He commandeered Diana and me to go up to Liverpool to help in the campaign. I murmured something about my dancing, which he imperiously pooh-poohed: politics were far more important. I adored him, so I went meekly – later enthusiastically – to help.

The political hustings were quite familiar since as children we had often accompanied my father on his campaigns. On this occasion my father watched Randolph from afar with a proud paternal eye, but desisted firmly from intruding, although he was obviously dying to. He confined himself to one appearance at an eve-of-poll meeting. He channelled his frustration into the construction, with varying degrees of success, of a series of swimming pools in the grounds at Chartwell. He started on a number of other 'improvements' all of which had to be covered up before my mother returned. Not having been well – for perhaps the first time in her life – she had taken a prolonged journey away from home on a cruise, somewhere in the East Indies, accompanying Lord Moyne who, was intent on looking for an almost extinct lizard. She was away during Randolph's campaign, so I kept her informed with two long letters:

22 January 1935   Adelphi Hotel, Liverpool

... I came up here last night to be with Randolph for his first meeting. It was very exciting. Sunday he was very depressed as he could get hold of no one, and everything was closed. Monday he wired for me and Diana to come at once to swell the size of his supporters that numbered five! – none of whom were actually voters in the Wavertree division. Diana could not come because of her [divorce] case – but I jumped out of my dancing pants, caught the next train to Liverpool and was met on the platform by a small deputation. They consisted of Randolph hatless, with an enormous muffler around his throat, Peregrine with his car, five or six handsome young men from goodness knows where, Miss Buck – Randolph's secretary – and a flashlight photographer. I stepped unsuspectingly from the carriage. A few unbecoming photographs of Sarah struggling with odd bits and pieces of luggage gathered at a moment's notice; then I arrived here to find the oddest looking collection of people, but all I discovered to be charming, sincere and hard-working. In an hour the first meeting was to be held. This was going to be very important for us, and we all felt very anxious – Randolph, of course, not at all apparently – and discussed having chairs put on the platform to accommodate the overflow. I wondered doubtfully if that would be necessary – but did not say so. At 7.30 Randolph told me to get on to the Town Hall and find out how it was filling up.

An incoherent child answered which wasn't encouraging. Finally I got hold of the caretaker, whose muffled voice seemed to come from under a pile of dust sheets. 'How many have arrived?' I gaily asked. 'No one,' he said and slammed down the receiver. I told Randolph – he went a trifle red and said: 'Sh! we never put any posters up outside the hall!' Still it was no use worrying. 8 o'clock – we must go. Randolph, me, Mr and Mrs Cannell (*Daily Mail* local), the *Daily Mirror* – a man called Watts, a marvellous two or three other people crowded into a taxi that groaned under our weight.

We shall anyway fill the hall a bit with our weight I thought. But it was amazing. The hall was packed and Randolph who had thought he would be alone on the platform found he hardly had room to stand on it himself. His stewards meanwhile had already organised an overflow meeting at the Women's Institute further down the road – which we went to later and which was even fuller and more enthusiastic. Randolph then said – if any of you feel like supporting me, please don't just go home, come now at once to my committee rooms and enrol. About 100 came which was surprising considering that the committee rooms were 1½ miles away.

Today more rooms are being got, and the organization is progressing well.

I honestly think we stand a sporting chance of winning. The first round is ours – but there are so many rounds – and can we keep it up. Randolph's voice is a great anxiety – he gets so excited and shouts much more than is necessary, and last night he nearly lost it.

It is his most valuable asset – he does speak brilliantly at times – all the women say he is a new F. E. Smith and sing 'Randolph, hope and glory!'

17 February 1935   Chartwell

... I told you about the first week at Wavertree more or less I believe.... All day we addressed polling cards, and then at nights went round with Randolph to the most enthusiastic meetings generally. On the whole he spoke very well, always he humoured his audiences and got them laughing and willing to listen, and what impressed them most was the way in which he answered questions afterwards. His answers, more than his speeches, showed that he really had an amazing depth of knowledge on a variety of subjects. There can be no doubt that he has a great power of rallying people under his banner. Young men and girls literally hero-worshipped the 'Fat Boy of Wavertree' as the *Daily Express* called him!

Also he showed an immense capacity for sustained hard work and generally infusing everyone with his energy. Randolph of course was the whole time confident of victory – the thought of defeat never seemed to cross his mind even in private. It was a horrid moment at the 'count' when we arrived and Orr-Ewing and Entwistle his agent told him he didn't stand a chance. He went very white indeed, and I wondered anxiously how he would take it. I must say he was marvellous – after that moment you wouldn't have known that he had lost! And certainly no one guessed how much he minded. It sounds pompous and horrid to say so, but losing Wavertree taught Randolph an immense amount, I think it would have been disastrous for his career had he won, because he would have been (naturally) so impossibly conceited. As it is, he has come out of it very well – shown definite ability and has gained general respect all round – if a certain amount of disapproval for splitting the vote. The 10,000 votes he got were due almost entirely to his speaking, as our organisation was really nil. The second week was slightly different. Randolph asked me to get hold of some of my 'boyfriends' and get them to come up to Liverpool and canvass. I had a sniffy telegram of refusal from one of my friends, but Harry Llewellyn burst upon the scene with his younger brother and proceeded to convulse me and Cousin Mop (who came to lend an air of respectability to the campaign) and indeed the entire electorate by their unconventional way of canvassing. They were up there ten days and Harry was a scrutineer at the 'count'. I think he thoroughly enjoyed himself although thoroughly disapproving of Churchill politics! He had a car sent up on Polling Day, and also his dog Lancer who did the most bewitching tricks.

I can't tell you how sweet all the people were and how much they loved Randolph. It really is a most romantic story. Randolph and his four friends from the tour he made in the summer in Lancashire decided by themselves to take this venture. His 'Gang' are all Lancashire men ruined by the penal tariff, one is actually a cotton-spinner who left his wheel to come and speak in broad 'Alfred and the Lion' accents for Randolph.

The day after polling day was sad, everyone returned to their jobs, Harry and David went back to Wales, Randolph back to journalism, me back to dancing. I am working for an exam – Wavertree was not a very helpful interlude for me exactly. Clerical work is rather trying for a would-be acrobatic dancer....

This was Randolph's first foray into the political arena where he had set his goal but which was forever to deny him any real success. Despite their disagreements, Randolph was to be everlastingly unhappy that he could not be as the younger Pitt to the elder, standing by his father in the House of Commons and fighting the battles with him. He did become a Member of Parliament very briefly during the wartime coalition government; but he had little luck in politics. I am sure, however, that as a renowned journalist towards the end of his life he gained great satisfaction collaborating with his own son, my nephew Winston, on their book about the Six-Day War in Israel. Winston was sent to cover the battlefield as a journalist while Randolph sat at home in East Bergholt – already quite advanced in his last illness – surrounded by telexes, recordings of broadcasts and copies of dispatches from his son in Israel.

Before Wavertree, Randolph, at the age of only twenty-one, had already made a remarkably successful lecture tour of the United States of America. Goodness knows what he was speaking about, but he certainly wowed his American audiences. Frankly, they must have been impressed by his name, of course, but also by his incredible good looks and his oratory. My father had had to teach himself to speak – the well known lisp which too many people have imitated was conquered, but he had to work at making himself an orator. By the time that Randolph was on the scene he had been brought up in the sound of that resonant, positive and riveting voice, and I suppose this is where family environment has a definite effect. If you are the son of a cobbler, you learn to make shoes just by watching; if you belong to a totally musical family, you will know about music – even if it is not your particular bent. I can only suppose that among my father's children it was a form of unconscious acceptance that made us speak 'the English rather good'.

There were two events during the Wavertree campaign which I carefully avoided mentioning in my letters to my mother. The first was that Randolph, descending the steps of the Adelphi Hotel, Liverpool, with his small entourage, was greeted by a man running up the steps with his hand extended. Randolph, thinking it must be an admirer – and remember, those were the early days when aspiring politicians were forced to kiss babies – naturally extended his own hand to the supposed voter. But as the man slipped away into the crowd, Randolph discovered he had been left holding a writ. Flashbulbs exploded for the opposition's publicity photographs, and Randolph became much more wary of supposed admirers. The writ, I must add, was for something quite innocuous, but it made a good picture and that, after all, is what newsmen are for – though in equally embarrassing situations myself, I have wondered just what they *are* for. But one has to remember the old reporter's saying: 'If there's no picture, there's no story.'

The second event was the time we were touring the dockland area when a brick was thrown into the car. No personal damage was done, but we were very near the water's edge and I remember thinking that if things got really nasty it would be a dirty and murky end to be pushed over the side. Apart from the verbal abuse – which, being children of a soldier and politician, did not trouble us – there was no further violence. But it was quite impossible for Randolph to do what he had wanted to do: stand up on the car and make a speech.

In some of the smaller halls where we had meetings, the noise was so great that Randolph simply could not be heard through the screams of violent abuse. On one occasion he even took a tremendous leap into the audience who were crowding the platform. They instinctively backed off and Randolph left the hall as we followed meekly – unmolested by the astonished crowd. Randolph appreciated on such occasions it would be impossible to put any policies before the crowd. But he did make it clear at every meeting, no matter how rowdy, that if he had no way of making them desist from their follies, he would at least assert the Englishman's right to free speech. He succeeded to a considerable degree; respect for him went up enormously, and at many meetings the audience became very attentive.

I notice that in one of my letters to my mother I quote the *Daily Express*'s reference to Randolph as the 'Fat Boy of Wavertree'. I simply don't understand this, because although he was beginning to fill out at that time there was nothing to suggest the somewhat lumbering figure which he was to have in later life. During his American lecture tour, one of Randolph's great friends, Freddy Smith, later Lord Birkenhead and the son of F.E. Smith, who was Randolph's godfather, adapted a stanza of Byron's to describe Randolph:

> A young Apollo, golden haired,
> Stands dreaming on the verge of life ...

was transformed into:

> A young Apollo, golden haired,
> Stands screaming on the verge of strife,
> Magnificently unprepared
> For the long littleness of life.

In his early days, Randolph used to ride regularly in point-to-point races. During one of these he took a tremendous tumble. Freddy Smith rushed across the field to see whether the fall was as appalling as it seemed from a distance. An ambulance was called and Randolph was shovelled into it. When Freddy returned to the waiting group of friends who were asking anxiously after Randolph, he remarked, adapting the famous quotation from 'Invictus': 'Unbowed, but bloody as usual.'

Youth, by its unique and mortal quality, is forgiven many things. But Randolph was to make many enemies in his life by his quite misunderstood apparent rudeness to people. His mind worked faster than most, and, like his father, he did not suffer fools gladly. He was a great fan of George Bernard Shaw and once wrote to him: 'Before I grow old, may I have an interview with you?' Shaw granted the interview simply because he was a young man. After, when anyone remonstrated with Randolph for his supposed rudeness, he would justify himself by saying, 'G.B.S. always spoke to duchesses and dustmen in the same language.'

About four years before his death, and two years before he was to become aware that the end was in sight, Randolph had an operation on a lung which was thought to be cancerous; post-operative medical reports made it clear that the growth had not been cancerous. This news was naturally greeted with general rejoicing. But Evelyn Waugh could not restrain himself from remarking, 'Randolph is better. They have just removed the only non-malignant thing in him.'

Randolph was very popular in the United States, as I would discover from taxi-drivers and doormen and the people I met in my own professional life. He was popular because of his real understanding of many of America's problems and because of his utter directness and outspokenness in interviews. This affected me personally after I had been charged with resisting arrest in Malibu. Randolph was due to be interviewed on a television chat show. He asked for a summary of the likely questions and topics so as to be properly prepared for the interview. He was given a very brief list; but as the interview began it became apparent that the only topic on which he was going to be interviewed was me. Randolph's response to this unscheduled change from the political to the personal was to turn the questions on the interviewer: 'Do I ask you about *your* sister? – I don't even know if you have one. Do I ask you about your father? – *if* you have one.' The interviewer was flustered and blustered until the control room intervened with some innocuous commercial. Randolph returned shortly afterwards to England where he was later threatened with a slander action for casting aspersions on the interviewer's origins. We never discovered the facts as the suit was never brought.

Throughout all the years I knew him, despite the usual occasional spats between brother and sister, he was a deeply emotional, affectionate and endearing person. Randolph once appeared on the popular American television programme, *The $64,000 Question* – the quiz game where you could choose your subject, from astronomy to Xerxes, be locked into a soundproof glass box and have questions hurled at you. Randolph chose general knowledge and, like the assiduous schoolboy he had never been, he mugged up his subject for six months. To the amazement of the world and to his own horror, when he went on the programme, he froze on the first question: what is the origin of the word 'boycott'? I hurried round to his hotel the next day and commiserated: 'Well, there have been some doubts about the authenticity of the programme, but you've certainly dispelled them. And you're a very popular loser.'

A grown man, mature in thought, he turned to me with a pathos I still remember: 'I don't want to be a popular loser. I want to be a popular *winner*.'

In later years, when Randolph had a series of black pug dogs as pets, he named them Captain Boycott 1, 2, 3, and so on.

Contrary to tradition, I did not become an actress because a burning ambition consumed me from the age of four. I was seventeen before the idea of a stage career ever entered my head – except for that casual remark to Diana in the flower room at Chartwell – and then it was because I was frightened by an insurance policy. I remember examining this brutal document at the moment when I was poised uncertainly between a happy childhood and an unknown future and discovering that my expectation of life was forty-odd years. 'Forty years!' I said to myself in dismay. 'Whatever shall I do with myself for forty springs and forty summers? I certainly can't go on doing nothing.' While I was pondering the harsh statistical realities of life and life insurance, I came upon the idea of going on the stage quite unexpectedly, much in the way one falls in love. As it happened – it was just around the corner.

3

Journeys Begin

After two years' study at the De Vos School and the acquisition of a diploma, I began to attend auditions. I would spend hours dreaming up exotic names for myself, a mental strain quite wasted on the callous sophisticates passing judgement on my ability. To them we were all quite anonymous. If you didn't answer smartly to 'Hey you!' or 'You there!' somebody else jumped into your place. None of these appearances made much impression; we accepted them as part of our training, an exercise in developing confidence. Inevitably perhaps, the only audition that really sticks in my mind was the successful one. C.B. Cochran who produced revues every year was preparing a show in 1935 called *Follow The Sun*. A notice was pinned on the board at school. It was an interview not a dancing audition and Miss De Vos suggested that Jenny Nicholson and I should apply. Dutifully, we hurried off to Cochran's office in Bond Street. Jenny went in first.

When my turn came, Sarah Michaelovitz, the impressive Russian name coined for the occasion, was forgotten and I gave my right name. I waited for Mr Cochran to tell me to touch my toes or turn a few cartwheels but instead, much to my astonishment, he asked, 'Does your father know you are here?'

'No,' I replied, 'I don't think he is particularly interested in dancing.'

'Have you thought seriously about a stage career?' he then asked.

When I assured him that I had, he said he would first have to find out what my father thought about it. I felt like a naughty child caught doing something wrong. Crestfallen, I left his office and met a jubilant Jenny outside who seemed sure that everything would be all right since she had been told to report to Frank Collins, the stage manager, to find out the time of the general audition. I told her what had taken place with me. She pointed out that this was silly. The fact that she was related to Robert Graves didn't interfere with her turning somersaults. Jenny was a natural and her bounding confidence imbued me with determination – and the patience to wait the outcome of the matter. Here is my father's response to C.B. Cochran's inquiry and a further letter in reply:

22 October 1935

Dear Mr. Cochran,

Very many thanks for your courteous letter. My daughter is very keen upon professional dancing and has been studying with great assiduity for nearly two years. I have found her so seriously bent upon it that I make no objection to her pursuing it as a career at this period in her life. I therefore give my consent to your engaging her in what you may consider an appropriate part. In the first place I should like you to give her the audition which has been mentioned. She wishes to be judged entirely upon her merit, and to play under a stage name. When you have seen her then we might perhaps meet and have a talk. I should be much interested to know whether you think she shows promise.

Yours sincerely,
Winston S. Churchill.

25 October 1935

Dear Mr. Churchill,

Very many thanks for your letter. I will arrange an audition for your daughter and will give you quite frankly the opinion of my experts and myself after I have seen her dance.

I was rather disturbed yesterday by a telephone message from the Theatrical Correspondent of the 'Daily Mail' that he had heard I was giving a dancing audition to your daughter. I told him that no such audition had been arranged, and he informed me that his information came through the Mail's office in Manchester.

Although you may rest assured that no capital will be made of your name as far as I and my staff are concerned, it is pretty certain that directly an audition is arranged for your daughter the news will, through some mysterious agency, find its way to Fleet Street.

I had instructed my Stage Director to arrange an audition for next Wednesday, but in the circumstances have countermanded it until I hear further from you.

Yours sincerely,
Charles B. Cochran.

It may not seem long from 22 October, when my father first gave permission, to 14 November when Frank Collins' letter arrived saying that I was to be auditioned. But when you are young a minute can be a lifetime. The actual private audition was delayed to my agony by C.B. Cochran's toothache which took him to hospital for a day. However, with parental approval secured, I was told to present myself at the Palace Theatre, between the matinée and evening performances of *Anything Goes*.

It was unbearably hot from the lights of the matinée which had been on all afternoon, and stuffy from the audience, which had just departed. I was scared, and to complete my discomfort the Palace Theatre had a steeply raked stage, on which it was extremely difficult to dance without experience. I struggled valiantly through three types of dancing: ballet, tap and modern. I started to sing but C.B. saved me from that ordeal with a wave of his hand after I had quavered through a couple of bars of the most difficult song I could have chosen – 'Smoke Gets In Your Eyes'. I waited for a few kindly words of consolation, but C.B., already badly crippled with arthritis, came up to the stage and told me that I had acquitted myself admirably and that I had a job. He said that in addition, he would arrange for me to understudy Clare Luce in a couple of her numbers. For the rest, Mr Collins would tell me where and when I was to turn up for rehearsals.

Cochran was to recall the event in pleasantly flattering terms in his book *Cock-A-Doodle-Do*, published in 1941:

There is a wrong and a right way of giving an audition. First of all, it helps if the practice costume is attractive, although it can be ever so simple. The hair tidily done is also a help. In fact, any aid that the applicant can give to the producer in his task of judging how a girl will look on a lighted stage is advisable, and helpful to her chances. Some girls arrive without a practice dress, without the right shoes, and without a piece of music to which they have learnt a routine of steps. Sarah Churchill, in the simplest of rehearsal costumes, looked attractive. She had carefully rehearsed her taps to a piece of music which she had brought. When she had finished she asked if she might have a moment or two to change her shoes. I gladly assented, as I always do to such requests, and saw another girl meanwhile, which served the double purpose of saving time and giving the aspirant a rest. Sarah's second dance was acrobatic, and as carefully rehearsed as the first. But she had not finished; she had brought her ballet shoes to show what she could do on her points. Had she been merely Miss Jones or Miss Brown, or far less good to look at, she would have been engaged.

Cochran communicated his decision to my father, and I recall the jubilation and excitement, and the congratulations from my parents, and of course from Mary – my first fan. I was once more summoned to Cochran, who wanted to know, as had been suggested in my father's letter, whether I wished to go under a stage name. Cochran saw my indecision and gave me some advice which he said I could take or leave. He said, 'Even if you change your name you will always be referred to as "Sarah ——, the daughter of Winston Churchill".' I saw the wisdom of this remark. Then he continued: 'Don't back down – try and live up to it.' And so Sarah Churchill, theatrical personage, was born.

Through the years I have often thought what name other than Churchill I would have chosen had I not followed C.B. Cochran's advice. It would have been Jerome, after my father's American mother, Jennie – a highly talented woman. Sarah Jerome has a lovely sound. But I am sure my decision was right. Very much later in my stage career I was to form a production company called, with my father's permission, Jerome Productions Ltd. Not, in all honesty, a notably successful venture.

The first test of my professional aspirations in *Follow The Sun* came, as so often in the theatre, not before an audience but one afternoon when I had to dance in front of the rest of the cast. We had just started rehearsals and Miss Luce had not yet learnt who in the chorus was to understudy her in her various numbers. It was in the nature of a Cochran show that his 'young ladies' of the chorus could 'stand-in' according to their particular talents, if the star should be unavailable or needed a rest. As this particular number called 'Dangerous You' was being prepared, Miss Luce asked the stage manager to tell her understudy to get dressed in her costume, as she wanted to study the effect of the lights.

I was numb with terror as I got dressed. I could hear the other girls all pattering from the dressing rooms and settling in the gallery to watch. When Miss Luce saw me she was taken aback – she was a good friend of Randolph's – and she kindly said that I need not bother unless I wanted to. I *didn't* want to, but knew I had to. When I finished, the applause from the gallery and stalls intoxicated me, for I knew that I was in. At the very, very bottom, but with both feet now on a firm rung.

Follow The Sun opened in a fog in Manchester, a real pea-souper that lasted three days and three nights. The professional wits had renamed our show 'The Daughters Of' because in the chorus – besides Jenny and myself – were Anne, the daughter of Mary Clare, and Pamela, the daughter of Gertrude Lawrence. The press were having a field day with us, and all the other current musical revues had written sketches about us into their programmes. One afternoon, during rehearsals, my chorus colleagues and I went to a revue matinée and watched the stars parody us. Cochran, recognizing how bad this could be for his show, had already, without saying a word to anybody, arranged to disguise us all in identically styled blonde, red and brunette wigs. My mother travelled up to Manchester for the opening of the show: an act of bravery which was more or less wasted because, as I didn't fall down, she didn't recognize me. In fact, a nice letter to my father proves she did spot me – and approved.

My first opportunity to go on as Clare Luce's understudy came as a result of her rather tempestuous nature. The number I had so carefully learnt, 'Dangerous You', required the star to dance with a series of partners, culminating in a duet between herself and Robert Linden. Each different partner was 'discovered' by follow spots. At the end of the final acrobatic duet, Clare had to be precisely positioned on a trapdoor through which, at the climax of the number, she would disappear in flames. At the end of the number on this day in the first house, she swept off the stage, demanded a glass of water from the stage manager and threw it into Bobby Linden's face, presumably for some lack of support in this extremely taxing dance. He stormed from the theatre, refusing to dance with her in the second house. She refused to dance with his understudy without rehearsal, and I was told to dress. I went to the still raging Miss Luce's dressing room, and asked her permission to make some very necessary tucks in the front of her dress, as I was afraid I might fall out of it during the backbends. 'No,' she snapped. 'You can fall out.'

It was not an auspicious preparation, but her dresser did some discreet business with needle and thread and later I heard from Cochran that Clare Luce had said I was very good. She was most kind to me during the Manchester and London runs of *Follow The Sun*, often asking me to replace her in a first-house performance.

I was never to feel alone or strange in the chorus line, especially with Jenny, Anne and Pamela, but I also made further friends among the other chorus girls. Being one of C.B. Cochran's 'young ladies' was like belonging to a lovely big family, and I never felt any resentment or jealousy from my colleagues because of my privileged background. We did two shows a day of *Follow The Sun* – we really were 'twice nightly'. It was a complex revue with thirty-six changes of costume. Our dressing rooms were on the fifth floor, no lifts, and as we scurried about the theatre my colleagues used to tease me and laugh at me – they thought it hilarious that I was still a virgin. As we stood in line, thirty-six 'young ladies', waiting for our entrance, one of the girls thrust into my hand the end of one of the guide ropes hanging from the flies. 'Here, hold this a minute. What does it remind you of?' Amid suppressed giggles and the opening bars of 'Love is a Dancing Thing', my mental virginity collapsed.

Nearly all the songs we sang in the show were given new lyrics – 'Love is a dancing thing' became 'Love is a damned good thing', and 'Love's in its heyday' became 'Thank God it's payday'. For one number we wore very short skirts and frilly knickers. At the end, we had to bow with our faces to the backdrop so that our befrilled bottoms were presented to the audience. The song preceding this display was 'How high can a little bird fly, Is there a limit to the sky?' Our version was 'How low can a chorus girl go, before she is called a so-and-so.'

At the beginning of the show, intoxicated and wholly entranced by my career, I had not noticed the man who stood silently watching me from the wings, Vic Oliver, the star. It was only as the result of a private party for the principals that I was to meet him. As a mere chorus girl I was naturally not there in person. Frederick Ashton (now Sir Frederick), who was the show's choreographer, took the opportunity to parody me, I believe not to hurt my feelings, but just to amuse the company. Vic Oliver was outraged on my behalf. The parody centred on a costume which revealed my navel. I had merely followed the designs that were pasted up in our dressing room. The others had hitched their dresses up as their Mums might not have liked the display. I, however, can be very liberal-minded, and wore my skirt on my hips. At the first opportunity after the Ashton parody, Vic came round to my digs, and formally asked me out to dinner. Unaware of his motive for his sudden offer and prodded by my girl friends, I accepted. He took me to the Midland Hotel where he knew most of the named cast would be, and we made a sweeping entrance – I was back on familiar ground as I had been taught how to enter restaurants and public rooms – and we were directed to the best table, where we commanded the limelight and interest.

From then onwards our relationship progressed mostly in long drives into the country, and it wasn't for a long time that Vic told me of the parody which had prompted him to appear so suddenly that day at my digs. After the very public after-theatre dinner at the Midland, Vic became very discreet about taking me out, and not a word leaked out to the press. My chorus colleagues either thought it had died or remained staunchly silent. The only acknowledgement that anyone was aware of anything came in the form of that song: 'How low can a chorus girl go . . .' The tune would be softly hummed whenever I was passing; even the call-boy would whistle it softly when he saw me. But I kept my own counsel.

It is difficult to remember exactly what we talked about as our relationship developed. Like most courting couples, we discussed our earlier lives – me with glowing descriptions of Chartwell and the black Australian swans. Vic said he would love to see it and I told him that when the show was over he must come down and meet the swans – and, of course, my parents.

Of his life, I learned that his father was a successful Austrian cloth manufacturer who had made many visits to Yorkshire and other English mill areas to study weaving techniques. He was a wealthy man and all doors were open to the young Victor von Samek. Vic was extremely musical and graduated with honours from the Vienna Conservatory of Music in both piano and violin. He had had a beautiful Viennese mistress. In those days, although it was understood, and indeed expected, that young gentlemen should enjoy the privileges of wine and women and all that these pursuits afforded, they were supposed never to walk on the same side of the street as their mistress, nor raise a hat to her. Vic brushed these conventions aside, incurring the fury of his father, who finally cut him off with the proverbial schilling.

Vic proposed to his lady, married her and they left together for America. He was never to return to Vienna, or to see his family again – except his sister, who much later was to emigrate to America. Vic's lady, I seem to recall, was well provided for, perhaps by former lovers, or by Vic while he was enjoying his inheritance, but he obviously had no fear of asking her to marry him in his financially deprived circumstances. With his musical talent, he was confident in any case of being able to provide well for them both.

This romantic episode, however, ended sadly. Neither of them could speak English, and loneliness descended on Vic's wife and broke her heart, as she pined for her Vienna. She pleaded with Vic to let her return. Sadly and regretfully, he let her do so, realizing that the hustling, bustling life of New York and America could never be for her. There followed a period of nerve-racking poverty for Vic. He used to make his living by orchestrating for small road companies, filling in as part-time conductor, violinist, pianist – or whatever was required. The companies were shabby, and the period not at all in tune with Vic's social or artistic capabilities.

He still had not mastered English, nor made much attempt to do so, for music is its own language, until he met a beautiful woman, a musician and dancer, who had also left a privileged background and taken to the stage. She had her own act, which consisted of playing the violin and dancing, and suggested that Vic team up with her and become her musical director. As he was not accomplished in English, it was fortunate that he was not required to speak, though they did do musical numbers together. The act would end in a climax that can only have been sensational, bringing gasps from the audience, as they both appeared in spangled dinner suits and equipped with stardust-spangled violins for the finale. Their friendship had evolved rapidly and she was to improve his knowledge of English considerably. I am told this is the best way of learning any language.

One day the manager of a theatre where they were performing came to Vic and asked him to make an announcement in the intermission for a charity collection. Then, perhaps, Vic and Margot would help some of the usherettes walk through the audience and collect the money. Vic protested: 'Why me? I do not speak the English good.' But the manager insisted it must be him as he was the only member of the company with a dinner jacket – the non-spangled one. Vic stumbled through the name of the charity, ending with the immortal words: 'I shall now come down and go through you all.' He was an instant success, there were delighted giggles from matrons and girls alike, and a record collection was made. The manager suggested he should seriously try to improve his English – but not too much – because he felt Vic had an inherent sense of comedy. Thus it began – and thus did it begin to fade for Margot. Vic did not rocket to stardom, but with determination and a sense of purpose he became a highly paid vaudevillian and, as it turned out, one of the last, for the end of vaudeville was clearly in sight.

By the time we met in *Follow The Sun* he was a well-established artist and star. I was in my first job as a chorus girl, and quite apart from my parents' probable reaction there was a general feeling throughout the company that the relationship should not be encouraged. I wrote an account of this attempted discouragement in my book *A Thread in the Tapestry*. I think it is worth repeating here:

Everyone from the call-boy to C.B. himself was to give me advice and tell me not to take this affection seriously. Even Mrs Cochran was induced to invite me to tea to discourage me from the folly of any serious commitment. She poured out the tea in an abstracted way and wandered vaguely about the room. Suddenly she plucked up courage: 'Cocky is most distressed at the news that you might marry Vic. You are so young. At the beginning of your career. Life is so long.' I felt she had memorized these lines. 'My dear,' she said, 'he is eighteen years older than you, and has been married twice before' – (this was not true as he never married Margot) – 'You are so young, so inexperienced ...' Her voice trailed away. Silence filled the room. I could not think of anything helpful to say. I was so sorry for her in her embarrassment that I wanted to join in and help her with her arguments.

Suddenly she smiled and said: 'Of course I ran away from home to marry Cocky and have never regretted it.' I bade her a smiling farewell.

The visit to Chartwell to introduce Vic to my parents (and the swans) was, however, awkward in the extreme once our intention had been explained to my father. The outcome of the request for permission to marry was the absolute insistence that 'Sarah must have time to think' – nothing must be rushed into – and Vic had to return alone to America for what turned out to be a seemingly endless nine months.

My parents still had a flat in Morpeth Mansions in Victoria as well as being rooted at Chartwell, for these were still the years of my father's political exile. I was free to come and go as I liked. In fact, no questions were asked, as I think they were nervous of doing anything that might provoke action on my part. It was a period of extreme loneliness. I had never been, except under duress, a social person – although I hope I have always been sociable. I always turned up at Chartwell for the weekends where young men were discreetly introduced and paraded before me at luncheons and dinners, although they were never asked to stay. I suppose my parents were subtle enough not to express a particular preference for any of these 'suitable gentlemen'.

I used to visit my mother at breakfast time, as we were both early risers. Many times in my life these breakfast sessions were to offer enjoyable and sometimes intensely fascinating insights into her character and her worries. But the breakfasts at Chartwell at this time were not happy; they were seriously constrained by the things we could *not* talk about. One day my mother made an extraordinary suggestion to me. I cannot quote her exact words but the meaning seemed clear enough: she said that she knew I was deeply unhappy, and that both she and my father were thinking of me. She went on to say that she had to tell me that with him, she deplored the step I was contemplating. There was a long pause before she continued bravely: would I perhaps like to have a flat on my own so that I could develop freely, as she believed I had a strong personality? My confusion was great. In other words, I interpreted, the

35

door to my freedom was open to any degree that I liked to choose – any-thing would be better than *marriage* to my 'clown' as Evelyn Waugh was unkindly to refer to Vic after our marriage.

Pre-marital relationships were still out of the question. Our strict education in morals and manners had meant that our chaperonage even extended to never being allowed on a train without the guard being given half-a-crown to watch over our safety. So, in this moment, my mother's suggestion seemed to make a travesty of our upbringing. How hard it must have been for intelligent, intellectual and liberal parents to under-stand, in an age of manners that were so rapidly changing. Their prime concern was for our protection and, I believe, it was totally unworldly. In retrospect this conversation with my mother shows her fond concern, although at these moments she remained an authoritarian figure with whom you could not argue.

This conversation, like the ensuing one with my father, only made me more determined to escape. I was summoned to his room at Morpeth Mansions, where he told me in robust and ringing tones, as if he were addressing a public meeting, what a mistake I was making: to have worked so diligently at my chosen profession and then throw it away in marriage to a – er – to an 'itinerant vagabond' with whom I could and should never hope to share in stage performances. I remained silent, having no defence for myself and certain that none was needed for Vic. My father then seized his British passport and, waving it dramatically in front of me, said, 'If you marry this man who is not a British subject and he does not take American citizenship, in three or four years you may be married to the enemy and I shall not be able to protect you once you have lost this.'

There was a long and stubborn silence from me.

He continued less formidably, 'I would prefer you not to marry this man, but if you do, promise me that you will not do so until he has Ameri-can citizenship.' I gave him my word, and I kept to it.

Diana was at Morpeth Mansions that day, unaware of the interview taking place. My father bounded out of his room, changing from the stern parent to the cherubic innocent and said to Diana, 'I think I have put her off!'

Diana, with her instinct and sensitive nature, said, 'On the contrary, I think you have chased her away.'

She was right. From that moment, my passive and somewhat negative attitude changed, and when, presently, I got news that Vic would not be able to return to England at any foreseeable date, I made my decision. In one of his letters he had sent me a ticket to America.

My clothes were mainly at Morpeth Mansions and I proceeded to start packing, to the accompaniment of insistent questions from a blonde, youngish and rather formidable housekeeper, who I seem to recall was of German extraction. I merely told her I was going on a holiday. I made up my mind that if either of my parents asked me directly what I was doing on the fateful day, I would tell them, but fortunately my seemingly passive attitude did not elicit such a question.

I did tell Mary, however, as the day chosen for departure was her four-teenth birthday, and though nearly eight years separated us, I thought with more concern of her dismay at the surprise news than I did of that of my parents. I trusted her completely to relay my love to my parents, and my regret that I should have had to make the decision. Mary, bewildered, but romantically inclined, as indeed I think all our family are, was intrigued and manfully and courageously carried out the unenvi-able task of being the messenger of doubtful news when the storm broke. My escape would inevitably break the continuity of our friendship from our rumbustious childhood days, but it became the foundation of our love for each other throughout our lives and despite our very different characters.

On the afternoon before the fateful day of departure I happened to run into Jenny Nicholson. She looked at me, convinced that something was up. She insisted on my telling her. I hadn't realized that my normally masked face was so obviously betraying my inner emotions, and sug-gested she should come home with me where I would tell her everything. She listened intently. At the close of the saga, I noticed there were tears in her eyes.

'I am rather jealous of you,' she said. 'I had a crush on him.'

I flung my arms around her, and said, 'Oh Jenny, why didn't you tell me? But you must *not* let my fortunes mar our friendship.'

It was at this moment I committed a folly. So that she should not feel excluded from my happiness, I entrusted to her the letter I had written to my parents and asked her to take it personally to Chartwell. I fumbled in my purse for adequate money to take her on the train. Jenny was impressed by this act of importance and responsibility, and said that she would do as I asked and that no one else should touch or read the letter. By now we were emotionally worn out and she suggested that she stay the night with me, thereby alleviating the pressure of what I now considered to be the spying housekeeper's eyes. I was already feeling like a ship putting to sea, the last ties were slipping from my hands. I was embarking on my own voyage, but I jumped at her friendly gesture when Jenny suggested she should go with me to the station. But it was to prove an indiscretion.

Although in all truth – and innocence – I made myself conspicuous enough by carrying an enormous chocolate-coloured doll given me by Vic, Jenny in the heady importance of the moment drew the attention of the crowd and the waiting reporters who always then used to attend the departure of the boat train from Victoria Station. With a sense of dismay and apprehension, I heard Jenny say in a loud and ringing voice, 'I will deliver your letter.' I was already in my seat and sat speechless as the train slid out on its way and I saw a crowd of reporters descend on Jenny. I believe she did deliver the letter unopened, but she regaled the reporters with everything that they needed: 'She is running away to marry Vic Oliver. I am her best friend [a sentence I have come to dread] and she has entrusted me with a letter to her parents.'

This was the letter I wrote:

October 1936

Darling Mummy,

I can offer no excuse – but things didn't seem to be working out so well – so I am leaving to join Vic in New York. I'm *very very* sorry to do it this way – I don't like backing out – but I think it is the best solution.

The blessing and 'consent' we were going to get in January were going to be very hollow – how could they be otherwise when both your hearts and minds are so set against it.

This way – I take all the responsibility – I have told no-one – no-one has helped me – I'm sorry it had to be Mary's birthday – but the decision was made in great haste when Vic's plan for coming back failed.

Please don't worry – please don't be sad. I will keep you fully informed of my whereabouts and plans – even though you may not feel like wanting to know.

My love to you darling Mummy,
Sarah

P.S. Please make Papa understand that I did not just wait till he was out of the country – it was a last-minute decision. I just have to go – I am sorry.

This was to be my first brush with treachery – on Jenny's part – and indiscretion – on mine. It was many years before I could bring myself to speak to her. Strangely enough it was Randolph who became our go-between. He had become friendly with Jenny when she had later married a journalist he knew. Randolph reported that Jenny was deeply hurt that I would not forgive her. If he were to arrange a meeting would I see her? I always have a feeling about forgiveness. I think it is divine, and I am not divine: I think God gave to mortals instead a power to forget. I asked Randolph to tell her I had forgotten and that I would love to see her. I am glad I did, for her husband was soon to die of cancer and she herself died barely two years after we had met again.

The boat train rumbled its way through the Garden of England, and the black and grey but always exciting Portsmouth took over. Suddenly there she was – the *Bremen*. I don't remember anybody harassing me as I clutched my ticket and my coloured doll and marched on board. Once installed in my comfortable cabin, first-class as arranged by Vic, I went up on deck to watch the departure – always a thrilling experience for me. While I was leaning over the rail, I felt a touch on my arm. It was Lady Astor.

'Sarah!' she said. 'What are you doing here?'

'I am going to America.'

'You're running away!' she said.

'No! I am running *to*.'

Nancy Astor, the first woman ever to take her seat in Parliament (in 1927), had never approved of my father, but she was to become my ally, not I think out of spite. After all, she was an American, and Americans do like immigrants. She was travelling with a niece of hers called Virginia Brand, who was the current companion of Harry Llewellyn. Lady Astor decided that Virginia and I would be good companions and said that any time I might wish, I could join her at her table. She declared that she was 'in the Ambassador's party' – Lord Lothian, British Ambassador to the United States. I thanked her and remained where I was at the rail, thoughts crowding and receding.

Another tap, and I turned around and looked into the eyes of a young, attractive, vital girl, who said she had just had a telegram from Harry wishing her a happy trip, and also saying she must look after me and sending me his love. So then I knew the news had broken. I confided to Virginia my fears of the two-hour stop at Le Havre. Where could one hide? In the cinema she said, brusquely and practically. What the film was I do not know, but we crouched in the ship's cinema for the two hours in port at Le Havre until we heard the lovely rumble of the *Bremen* getting under way.

The first two days of the voyage were enjoyable and Virginia was an enchanting companion. We occasionally paid our respects to the élite upstairs and other times would eat by ourselves in the main dining room. The *Bremen* was a German liner and the after-dinner cabaret tended rather unnervingly to consist of the massed voices of the predominantly blond and blue-eyed crew singing 'Deutschland über Alles'. But another personal bombshell was about to explode. A steward brought me a wireless message. 'I AM ON THE QUEEN MARY. DO NOTHING UNTIL I ARRIVE. YOUR LOVING BROTHER, RANDOLPH.' The chase was on.

It was a race indeed between the *Bremen* and the *Queen Mary*. How could they make up our two-day lead? I was confident we would get there first. But we were delayed by a hurricane and precious time was lost. The hurricane was terrifying and the *Bremen* had to heave to. I had hardly ever travelled unaccompanied, even though I was over twenty-one. Certainly I had never had to make any serious decisions or fall back on myself for resourcefulness. All the emotional upheaval of my painful decision and my first contact with publicity seemed suddenly part of the storm around me. The hurricane held us up for a full day, anchors down and engines in reverse. After what seemed an eternity and a terrifying experience we nosed our way through and arrived a day late in New York – but still two days ahead of the *Queen Mary* as, naturally, the hurricane was impartial. My own hurricane was about to break over me.

When it was past and I had collected my thoughts a few weeks later I wrote to tell my mother all about it:

Briefly this is the position. You know the American press, Vic never said all those hurtful things, but during the five days I was on the boat, they never stopped questioning him even at night – and as there was some delay in getting into touch with me, he continued to deny reports of our impending marriage – specially after Randolph sailed because he thought if he said, 'Yes I intend to marry her on landing' which was our original plan – Papa might bring out some opposite statement, which would have made a public scandal, or even have me stopped at the immigration place which would have been quite simple.

Whatever mistake I made – Randolph's sudden departure like that put 'the lid on it'. There would have been publicity of course – but little, and it could easily have been made to seem quite natural had you wired cousins to meet me on arrival – but Randolph's departure confirmed all the rumours and gave them a five-day story. 'Dash across Atlantic'. 'Brother chases Cupid' etc. You can imagine – But I'm hardly the person to talk about mistakes – and it's always easier to see what should have been done in retrospect.

Vic met me at quarantine where I had locked myself into my cabin. He fought his way through 50 reporters and we had 4 mins talk – he had brought a man with him who took charge of my luggage, passport, everything – Vic was totally marvellous, he wanted me to leave the boat privately which he could have arranged after having seen the reporters (which is essential or they write worse things) and for us to go and get married right away – but we both realized after a rapid discussion interrupted by loud cries from reporters outside – that would make Randolph's arrival ridiculous, and as Randolph had already cabled to that effect – we decided it was best to wait.

The old saying 'Journeys end in lovers meeting' I prefer to change to 'Journeys begin with lovers meeting'. I had told Vic briefly of the journey and he had produced a ring. He said, 'We must get married right away.' I said, 'No, we can't.' I told him I had promised my father I would not do so until he was an American citizen. I suggested that his lawyer, who was the man with him, tell the press I would meet them in Lady Astor's stateroom to answer their questions. Before we had docked, Lady Astor had asked me what I intended to do since everyone would know of my trip. 'Get off the boat,' I had said, and didn't mean it cheekily. 'I don't think you are accustomed to this kind of situation,' she had replied and had insisted that she would call a press conference for me when we docked and suggest I met them and that she would introduce me to America. I looked at her gratefully. She had taught me an important and lasting lesson: Never sneak or hide from the American people. They love an adventurous spirit.

Vic left, and Lady Astor sent her steward and my steward to escort me to her stateroom where the press were gathered. As I recall, with Lady Astor's prior approval, I managed my own statement. I do not remember my exact speech except that I had nothing to say about my personal affairs, rather that I was in America to pursue my professional activities, to see my American cousins and the land of my grandmother, Jennie Jerome. After that the way was clear.

I said goodbye to Lady Astor, and to Virginia, neither of whom I was to see again. They like so many in my life had been midwives in my time of need. I walked down the gangplank to be confronted by the Raymond Guests, my American cousins. The Guests wanted me to go with them to their home in Long Island, insisting, 'We will look after you.' I felt I had been looked after long enough, thanked them politely and asked whether I could come at the weekend. 'Where will you go now?' they wanted to know. I replied with great aplomb, 'To the Waldorf Towers, to Mr Bernard Baruch,' whom, incidentally, I had not informed. At that they gave in, knowing that I was safe and that they could contact me. Courteously they assisted me through disembarkation, put me in a taxi, and off I went. Bernie was not in the least surprised to see me, welcomed me and told me I had shown sense. He had already been on the transatlantic phone to my father and said I could speak to him later. He had engaged a suite for me so that I could come and go as I pleased.

I met Randolph next morning with a sisterly glint of satisfaction in my eye, at having arrived first and found my own way through throngs of reporters to the pier. When Randolph saw that I was determined, safe and happy he went about his own business which was to cover the presidential elections. Once I had reassured him of my intention to keep my promise to my father Randolph felt that his responsibility to me and to the family was complete. Time has dimmed my recollection of the day-by-day sequence of events, but Vic and I saw each other every day, discreetly.

The weekend came too soon. I told Vic I felt it would be ridiculous for him to accompany me to Long Island – not that he had been invited. My father used to say, 'It is always good to turn down an invitation, but it is preferable to wait until you have received it.' Vic, now sure of my purpose, agreed, and went about the complicated business of securing the necessary papers to permit me to work. We had decided that the best way for me to spend the time until we could be married was for me to join him in his new show *Follow The Stars*, in Boston. So he was to arrange permission with Equity for me to work for a limited time with him.

I went off on my weekend with the Raymond Guests. They were delightful people, particularly Raymond, who had a sensitive understanding of my predicament. They were all beginning to understand that I knew what I was doing, that my father's old and dear friend Bernie Baruch was in constant communication with him and that they need not feel too responsible for me. Quite naturally, however, they wanted to introduce me to the Long Island Four Hundred and asked me to join them at a ball. I declined this invitation. I did not wish to be paraded about unnecessarily and claimed fatigue. Raymond supported me and I stayed at home. But the next day I was introduced with my willing acquiescence to the all-important country club life of America. This I felt was a reasonable ground to choose because it was at a polo match, and Raymond was playing. He was a great horseman and horse owner. Here I felt I could be sure of myself, as my father had been a great polo lover and player, and I had a background in the sport.

All was absolutely 'hunkydory' – everybody was delighted with me, I was delighted with everybody. I said all the right things, did all the right things, and looked all the right things in my well-cut clothes, depicting not the runaway, but the well-dressed English girl meeting her American cousins. No questions were asked about Vic, conversation was astutely steered away from any sensitive area, and I responded to their good manners with my own. I felt I was acquitting myself well – why should I have been aggressive? Relieved, I thought: 'I have jumped Beecher's Brook the first time around.'

Then, during the interval in the match, all this immaculate effect was suddenly marred. From the other side of the ground, 'halloo-ing' with delight, appeared several familiar, if bizarre figures – Circo Rimac's Rumbaland Muchachos, the Cuban band who had played in *Follow The Sun*. They rushed up to me right in front of the clubhouse stand. I was delighted and touched to see them, but I think it better to draw a veil over the next few moments. When we returned to the house I asked to speak on the phone and called Vic to come and get me at once. Affectionately, the Guests and I agreed that since there were no more social engagements to fulfil perhaps it would be better if I went on my way, back to New York to sort out my professional life.

On our drive back to New York, Vic told me of his progress with my work permit. He was confident that all would be well, but we would still have to wait a few days, which meant that he would have to go on ahead to Boston. But before he left he took me round New York. He bought me a beautiful dress, saying that it came out of 'professional expenditure', and strangely enough this one too was cream, copper and gold. We went to such restaurants as Longchamps and Childs, sadly now vanished, which were not social places and we were left more or less alone. Once he took me to the theatre where we were photographed sitting in the stalls. The picture appeared in the press, and underneath a witty reporter wrote, 'Alone at last – with 500 others'.

Eventually, work permit secured, I could join the cast of *Follow The Stars*. That job made me want to give up the theatre forever. I had no time for rehearsal and I was under an unsympathetic chorus mistress. The Boston papers had headlined me 'England's Dancing Debutante', making me such good publicity value that my name went up in lights on the marquee. This did nothing to endear me to the other girls in the

43

chorus. I could scarcely endure it when I was told to do a few dance steps before that unsmiling line of chorus dancers, against the headwind of cold hostility. On my birthday – the only one on which I received no telegram or card from my parents – Vic gave me an enormous cake, and insisted I should take it to the chorus dressing room to share it with them. I stood in the door to offer it to them, and was received in total silence. Putting the cake on the bench, I said, 'I'm sure that if you don't want any you can find some use for it'; and left before I could hear the inevitable scathing replies.

But the worst was yet to come. I hadn't brought my own ballet shoes and the pair I was given had unfamiliar steel arches. Just before the show, I strained my foot trying to break them in. To add to my misery, my costume was a hideous colour called American Beauty. On a rose, this colour may look good, but duplicated in fabric it's terrible, particularly next to red hair. And as if that weren't enough, the dress itself was unbecoming. I was in despair when I looked at myself. Then I discovered the signwriters had spelt my name wrong. It was just too much. Under ordinary circumstances I might have mentioned it casually a couple of days later, but these were far from ordinary circumstances. I demanded that it be changed at once or I wouldn't go on. It was the last desperate stand I could take and it forced my stock even lower. After all this I could hardly plead that I was lame – nobody would have believed me. My foot hurt, but I just had to grit my teeth and get on with it. The only consoling thought was that *nothing* could be worse.

After the first performance, I went off stage in agony to be swept up in a crowd of reporters and photographers. They were friendly and pleasant, but I was nearing the end of my rope. Finally, they went away and as I limped towards the dressing room I heard somebody hurrying after me. I knew I couldn't endure another word.

'I simply must go,' I said, turning on him in a rage, 'I have nothing more to say.'

'But I'm not a journalist,' he protested. 'I'm a chiropodist and I want to look at your foot. I've been watching you and I know you've injured it.'

The dam burst. I wept on his shoulder as he helped me upstairs. He got to work and the toenail was removed in little strips, bit by bit, without any cocaine – as that would have apparently prevented me dancing on it. We had to do four shows a day. It was the most agonizing thing I can remember happening to me, and twice I was sick after coming off stage.

Through all this, Vic, who wasn't enjoying it much either, was stalwart in opposition whenever I mentioned quitting. 'If you give up now,' he said, 'you'll give it up for ever. Don't.' So I stayed.

During these months that Vic and I worked together, he became my link from knowing nothing really about stage life or vaudeville to suddenly knowing a great deal. Through him, I discovered a completely new world. It was not always easy. Sometimes, to assist Vic, I would sit in the auditorium with a stopwatch during his act and time the laughter and the pauses. Like many comedians, Vic had script writers, some amateur, who would send him jokes. They were all tried out if he thought them worthwhile, and they were given three shots. If they failed to raise a laugh they would be politely returned by his secretary, and suitable remuneration was arranged. He kept a catalogue; if there was a joke about a dog, it would be cross-referenced under 'Trees'. Thus I learned what a very serious business comedy was.

Working, as you could then, for fifty-two weeks a year, doing whistle-stop tours and one-night stands, material could remain much the same since you would have left town before repeating any joke. Now I watch with amazement the comedians who have to face the devouring monster of television, where new material is insatiably demanded. Watching Morecambe and Wise, Tommy Cooper, Charlie Drake, and so many of those enlightened and enlightening players who have made the transition from theatre to television, I admire them enormously. Knowing for myself the serious business of comedy, I wonder if this may not be the reason comedians are often not such funny people off stage. I also learned from Vic something I have not been able to achieve in my own life – how a four-show-a-day, one-night-stand performer packs up as he goes through his last show of the day; so that by the time his act is finished and he has to hit the road, all that is left in his dressing room is a piece of Kleenex and a jar of cold cream.

Till this time with Vic, I had been afraid I would not find enough to do. Now I was afraid I would never have time to do everything. *Follow The Stars* ended after a short run, and Vic was to return to New York with a single vaudeville show at the Loewe State on Broadway, then the mecca of vaudeville, which exists now only as a cinema. Vic insisted that, with the damage to my foot, it was ridiculous for me to continue with the ballet, and found a charming partner for me, James Struthers, with whom I would do a ballroom dancing number in his show. Once again we did four shows a day, sandwiched between the clowns and tumblers, and a female

45

impersonator who took his role so seriously that when in costume he used the ladies' cloakroom. I thought this highly amusing and told Vic. He was *not* amused.

Despite the excitement and involvement of my new life, the personal worries for my parents and legal intervention continued to prevent my marriage to Vic. A long letter to my mother was full of this.

I wouldn't dream of trying to excuse the step I took – but I have also given up any hope that you and Papa can ever understand or have any conception of what I have been through these last 9 months that I have loved Vic – to be in love and know the weakness of your love – to have to realize not only the incongruity of the situation, but that the man is despised – by those who say they love you – continually and perpetually to have him insulted and treated as a low adventurer – to be made to feel you have committed an error of taste, and finally even to have your sincerity questioned – and then when he went away – no one ever spoke of him, except to abuse and bring back to me ridiculous and untrue stories – when he was not there to defend himself – no-one ever asked if I was sad – or how the long days and nights at Chartwell, with nothing to occupy my mind, ever passed....

Looking back on that time with the help of my letters to my mother, I think now that perhaps I was too upset to be really fair to my father. He must have been appalled at the prospect of his daughter going off with an Austrian, eighteen years older, whose background was a mystery and was the opposite of what a father would have thought desirable. At that time, however, I was miserable and bitter, and it was made worse when my father seemed to start acting like Mr Barrett of Wimpole Street (a play, ironically, in which I later had a part). I found it all outrageous and went on in my letter to my mother:

For the rest, what can I say? Papa has the best lawyer in America working for him – in an informal moment he as good as admitted that if we (Vic and I) were paying him to get us married – the legal difficulty could have been straightened out in a few days – but I suppose it is his job to prolong the thing as long as possible – to stall and stall and to play for time – in the hopes it may die – or that at last, circumstances *will* divide us. Then I had a feeling Papa was not playing quite straight with us – it seemed an ominous silence – was this waiting just a test for our affections – or was it just a playing for time in the hope that lawyers working night and day might unravel something in his past to prevent us marrying.

I don't know if you know what —— has resorted to now :– failing to find anything on Vic – he has turned his activities to Vienna and in a delicate and for him safe-guarded way – he has had men suggest to Vic's wife – to contest now – at the ninth hour with the first decree passed – to contest the case. All her expenses will be paid for her, etc.

I refuse to believe that Papa knows of this – and that —— is just over-zealous – those are apparently just the usual American tactics – he is the smartest lawyer – and can delay the marriage for some months if Papa asks him to – equally if Papa asked him to speed it up – we could be married so soon.

Considering the situation – and the publicity – I should have thought it preferable, to me being out here unmarried and still a subject of mystery, gossip and rumours.

Finally though, all the confusion was resolved; the lawyers could find nothing to prevent us. Vic's former wife of so many years' separation nobly refused to contest the decree, and so, on Christmas Eve 1936, Vic and I were married in City Hall, New York. Our witnesses were his lawyer and, to represent me, a cleaning lady who was polishing some brasses. Three hours later we were on the *Aquitania*, rolling back to England, Home and Duty.

4

Separate Ways

The ss *Aquitania* was a long and narrow ship and even from our cabin on the upper deck it seemed to me that the water was impossibly near. When I say that we were rolling home the words are not carelessly chosen and once again I must say that I was frightened. What a place for a honeymoon, as the ship heaved and rolled through the waves! I looked out of the window of our suite – not a porthole, because this was upper-deck travel. (Even when we were without a bean, as then with only $200 between us, Vic was always careful that we should live well.) I saw that directly outside on the deck a seaman with a broom was steadily brushing the Atlantic away. This was, I suppose, an attempt to reassure the passengers. My shaky mathematics told me that the ship could only tip forty-five degrees, and I knew that most ships were built to be unsinkable. The *Aquitania* proved to be no exception – I discovered later that she was carrying water ballast – and Vic and I surfaced for lunch, dinner and tea and all that the human frame requires, until the rolling finally brought us home.

We disembarked at Southampton, unloading our goods and chattels which were many in spite of our impecunious state. We got on the train, and never has a cup of tea and a slice of British Rail plum cake tasted so good. When we arrived in London, true to character, Vic hailed a taxi, and we drove in state to the Carlton – which alas is no longer, having been hit by a bomb during the war. We were escorted to the bridal suite, where Vic called his agent, Henry Sherek, and said, 'I'm here.' Then he looked round the room and said solicitously, 'Are you comfortable?' My mind, like a machine, was already worrying about the cost of this sumptuous temporary home. I remembered the play by Noël Coward about a couple who ran out of money and had to stay in their hotel suite until they were finally ejected by the management (with the usual Coward aplomb). We were ahead of time – Vic's first date was not for a while – so we had a few days to spare. I rang my parents and we spent the day with them at Chartwell. If the reunion was joyful, it was still somewhat restrained – but my father was a great believer in 'those whom God hath joined together let no man put asunder'.

At the end of that day, we returned to our suite at the Carlton, and Vic settled down to preparing his act for his onslaught on British music halls. He became fascinated by one of the Carlton's page-boys – not, I assure you, that he had any homosexual tendencies – but to complement his elegant image he felt that he needed someone to carry his by now voluminous amount of music and his violin. Frank Cox, the page-boy, was small but sturdy. His parents were approached, their consent given for him to be released from his apprenticeship in opening and closing doors, and he was duly instructed in his new duties, carrying Vic's violin and music to the orchestra pit. So, with his new minion trotting behind, Vic started work, and he worked continually, for in those pre-war days there were still plenty of music hall dates available. Frank Cox was to work with Vic for more than thirty years.

In the midst of all this activity, Vic also looked for a home for us, and after a certain amount of deliberation we landed up at No. 66 Westminster Gardens. I didn't know it then, but it was to be the last permanent home I was to know for many years. Also within the block lived my brother Randolph and C.B. Cochran. Whether this factor influenced our choice of the place I am not certain, but I am fairly sure that Vic's concern for me was expressed here, thinking that I might feel happier to be near familiar faces. Later, my sister Diana and her second husband, Duncan Sandys, were to have a flat there. Something else that we didn't know when we took the flat was that on the opposite roof very close to our windows, was an air-raid warning siren. When the war really began I was shocked into near insensibility when it first roared into action, and leaping from bed, stubbed my toe agonizingly on a piece of furniture which affected me far more than the siren's warning. When I recovered my composure after this false alarm, I discovered that I was clutching a volume of Shelley given to me by my brother Randolph. I had obviously decided that was my most critical possession in an air raid. Shortly after the new flat had been organized, my mother's former lady's maid, Ada Jeffries, suddenly arrived to see me. She told me that since leaving my mother she had started a small dressmaking establishment which had proved not too successful and she asked, 'Do you have a place for me in your household?' I was delighted, and so we started our family life. Jeff was to be with me for many years and has remained a great and valued friend.

Quietly sitting on my little white rug like a pampered Persian cat, I was fretting for action. So, one day, I summoned up courage to tell Vic that I wished to return to my trade. He was probably somewhat dismayed that the love and care he had lavished on me still left me dissatisfied, but with his usual zest and enthusiasm for my happiness, he plunged in to find what suitable repertory companies would employ me. There turned out to be more than enough – and I began again on the bottom rung, as Assistant Stage Manager, which meant teaboy and bottle-washer, occasionally walking on, with two companies that alternated between the Festival Theatre in Cambridge and the Royal in Brighton. I remember this time well and with affection. I was to meet and work with many later well-known people, among them Ronnie Waldman, Judy Campbell (of later wartime fame with 'A Nightingale Sang in Berkeley Square'), and a young man called Val Blanchard, better remembered now by his real name, Macdonald Hobley. If I have forgotten any names it is because I was again totally immersed in what had come to seem my mission in life – the theatre.

I now had a little red Standard motor car, and rushed after the last house on Saturday night to be with Vic, who was also working either in London or the provinces. For the next two years, I worked for several companies, rising from ASM, where my duties included at Cambridge the responsibility for keeping the back doors shut as there was a rather fragrant pigsty at the back of the theatre, to the heights of being guest star and appearing as Juliet with Arthur Lawrence at Northampton. Although in retrospect this all happened very quickly, I remember how slow the progress seemed at the start, and my excitement the first time I was actually asked to go on stage, filling in for someone who was sick. It was a small part, but it meant that I was included in the line up for curtain calls, and so intoxicated was I by the headiness of the applause that I quite forgot my other function as ASM until I was reminded by a nudge from one of the cast that unless I did something about it quickly, the curtain would stay up all night.

I first began to suspect that I might be a comedian when I was at Cambridge. I was appearing in a Mabel Constandouros play, *Three for Luck*. The stage was set as a breakfast room, a sideboard groaned with the conventional silver platters, and I proceeded on stage, languidly lifted the lid of a silver dish, looked moodily within and spoke my opening line: 'Lord, I feel like a struck match.' It was my first laugh. I could see the cast laughing too in the wings – and felt a surge of excitement. From this first essaie I was allowed to play Lavinia in Noël Coward's *Family Album*. I had to have a lisp and an inability to pronounce my Rs for the part, which quite suited my actual capacities, and I had a classic line as the family gathered round to hear the will; when no will is to be found, Lavinia, referring to the butler, Burrows, lisps: 'Bowwowes and I burnt it.'

These theatres and companies were the best training ground anyone could have had and the experience I gained was invaluable. Much later, when Hollywood was to fall in front of the child television – then known as the 'bastard' – those who found ready employment were the ones who had had stage training, as we not only learned our lines but remembered whole scenes. The theatrical discipline of 'the show must go on' was another lesson – it was considered part of the duty of the members of the profession to do our best with a play, however tedious it might have been to perform, to keep it going through the required 150 performances to enable it to be printed in a French's edition. These copies of the plays, printed with lists of the original cast and with detailed stage instructions and lighting plots, were the basis of the playwright's bread and butter, being available for all time, and for amateur companies throughout the country.

My first and unexpected experience of making up my mind about my career was forced upon me when I had to make the decision to leave my job with the rep company. I get fond of people I work with and find it very hard to make a break, but when I am not given parts which I deserve I must take the next logical step. This was beginning to happen to me in repertory: I was not getting the parts I knew I was ready to play and so, naturally, I felt again dissatisfied. It must be said, once more, Vic's own feelings about my working at all were pushed aside, and his concern for me prompted him to say, 'It is time for you to leave.'

Finally, in blubs of tears, I kissed my friends goodbye and set out on my own. Precariously at first but, inevitably, with increasing assurance, I began on a series of 'guest appearances' not attached to any specific company but working all round the country in a variety of plays. As a young actress, and inexperienced, I often found myself to my surprise playing older women or character parts, although I did play Juliet for the first time at Northampton. I came to believe that an actress will always be too old or too young for the part which happens to be available; but a part I particularly remember from this time was in *Dr Wu*. I only had a small part but it required an elaborate and beautiful make-up: indeed, I spent more time in making up than on the stage, where I was, to my delight, carried on in the arms of a young and handsome actor. I also remember an occasion in Southampton playing in *The Outsider*. The fleet was in, the audience full of sailors, and when I delivered my line – 'I don't want a good man's love – I just want a young man's passion!' – there was an uproar. Quite definitely the fleet won that one. I played in *The Constant Nymph* in Birmingham, met Ronnie Waldman again in *Dr Clitterhouse* in Weston-super-Mare, and also, during 1938, played for several months in London at the Haymarket and on tour with Vic in the play *Idiot's Delight* by Robert Sherwood. Like most artists, Vic wanted to extend himself by working in something that was not strictly his field – the clown always wants to play Hamlet and Hamlet the clown – and in this play he starred with Judy Campbell, my friend and colleague from earlier rep days, while Michael Gough and I played the unenviable parts of a pair of milkwashy honeymooners. Neither of us has been able to forget Mr and Mrs Cherry. I had the audacity many years later to draw our feelings about the parts to Robert Sherwood's attention. He heartily agreed.

In 1939, I was given the part of Mrs Manningham in *Gaslight*, my first really strong dramatic role, and one which was to become very important in my acceptance as a name in my profession. But this was August 1939 and we were all aware of the imminence of war.

As my first solo steps continued, I was growing and developing almost without realizing it, and my marriage with Vic started on a steady decline. We worked together quite often, I quite often worked alone; but the inevitable separation caused by my growing up had begun – Vic would have liked me to remain the protected child forever. Such separations, however, are not sudden: the thread that holds couples together is very elastic and stretches, retracts and stretches again for a long time until the elastic finally wears out.

On Saturday 2 September 1939 I was in the play, *Quiet Wedding*, starring David Tomlinson at the Coliseum. The cast appeared at the theatre as usual, all having heard the well-publicized announcement that the Prime Minister, Neville Chamberlain, had asked us to be at home by our radios at eleven the following morning. We knew that this must be the formal declaration of war. Before the last show, we checked the 'house' – there were four people in the audience. The stage manager went to the manager and said could we not at least suggest that the audience might sit together – the answer was no, they must stay in the seats they had bought. In the circumstances, the atmosphere was already highly charged, but this decision determined us on a performance to remember. We chatted to the audience between lines – suggesting that we should all share a taxi home. I lost my false bosom at one point and, at another, David Tomlinson chose to appear for our intimate love scene wearing a fireman's helmet. Years later, I was searching for a gallery in which to show a friend's sculptures and since finances were small I was asking in antique shops if they would find room to mingle the sculptures with the furniture. One woman I asked was unable to help but said, 'Do you remember *Quiet Wedding* at the Coliseum ?' She had been one of 'the Four'! After the show, we kissed each other fond goodbyes, knowing what was to happen – and after the next day's broadcast the London theatres were all promptly closed. It had been our last night, but it was indeed a night to remember.

The provinces were still very much there, however, and for the next year, all through the phoney war, I went back to my guest appearances. After having seen Gwen Ffrangcon Davies' West End performance in *Gaslight* of that frail figure, driven near to insanity by fear, I was determined again to play Mrs Manningham and from January until May 1940 toured the country in it, with good reviews for the show and accepted recognition. In July 1940, I was back in London, this time playing at the 'Q' near Kew Bridge in a variety of roles, the prime of which, perhaps, was *Mary Rose* by J.M. Barrie. By now some of the London theatres had started opening again – the Windmill, of course, never closed – but the performances were always under threat of bombing so that, although we still played twice nightly, the second house was timed to finish before dark. If you couldn't get home you had to stay put.

I was naturally thrilled to be asked to play 'one of the suicides' in *Outward Bound* at the New Theatre. Once again I was to be in good company: including the gracious Louise Hampton (known to most of us for *All My Sons*) and Terence de Marny, who was to be a friend for many years. He used literally to back onto the stage and I asked him why. 'Oh,' he said, 'you must never go on stage without looking as if you've come from somewhere.' One night during the show Terence's character had just given the line, 'We are all dead.' Then the sirens went off – for the first time seriously. The English audience burst into laughter.

The manager appeared on the stage and asked the audience to remain in their seats, which they did. The cast belted up onto the roof to watch the first blitz on London docks. It was strange and ominous; the real war had finally begun.

Soon after this, I was asked to appear in *Spring Meeting*, a film with Margaret Rutherford, Michael Wilding and Nova Pilbeam. As the theatres plodded on carefully in town, the film studios moved out to the suburbs and beyond. The film was to be made at Welwyn Garden City, and those of us who lived in the centre of town were asked not to go home at the end of the day, but to stay in the studio. I do not remember how many people accepted this general offer. I know I did, to lessen Vic's worry, and so did Michael Wilding. Our dressing rooms had proper beds put in them; the blackout was by now fully operational and heavy curtains swathed the windows. There was an old man in charge of us, the stage doorkeeper, who was probably fire-watching as well as seeing that we behaved ourselves. When returning from a walk in the evening – probably to the nearest pub, but not without observing the the distant blitz on London – we would knock on the door and he would let us in. Our nightly conversations with him delighted us because of his disturbing tic, which became reassuring eventually; he had the disconcerting ability to answer questions with a 'yes' while shaking his head and with a 'no' while he nodded. As all film people will know, we are early risers, and in the hours while we waited for the rest of the cast to arrive, Michael and I would ride bicycles in some nearby sandpits. It was a desperately poignant moment when Nova Pilbeam's husband was killed in action – but she finished the film; and Margaret Rutherford, that beloved and enchanting lady, wobbled her already apparent chins through this mild but pleasing comedy. It was on the occasion of my father's death that she sent me a kind message remembering our adventures at Welwyn Garden City.

Among other memories that come to me of this early wartime period, although I cannot pretend to be chronological, was a tour that I did with Vic in *Words and Music*. By now the bombing of London had ceased and the famous Baedeker raids had taken over. It began to seem that the bombing of towns took place the week after we had been playing in them, as though the Germans were following us around the country. We knew we could not have been any kind of a target for them, but as the weeks went on, it began to be something of an embarrassment. At this time we had a small country house at Eythrop on the Rothschild estate. On one

Mary (*right*) and me helping my father build the wall at Chartwell.

On Budget Day, 1929, with my father, who was Chancellor of the Exchequer, my mother and Randolph on my left.

Me at 17 – a photograph my mother loved.

It took me two hours to do my make-up as Little Lotus Flower, but I only had one line.

With Vic in *Follow the Stars*, USA, 1936.

Home to England with Vic; Randolph meets us at Waterloo Station.

With Vic in Noël Coward's *Tonight at 8.30*, which we performed at 5.45 p.m. to avoid the Blitz.

Section Officer Oliver.

With my father as ADC.

Shaking hands with Stalin at Tehran, 1943, observed by Molotov (*partly hidden*) and Roosevelt (*centre*), Harriman, Eisenhower, Andrew Kerr, my father and Anthony Eden.

LEFT Mrs Manningham in *Gaslight* with John Sykes in 1945.

Mario Soldati working with his heroine in the film *Daniele Cortis*.

Cutting the cake with Anthony at Sea Island, Georgia.

Classic studio publicity shot: the new starlet's first day on the MGM lot.

A celebration dinner in New York: Diana, Anthony and me.

LEFT A fact *is* better than a dream: rehearsing for the film *Wedding Bells*.

RIGHT Comparing notes with Fred Astaire.

A special backstage visitor: President Truman.

To Miss Sarah Churchill with kindest regards, and appreciation of a lovely and most talented actress. Harry Truman

occasion, we were staying at Westminster Gardens in London when a bomb fell on Eythrop, and we were at Eythrop when a disobliging bomb fell on Westminster Gardens. We were frequently visited at this time by an American journalist, Paul Manning. Although America had not yet joined the war they were more than half-way with us and Paul had come over to write a piece on how the British were standing up to the blitz. One night, he was with us when we were working at Golders Green Hippodrome. This was a theatre Vic had often played in the pre-war years and where, if he did not get an expected laugh, since the Hippodrome adjoined the Crematorium, he would say with a charming smile, 'Perhaps I have come to the wrong building.' On this particular night, we were folding up for our headlight-hooded journey home after the show and saying goodnight to the rest of the cast when the theatre shook and there was an explosion. Immediately, it seemed, the street was filled with air-raid wardens. They told us that the famous Jack Straw's Castle pub at the top of Hampstead Heath had been hit, but that there was no serious damage and no casualties and that anyone driving home across the Heath was safe to go. I was glad that Paul Manning was with us then. He followed our fortunes and luckily he never had to witness any serious misfortune. I am much in favour of war journalists. This may be a matter of heredity, or it may be that other types of journalist have occasionally given me a hard time. I am proud to have been the daughter of a war journalist and later the wife of a wartime photographer.

The touring show *Words and Music* tried to combine Vic's and my talents. In it, I did the balcony scene from *Romeo and Juliet* with Robert Sansome. I came on right after Vic's act. I used to stand in the wings and listen to the thunderous applause for him and wonder if anyone would ever listen to me. But they did – and when we played Streatham I got the kind of notices you would write yourself. C.B. Cochran, who had been following my footsteps the whole way, rang me in great excitement. It looked, he said, as though I was ready to advance and he thought he could do something for me. He wanted to do a full-scale production of *Romeo and Juliet* with me as Juliet. His and my elation were premature – horror of horrors, the Sunday papers burst the idyll with a blistering, scathing notice from James Agate in which, among other things, he said that my voice was like a croak, impaired by too many cigarettes smoked in darkened nightclubs. I didn't smoke then, and now only puff at one nervously. I can't remember Vic ever taking me to a nightclub. But this was too feeble an excuse, and I remember thinking as I climbed the stairs to Cochran's office to keep our appointment, that James Agate had blighted my hopes. I was right.

'I'm sorry, Sarah, but I just couldn't afford to put you in a show after that.'

I said nothing. I just longed for the interview to end quickly, because I could see that he was hurt and disappointed for me. There was nothing to do but accept his judgement and press on. However, that's the theatre for you. I was later to appear in his radio programme *Cock-a-doodle-doo* where I did do the balcony scene and with none other than Leslie Howard. The review after that was rather more encouraging: 'Have we a new voice for the radio?'

Later in 1941, I joined ENSA. Diana was already involved in war work as an air-raid warden – an unlikely sight in those days in trousers and high-heeled shoes. I was disappointed that ENSA did not feel as I did about what the troops wanted – I had played *Gaslight* in Portsmouth with the fleet in and felt sure the soldiers would like it. But I became increasingly aware that in the early stages of the war it was the music-hall talent and guts that were more successful and of immediate assistance to the war effort.

Of course, by the middle and close of the war, strong dramas had become popular and beautiful classical concerts were the much-needed fodder for the troops because, by then, all England from sixteen to sixty was involved in the gigantic struggle. Foremost among those who gave freely of their services in the classical concerts were two close friends of mine – Moiseiwitsch and Malcolm Sargent. I had crossed their paths in my touring days. Shakespeare too became extremely popular with the troops. At the risk of offending my American cousins I must recall an occasion when, after a performance of a Shakespearian drama, some of them were asked if they had liked it. 'Oh yes,' they replied, 'particularly the quotes.'

What can one say about a break-up? It is as intangible as falling in love. The tugs and ties of a relationship are not easily explained – it must of course lie in the personalities of the two people involved. I had needed to get away from my happy home for it wasn't a question of having one strong parent but, as the world now knows, two great and strong parents. So it was perhaps natural, having been brought up with adults, that I should choose, at twenty-one, a man eighteen years older than myself. Maybe I was looking for a substitute father; indeed, I have sometimes thought that I was trying to marry my father. I had been loved and protected through my early years, but now I felt the need to give up the beloved chrysalis of my early days and find what it was all about and what I was to become. This you cannot do in too protected a surrounding.

Vic cosseted and loved me as the child that he found me; but he was to lose me when I found myself. He had in him a Svengali quality and never learnt that some people must find out for themselves. First, he didn't want me to stay on the stage, but how would I have met him at all if I had not followed that instinct? I can remember no dramatic scenes or bitterness with Vic. My delay in deciding that the answer was for me to go into the Forces was brought about by my severe self-questioning: why did I have to leave this delightful man? But the urge for self-expression was steadily growing in me.

I suppose the fact that Vic had waited to marry me until he was an American citizen, as my father asked me, produced the final climax. As an American citizen, he was ordered to leave England and return to America as the US Government would not take responsibility for the safety of American citizens – indeed, I recall they were told they could lose their citizenship. The late Joseph Kennedy, then the American Ambassador, had pronounced publicly that England would not survive two weeks. My father was of course Prime Minister by then, and as he commanded the affection, respect and endurance of the British people, how could I leave and live in America, even though it figured so largely in my affections as well as my blood, while the house was on fire!

To Vic's eternal credit, when I announced my decision that I would not accompany him to America, he stayed on, waiting and hoping that I might change my mind and working with two other fine Americans, Ben Lyon and Bebe Daniels, who lightened our blackouts with their gutsy radio shows. He stayed, not without a certain danger to himself, for remember, had the Allies lost the war, there is no doubt that the Germans would have dealt abruptly with any Churchill or any of our close friends or relatives. So it was then that I went to my father for perhaps the only time to ask him a favour.

5

Churchills at War

I think the only time I asked my father to exert his influence on my behalf was, ironically, to get me *out* of the theatre. I informed him that my marriage had now reached breaking point. He, like the rest of my family, had become rather fond of Vic and was flabbergasted at the news, because once again I had kept my own counsel and no one was really aware of things having gone so wrong. My mother was dismayed, as she too had become fond of him and Mary wept – she after all had been part of the beginning.

My father said, 'I hope he is going to be a gentleman and give you a divorce.'

'Of course not,' I said, 'I am leaving him.'

'You cheeky bitch – I wouldn't let you leave me!'

I told my father firmly that I didn't want his advice, but that I did want a favour from him. I had decided to join the Services and asked him to arrange it as soon as possible. I was in the WAAF within forty-eight hours.

To all appearances I remained with Vic throughout the war years, and went to his shows when my leaves coincided with them. In fact, the war years were to guard our lengthy separation. Neither of us blamed the other and, when the divorce came, it slipped through with no publicity. Vic, who had to go to court, came out with a gallant and gentle sentence: 'We were very happy at first, but then a rift appeared in the lute.'

In October 1941 I became an Aircraftswoman Second Class. My choice of the WAAF was influenced by the colour of the uniform. I was enrolled and despatched on a long train journey to Morecambe for the inevitable 'square bashing' and wrote plaintively to my mother about the first few days, largely concerned, as always, with my appearance. The shoes were a particular horror – not a pair fitted, all were hideous and you simply could not do anything but 'clump' in them. We left for Morecambe at four o'clock in the morning to catch an eight o'clock train. We had to carry full equipment, including gas cape and gas mask strapped on one's back – full-sized kitbag on one's shoulder, smothered in an enormous topcoat and clutching a suitcase with civilian clothes in the other hand. I never imagined an eight-hour train journey could be a rest cure! It was a wonderful system though, watching a straggly bunch of nervous civilians change in about forty-eight hours into fairly passable looking WAAFs. Another forty-eight hours saw a change in deportment and manner, and one would march away with a look of pity towards the next bunch of sad-looking individuals being herded in the entrance gate.

I quickly became involved in my new life and the worries of the last year began to recede in gentle proportion. But I wrote to my mother: 'I am unhappy about it all and yet greatly relieved in a way – it is rather as if I am slowly and painfully beginning to breathe again – and the great thing about *this* life is that there's no time to give way or brood! I've 59 pieces of equipment to remember!'

Having thus far got away from my old life, it was perhaps inevitable that I should be asked to give a reading at a recruiting concert perform-ance, and so I rendered Rupert Brooke's 'If I should die ...' It was, I suppose, another military way of identifying and using talents.

I was first enrolled as 'Clerk Special Duties', a rather unspecific title, until it was decided into which branch I should go. At the interview at Morecambe, the authorities wanted me to go into Administration. I think it was because they were short-staffed and because Clerk SD and Photo-graphic Interpretation, which interested me, did not lend itself to quick promotion. There were officers in that branch, but apparently only a few. I explained that I was in no hurry to become an officer – on the contrary, that a job I could specialize in would interest me more than office work and organization – so I remained Clerk SD but felt that the powers that be were not quite happy about it. I was interviewed again in the camp at Morecambe and I tried to find out more. I thought administrative work might be interesting if it were abroad – I understood they were beginning to send WAAFs to the Middle East, which I would have loved. I found the most exciting part was all the etiquette and discipline being the same as for the men – I must say one felt ridiculously proud of one's uniform, and all it stood for.

I wasn't under pressure only from the WAAF to aim for the quick promotion that they seemed to think my family connections warranted: my mother wrote to me at this time to say that my father had discussed me with Air Marshal Sholto Douglas, who said he would like me in Fighter Command, working on plotting, which was pushing models of invading and home aircraft about in the Operations Room and which was an important, if not especially exciting job. I think her own concern was that it would mean my being stationed half-way between Chequers and London. But I had decided on Photographic Interpretation, and went on a course with a mixed collection of trainees from all the services – Canadians, Americans and British – and of all ages. The course was held at a country house, Nuneham Park at Nuneham Courtenay in Oxfordshire. We were on only the second course held there and I wrote home:

They are still sealing up the tapestries and the panelling. We sleep about eight in a room and have one *batman* to look after us! He is terribly sweet and very proud of his girls! – lights our fire for us, brings us hot water, etc. The bathing situation looks gloomy – only one a week.

I was promoted to Assistant Section Officer, then to Section Officer, and found myself with the Photographic Interpretation Unit at Medmenham where I was to serve for the rest of the war. The work was basically in three phases. The first phase took place at the fighter station: survey pilots would return from their flights at about four in the afternoon – in winter, just before dark – and their photographs would be developed immediately while the pilot was debriefed by the first phase officer. From the pilot's estimation, and the actual photographs, the position of the pictures would be plotted and initial information put into a report. By eight o'clock in the evening, when we started our shift, the photographs and plotted positions would have to be at Medmenham for the second phase on which I worked. Within twelve hours – we worked until eight in the morning – the photographs had to be interpreted and a fuller report made, which was then rushed to the Air Ministry. Each area was allocated to a specific interpreter – one of mine was Kiel Harbour, from the photographs of which I had to plot the movement of shipping, estimating, for instance, when they were shifting smaller craft to make room for a battleship or destroyer. I still have the scraps of paper on which I wrote the measurements of the enemies' ships, their number of gun turrets and other features – the only means of identifying each ship from the air.

The third phase of the operation involved the regular collation of information about various suspected sites of activity – for instance, when it became known that, on the Atlantic coast of France, the Germans were constructing underground submarine pens, a close, systematic watch was kept on their progress. So there was always a large library of background resources. When the Americans first saw our work, they thought that this background was unnecessary, until it was explained to them that a doctor can hardly know what is abnormal in a patient if he does not know what is normal.

Where I worked, in the second phase, there was a great feeling of urgency. The need for accurate information to be fed to the Air Ministry and thence to the bomber squadrons as swiftly as possible meant that we worked under considerable pressure. When the doodlebug raids began, along with many others, I spent much time trying to identify their launching sites, by spotting what we called track activity. As soon as a site was identified, Allied bombers would attack it, though within forty-eight hours another would spring up. In this race against time we worked on the simple assumption that where there are people, there are going to be latrines – and the sight of that little oblong, where there wasn't one before, was often the definite indication of another site. It was concentrated and fascinating work. Our eyesight was under constant scrutiny with two-monthly check-ups. On nights, we worked twelve hours on and thirty-six off, so that we would be fresh for each shift, though day shifts were worked to more normal hours.

Puzzling and tedious as it often was, there were moments of terrific excitement and discovery. One American interpreter had been watching a particular mountain in his regular checks on an area. Suddenly he noticed a change: it appeared that the top of the mountain had been shaved off. At the mountain's base a railway line disappeared into it. There was no apparent reason for this, but we were never allowed to 'assume' anything. He had been allocated this area so he must survey it constantly. I was in the room one day when, after weeks of unrewarding scrutiny, there was a shout of delight – there was a photograph of a plane being winched up the side of his mountain! The Germans had built an underground factory. Aeroplanes were winched to the top of the mountain, then the 'shaved' mountain-top was used as a runway.

The most exciting job I had was working on the preparations for Operation Torch, which was the invasion of North Africa. There were only six of us in the room. Villiers David was in charge of this small company, sent to keep us in order and generally collate all the material – not that with such distinguished company there was much need for disciplinary supervision. There was Murray Thripland and Dorothy Garrard, both leading academic archaeologists, Glyn Daniels, another archaeologist who was our contact with ground intelligence through Villiers; and, to show the variety of talent assembled, the fifth member of the group was Robin Orr, composer and organist to St John's College, Cambridge, and I can't think how I ever got into such erudite company. I was suitably awed and impressed, having never passed an examination in my life apart from lower certificate.

Quite unconsciously, however, I made a strong impression on my colleagues. In the basement of the house were the workrooms of the modelmakers. These of course were secret and we were only allowed to see them well after an operation was concluded. But I made a friend of one of the modelmakers, David Strachan, and when faced with the complexities of setting a slide rule, I would tiptoe downstairs and get him to do it for me. In fact, I got two slide rules, so that I wouldn't have to change the setting if the photographic sorties used cameras with different focal lengths. David would set them both, once I knew the areas I was working on, and I would carry them gingerly upstairs. After two or three weeks of Operation Torch, we had all relaxed in each other's company and conversation flowed.

I think it was Murray Thripland who said one day, 'Sarah – you've got us all bewildered. Why do you have two slide rules?'

Like a fool I told them the truth.

Villiers David was delightful – as they all were – but Villiers was our own private 'don' and used to keep us amused when we began to tire. He wrote a small book for us called *Advice to My Godchildren*, which is absolutely hilarious, though now unfortunately I no longer have a copy. To this day I remember the opening phrase: 'Always eat your rice with a spoon.' And the last one: 'You must be a snob in life and appreciate all its variety and brilliance. Try to be famous, because that will ensure you the best cook, and the best table and service in the best restaurants.' With these aphorisms he used to regale us in our breaks to keep his 'godchildren' alert and amused. Dorothy Garrard did her share of enlightening us, mostly by tripping over when we were walking in the garden, once falling at Villiers' feet. Gallantly helping her up, he said, 'Dorothy, I do not approve of women falling at my feet.' But I rather think he did!

It would not be possible to speak of all the inhabitants of Medmenham – or the 'Mad Men of Ham' as we were known locally – without mentioning our commanding officer, Wing Commander Douglas Kendall. He was brilliant, a wonderful co-ordinator with the Americans, kind, slightly shy, but he held his medley of personalities together. Many fascinating people passed through the station from all the services and all our allies. The most colourful and probably one of the most beloved characters was Charlotte Bonham-Carter (Lady) (Section Officer). As her name implies, much privilege and indeed ease could have been afforded her, but she chose to join the ranks at the age of sixty-two. Living in a world of her own, she had an acute social, political and historical sense, which was of great value. Her eye may have been acute, but she herself remained a confusion. She conformed, yet did not conform. She wore the uniform in her own particular style: from beneath the WAAF cap flowed grey strands of hair which would obey no one. She went on parade with a string bag containing her luncheon as she preferred to eat her own food, which was vegetarian, rather than the sludge food of the cookhouse. This was not an act of snobbery and she became, certainly for me and I think for most of the station, an example of obedience tempered by individuality. She would hitchhike her way to London when duty called, trailing the clouds of her grey tresses. As she was standing at the gate, waiting for some suitable jeep, the corporal on duty would ask her where she wanted to get to. In a bell-like voice she would say, 'To the Air Ministry, please, young man.'

Once, one of my great friends, the concert pianist Moiseiwitsch, agreed to give us a concert. We were concerned that the thumped-out canteen piano would not be a suitable offering to the maestro. Since I had engineered his appearance through my mother, who was the head of the Red Cross Aid to Russia Fund and for whom he gave a weekly fund-raising concert, I went anxiously to Charlotte for advice. 'Don't worry, I have a lovely grand piano stored away, and if suitable transportation can be found I will see that it is disgorged from its wartime imprisonment.' Anticipating my next question she said: 'There will be no trouble in tuning it – Robin Orr will assist, I am sure.' So it was all arranged and the great day came. All who could leave their duties were massed together and the leonine-headed Moiseiwitsch appeared on time. Benign, suave, enchanting, he greeted everybody graciously and expressed with upraised hands his amazement at the beautiful piano. I puffed with pride. They say it comes before a fall – in this case it came before a string. After a few crashing chords of, as I recall, Beethoven, a string chose to leave the piano and wave like a daddy-long-legs in the air. Moiseiwitsch did his best, but once you have one note out of order it is impossible to avoid

63

it. He struggled valiantly with this difficulty, but whatever he tried, going rapidly to the softer tunes of Schumann, the tentacle of that note would appear, beautifully illuminated by the harsh lights of the hut in which he was performing. I didn't know whether to go AWOL and disappear into the shades of the wood, or to stick it out miserably. Moiseiwitsch went red in the face at first and then became statuesquely calm. The concert ended, we naturally all applauded, he stood up and bowed and Charlotte swept onto the scene.

'Thank you, Mr Moiseiwitsch, for *ruining* my piano.'

The tension broke and he said the Russian equivalent of *C'est la guerre.*

Another time, I persuaded Malcolm Sargent to come down. We were not so ambitious about a piano this time, but he turned out surprisingly to be an excellent pianist – at least, surprisingly to me, for in my ignorance I had thought that conductors just waved wands. At the end of the performance, we gathered round the stovepipe fire and had a pleasantly relaxed conversation. Malcolm told a well-known musical anecdote, briefly and succinctly. Charlotte, not to be outdone, told exactly the same story with different emphasis and at greater length.

Malcolm said with much charm, 'Charlotte, I have just told that story.'

Charlotte turned to him with a beaming smile. 'Oh, in that case I now have *two* musical stories!'

The conditions at Medmenham were, to say the least, strange. Medmenham was really a small village. We worked in a large, white house that belonged to a Mr Weston who made biscuits, though he had tactfully vacated it for the duration. It used to occur to me to wonder how such a secret station could be so blatantly visible, but I suppose security was good enough because nary a bomb was dropped on it or anywhere near the grounds. Nobody actually 'lived' in the house – it was all given over to workshops which were manned twenty-four hours a day. The personnel were in huts under the beech trees in the grounds. They were damp in winter – I found rust marks from my suspenders imprinted on various items of underwear – and in summer the huts were full of wood spiders with long wobbly legs. I used to capture them in my toothglass, slide an envelope beneath it and eject them. Other visitors were the mice, who would appear at regular intervals when we were on duty in the big house. Scrambling down the chimney they came for crumbs from the sandwiches which we had in preference to the cookhouse food. Even on duty we would know it was time for the midnight tea break by the scrabbling of little feet. But on the whole, the accommodation was comfortable – wood was brought for us to make our own fires in the huts and the bathhouse was supplied with lots of boiling water.

At first one would share a hut with only one other and here I was to meet a sweet Irish girl called Jan Magee. It was the start of a friendship which endures to this day. After being shown round the place and taught to familiarize myself with the library of information, maps and useful things like dictionaries, I went through a brief period of plotting and it was to Jan that I went when I could make neither head nor tail of what piece of terrain I was meant to be looking at. We had trained at different stations and she was already at Medmenham when I arrived. Though she had never travelled, she had an acute instinct and a mind that once it had learned a certain terrain never forgot it.

When the Americans, commanded by Eliot Roosevelt, the President's son, arrived in force at the station eight miles away, I met several of their officers, principally Harvey Brown, who came to help with the co-ordination of the two stations, William O'Connor from Washington, and Pleasant O'Neill from Texas. Harvey, O'Neill, Jan Magee and I would go about together as often as possible. We had hilarious leaves when we would congregate at my tiny flat at 55 Park Lane. The ever-generous Americans would raid their PX, equivalent to our much less luxurious NAAFI, for the parties. In my experience, my American friends were un-failingly generous during the war. Of course, in wartime, true soldiers always share what little they have. But in war, or peace, there has been for me something special about Americans: and I don't believe it is just because I am part American myself. There were many happy occasions at 55 Park Lane – often only forty-eight-hour leaves snatched in between long spells of duty, and often to the accompaniment of the thunder of z-guns from Hyde Park. When my friends discovered that my sister Mary was on duty at the Hyde Park battery, they would pretend amazement that I couldn't keep the guns quieter.

Chequers was near enough for me to go over on my leaves. Sometimes, I would go on a borrowed army motorcycle – so heavy that I had to have a hand to get me started. Goodness knows what would have happened if I'd ever fallen off. Luckily, there were regular van deliveries between the three stations in the area and I could hitchhike most of the way to Chequers. On arrival, I would normally go straight up to see my father as, being in uniform, I did not have to dress for dinner. On one special occasion he was in his bath, floating full length with an enormous sponge strategically placed.

'Come in, come in. What have you been up to?'

'Just the usual routine.'

'Ah.'

He yelled for Sawyers, his valet, who wrapped him in an enormous Turkish towel. I waited discreetly while drying and dressing occurred. Then came the final touch, combing his hair and then brushing it with two ivory hair brushes. He used to part the two or three remaining hairs across the dome of his head with meticulous care, splash on some cologne and then we would go down to dinner.

On this particular evening, while this elaborate hair-dressing procedure was taking place, he said, 'At this very moment, sliding stealthily through the Straits of Gibraltar under cover of darkness, go 542 ships, for the landings in North Africa.'

I couldn't resist it. I said, '543.'

'How do you know?'

'I've been working on it for three months.'

'Why didn't you tell me?'

'I believe there is such a thing as security.'

He looked at me with what I feared would be a blaze of anger at my impudence. Instead, he chuckled, and we went down to dinner where he told the story delightedly. Later, when Mrs Roosevelt came over to England to see how women were faring in the services, my father proudly repeated the story to her. Mrs Roosevelt, a remarkable woman of whom I became very fond, returned to America to give her account of English women's work in the war machine and she recounted this story to illustrate the importance of security, even between father and daughter. It went down very well, I am told, but not for me. I was summoned to the Air Ministry for a carpeting for breach of security!

'Who told Mrs Roosevelt this story?' I was asked.

'My father.'

'Winston! Really. Oliver – dismissed!'

It had been decided by my parents that one of us should accompany my father when he went abroad to act as a sort of family ADC. Mary and I delightedly alternated this pleasant duty. She went with him to Quebec and Potsdam, and my first great wartime adventure was when I accompanied my father to Tehran. There were great highlights on the trip.

First, the Straits of Gibraltar seen from the bridge of HMS *Renown* in the failing light of late afternoon, and Gibraltar herself emerging from a falling twilight mist with a necklace of lights. From an England blacked out since 1939, this was an incredible sight. I had never been on a fighting ship and the *Renown* never looked more magnificent. I went up on the deck and felt completely alone – but as my eyes grew accustomed, I found that I was far from alone. A and B turrets and then the bridge rose in grand echelon to the stars, and the silhouettes of men arming the guns became suddenly apparent. Port, starboard, for'ard and aft the black shapes of our escorts glided. The HMS *London* at our stern seemed so close you felt you could pat her nose. I thought of their wives and sweethearts, who had not the privilege of accompanying their men to war.

We had been supposed to fly from Gibraltar, but the weather was not good, so we went on to Algiers, where the women – code and cipher officers and myself – all in uniform were battened down, because women in uniform were not allowed to be seen in this area. Incidentally, Harold Macmillan, who was the Minister Resident in Algeria, had a conference with my father between Gibraltar and Algiers. We finally arrived in Malta on the evening of 17 November 1943.

The palace on Malta, where we all stayed, was a lovely place. The gardens were magical – five of them, all walled – lovely paved courtyards, wonderful flowers and fine red earth. There we had to wait until we were joined by the United States delegation. My father didn't mind the wait, as he had not been well on the journey and had many things to think about. On one of these days, he paid a visit to the naval dockyards. The people were warm and quite thrilled to see him; he was completely mobbed. Many of the Maltese police forgot that they were supposed to be there to protect him and simply joined the crowd, following him everywhere.

I was taken on a flight in a Mosquito, then perhaps the best and fastest aircraft of the RAF. I remember we flew around the whole of Sicily, over all the bits I knew so well from sitting at a desk at Medmenham gazing at photographs. It was an unbelievably exciting experience. I knew it so well, I didn't need a map. The only unfamiliar aspect, of course, was the colour – I only knew it in black and white, and it was all lovely pink earth. We flew around the slopes of Etna, which was capped by snow and cloud, and then back to base, chasing a Walt Disney sun that refused to set. I confess that the flight made me feel a little sick. As we twirled about

Etna, dropping and climbing some hundreds of feet, my ears hurt and that awful feeling in the joint of one's jaw, as if everything was turning to water, overcame me. I had to use an immense effort of will and concentration not to shame myself or my uniform. We had a bevy – or perhaps a 'sting' – of Mosquitoes. They only held one passenger, normally the navigator. The passengers were the United States Ambassador to England, John Winant, Air Marshal Portal in another, the AOC of Malta, Air Vice-Marshal Park, in another and me in mine.

One of the highlights of these journeys with my father was the constant change of plan – orders, counter-orders and disorders. The US President, for example, didn't want to go to Cairo at all after an appalling security report was passed to him. This, of course, created a great flurry, but due to the considerable numbers attending the conference, it was virtually impossible to find alternative accommodation at short notice. Amidst all this, my father remained serene. He had had to have an injection which knocked him out rather, and then he caught a cold. But at intervals he enjoyed himself and played a lot of Bezique with Randolph.

First stop Cairo, before the conference began at Tehran, and I wrote to my mother:

Well here we are at last! It is perfect weather – though WAAF uniform is a bit trying! How lovely it is to wake each morning to this light gay sunshine. Everything is too beautifully arranged and we live in palatial splendour and luxury. I don't know that I think Hollywood sets are always exaggerated anymore. The villas I have been to so far surpass anything I have seen – except on the films! Then suddenly in the midst of this oriental-cum-Hollywood fantasy, you find yourself in a room that reminds one of a dentist's waiting room in Wimpole Street! Now some order to this letter: –

We arrived 3 o'clock Sunday afternoon, having flown from Alexandria – only a short trip of 40 mins. We went straight to our respective villas – and the ADCs were summoned by the captain in charge of us. We sat obediently in a circle while he told us in words of one syllable how to work the lavatories and telephones, etc. I must say straight away his arrangements were flawless. The security of course is so terrific that it is laughable – no matter where you turn, you come across a palsy of plain clothes detectives – Marines – Egyptian police – good old Cockney soldiers and carpet-slippered Abduls. I spend my time trying not to be overheard by lurking sentries beneath the windows or to overhear little clusters of VIPs dotted in every room....

Off we went to visit Monsieur et Madame Chiang. This was rather thrilling – having again draped ourselves in an ante-chamber, making spirited conversation with the Chinese ADCs, I was sent for and we sat in a circle with two interpreters and had about 15 mins. conversation – Papa with Chiang and me with Madame Chiang. She was looking very ill and tired and is suffering from, among other things, 'pink eye'! Papa was impressed by her – and there is no doubt that she is far and away the best interpreter!

Papa is better and in good spirits now that he is here and can get his teeth into the problems. I am off to Cairo to a hairdresser – most necessary!!

Later, on 23 November 1943:

Today has been very exciting and exhausting. I was yanked from underneath a hair-dryer in Cairo at about 12.30 and told that I had been invited to lunch with the President. Unpinning my damp locks and hot in the face, I leaped into a grand car and was driven off to his villa. There I was greatly relieved to find Papa – who I thought was lunching with General Marshall alone – hence my departure to a hairdresser in Cairo. There was just Harry Hopkins, the President, Papa, myself, Admiral Ley and Tommy and John Martin. I find Harry Hopkins rather difficult to talk to.

After lunch – rather disconcerting American lunch – you know, you help yourself to a quantity of what looks like delicious fruit salad and find it all covered in salad dressing!?! – Papa and I went on a reconnaissance visit to the Sphinx and Pyramids to see how close we could get with a car. Finding we could drive right round them, we went back and got the President and all three of us bumbled along for a second tour. It was a lovely drive and the President was charming – simple and enthusiastic. I think he enjoyed himself – I think he appreciated the trouble Papa took. Papa loved showing them to him. It really is wonderful how they both get on – they really like and understand each other....

Madame Chiang has sent for Lord Moran concerning her pink eye. I suggested Optrex and golden ointment!

There was a surprising amount of waiting during these conferences. In Cairo, I had some time off and promptly went shopping. Francis Stonor took Charles Moran and me to lunch at the Ghezira Sporting Club, which was very British. Afterwards we deposited Lord Moran, minus shoes, in a mosque and went off to the bazaars. It was an experience I was in no hurry to repeat. The squalor and smell and flies were appalling, the goods on display seemed trashy and gaudy, and I wanted to plunge into a bath of disinfectant. Afterwards we visited some of the large department stores, which provided a wonderful comparison, cool and air-conditioned. I lingered at the toilet water counters dabbing experimentally to get rid of the bazaar smell. In the end I bought three face flannels and a hot-water bottle – so much for shopping in the mysterious Middle East.

After the conference proper in Tehran, we returned to Cairo and I, of course, wrote to my mother:

4 December   Cairo

Francis Brown handed me your sweet letter as I set foot on Cairo West air-field after returning from four completely thrilling and highly successful days at Tehran. The journey has been steadily rising in crescendo and excitement and there has been little time to write and now, looking back, it is going to be hard to remember what happened when. But here goes –

The flight was absolutely lovely. I think flying is probably the best way to see this type of country. Miles and miles of sand desert – thorn rock desert – all of which might be alternatively monotonous or forbidding by horse, camel or motor car, but is magnificent when seen as a panorama. Particularly the wilderness just south of Jerusalem (How could they ever have called it the land flowing with milk and honey?) and then, of course, the great range of Persian mountains we had to cross. That was absolutely thrilling – we flew at about 12,000. Mountains came up to meet us – then slipped away again (never of course – to reassure you – very close; 12,000 clears most, and the one or two higher ranges were given a wide berth!). But how brown it all is. They say in spring there are lovely flowers and touches of bright green – but this time of year the only colour for many miles is varying shades of pinky sepia. Occasionally there is a sudden slash of a red or aquamarine seam in the rock formation – like the Gunters layer cake we used to have for our birthdays – but no life, no trees, no green grass, just swirling desolate mountains.

The airfield at Tehran is very impressive, a great stone plain with snow-capped mountains rising straight from the fringes of the plain.

We were met by Mr Bullard, the minister, and driven to the [British] legation. A gloomy evening followed! First the night before the flight, Papa had stayed up too late and talked too long with Anthony Eden with no afternoon sleep, result: laryngitis next morning. The plane is very noisy so more throat strain. Then the security precautions were very idiotic and Papa lost no time in saying so. The climate though sunny was much cooler and the legation all lined with tiles struck chilly – and anyway, 3.30 is a dismal time to arrive! Everything was a bit gloomy. Papa was really very tired and his voice almost completely gone. Uncle Joe [Stalin] was already there and he – Papa – wanted to start right there and then. However, Moran and I went into action, got our heads bitten off; but finally, luckily, no meeting and he had dinner in bed like a sulky little boy and was really very good. He was nervous and apprehensive, I think. After all, this *was* the high jump and it was frightening not to be feeling well and to have practically no voice. Still, they say a bad dress rehearsal = a good performance and after a good night's sleep, he never looked back. The voice grew steadily in volume – and his spirits picked up – and before long, it was evident that all was going well.

On his birthday, he gave a wonderful party. I enclose the dinner list. It is difficult to tell you, but of course it was the high spot; not only because of all the 'great' that were gathered, but because of why they were gathered, and most of all because of how they really get along. Uncle Joe is a great man – of that there can be no doubt – he also has a great sense of humour as darting and as swift as Papa's. I think perhaps he made the remark of the evening. When Papa during one of the many toasts remarked: 'England is getting pinker,' Joe interjected: 'It is a sign of good health.' There was a great roar of laughter, the kind of laughter that is only heard among friends. Whatever follows, one couldn't help but feel that a genuine desire for friendship was sown that night. Nothing of course flourishes without care – constant care – but in the unreserved laughter that constantly filled the room, one felt that there was a real urge to make things go, now and in the future. I also knew that it was Papa who made all this possible. His buoyant vitality and directness compels and infuses all these meetings with this feeling – meetings that otherwise, for all the different and true greatness of the other two, would be just 'talks'.

You know, I have noticed a curiously touching thing about the President when he is with Papa. He forgets he cannot walk. Once after some lunch, Papa sprang from the table to go and arrange something (I think it was the tour of the Pyramids) and the President very nearly got up too – he leant forward on the arms of his chair, just like a man about to rise quickly. It's this feeling that Papa gives to everyone – this quality which he takes with him everywhere.

But now to the dinner: almost one of the first toasts that was drunk was mine! This was proposed by the President. It was terribly sweetly done. I was particularly touched because he couldn't see me – but he has twice remembered me when I wasn't around – which I think is wonderful. Stalin got up and came round and touched glasses with me; and I went to the President and thanked him, and he said: 'I'd come to you my dear but I can't.' I love him. Well then the evening went on and there was never a moment when someone didn't spring up. I terribly wanted to get up and propose Papa's health. Everyone toasted him as a great man and a Prime Minister; I wanted to tell them he was a nice father too – and more. But the old restraint kept me rooted and a new restraint kept Randolph seated too – and I couldn't help thinking how a few years ago he would never have been off his feet! He is trying you know – there is a big change in him....

The other great wartime adventure with my father came when I accompanied him to the Yalta Conference in February 1945. I turn once again to my letters to my mother. The narrative wanders here and there, as I believe it does in most people's letters, but this is how she learnt the story. The only additions I have made are to explain more fully now who the people I refer to are.

31 January 1945   Malta

What a rush, needless to say I have forgotten hundreds of little things – in fact everything but my precious shirts and collars washed in the dead o'night with loving care! We had a miserable trip. The plane was perfect – a wonder of comfort – silent as a ghost, and leapt off the ground like a gazelle; but no sooner were we on board all puffing and blowing and out of breath, than worry set in. We had a delicious dinner, but as usual, at first the plane was cold – so everything was turned on and Papa sat huddled in his great coat. Then it began to get hot and in a minute we were all as pink as tomatoes screaming for air. More re-adjustments; but Papa looked like a poor hot pink baby about to cry! He took his temperature – and it was up and, 'Oh Lord!', I thought, 'there we go again'. It was about one o'clock before we settled in for the night but nobody slept much, if at all.

We landed at 4.30. Tommy [Thompson] tumbled out of his bunk where he had been lying half dressed and tottered forth bleary-eyed to check with the airfield station master that we had cancelled the reception. Had? Well, to his horror, everything but massed bands greeted him. The tarmac was literally laced with gold braid: something had obviously gone wrong, and some very angry scrambled eggs rumbled off back to their beds! I found it even harder to sleep in the silence of our grounded aircraft, where every rustle and sigh could be heard, so I dressed – a feat unparalleled in the history of contortionists – in my bunk, doubled up. Somehow the long hours crept by. I pulled back the black-out from my window and saw the sun rise over the hangars of the airfield. The pale blue rarefied sky grew warmer and the grass was emerald green and there was no snow.

His temperature went up to 102 in the night; it was a 100 still in the morning. What to do – he was miserable and convinced he was in for something. Sawyers – he is a miracle of devotion – muttered to me: 'He's always like this after Lord Moran's pills!' I meditated on this profound statement and passed it on to Papa, who grunted and said 'True!' So I followed up with: 'I'm sure it will soon go – it is a pretty powerful drug, and when we get out of this hot plane I'm sure you'll feel better.' It was touch and go between the ship and the hospital for a few hours. The hospital was laid on – the ship was cancelled – the hospital was cancelled, and the ship laid on. We said we would be ready in two hours, and were ready in half an hour. I don't know who met us – I didn't dare look. Though much warmer than England there was a brisk wind. The ship was cold – and the bed round the wrong way; nevertheless, he was very good – but sat in a dejected lump while Sawyers redesigned the ship. My heart sank lower and lower: bed, hot water bottles, and before he could tell Tommy that he would see Alexander, Marshall and the CIGS at lunch time he was asleep. 'Sleep that knits up the ravelled sleeve of care – the balm of this life's woe!'

The 'Entourage' collapsed into baths and shaving bowls – and emerged feeling much better at lunch. We lunched without Papa who slept on like a lamb. Finally, old Charles [Moran] decided to wake him. Miracle of miracles: the temperature was down, the sun shone. It was still down in the evening. The Governor [of Malta], CIGS [Field-Marshal Sir Alan Brooke], Alexander [Field-Marshal Sir Harold Alexander] and Anthony [Eden] arrived in quick succession – and Anthony and Alexander Cadogan [of the Foreign Office] and Averell [Harriman] came back for dinner. He was in wonderful spirits and I really think all is well. Isn't it wonderful. At 12 o'clock the well trained guests left – and 12.30 found me unconscious in my bunk!

The Governor's wife and daughter are calling any minute now – Spitfires are beating us up at 11.30 – and General Marshall arrives at 12 o'clock. I must away and breathe on my buttons....

4 February 1945   Yalta

Today it is difficult to know where to begin – so much has happened these last two days. The President arrived at about 10.30 and steamed in his cruiser (USS Quincy) – a great ship about the size of a battleship – past our more modest cruiser. It was a lovely sight. Everybody turned out on deck, and the Maltese thronged the roof-tops. 'God Save the King' and 'Oh say, can't you see' were played, and we were so close you could even with my moderate eyesight, recognize familiar faces. The person who seemed to know most people on the President's ship was Sawyers who bowed gracefully in acknowledgement continually. Very soon afterwards a formal call was made and I met Anna [Boettiger – Roosevelt's daughter]. I thought at once how amazingly like her Mother she was although of course so much better looking – and immediately after that thought – I suppose strangers think Diana and I to be like you, only not so good looking! She is very easy and I like her, but I think she is quite nervous about being on the trip. I like the American military men – Navy, Air Force and Army – they seem very superior creatures!

We had a wonderful flight, starting at 3.30 a.m. and arriving (at Saki) 10.30 February 3rd – which was really 12.30 as we were flying towards the sun. Everyone is very grieved about the occupants of one of our Yorks that crash-landed off Lampedusa – 13 out of 19 lost, including 3 brilliant young men all specially briefed for the Conference.

Papa was met by Molotov and Vyshinsky and there was a miniature parade and revue, and then we clambered into our cars for the 6 hour drive.

Darling – really! Averell must be mad to make his poor President endure that endless and very boring drive. It was not as bad as painted, but tedious. One had to travel so slowly because for the first two hours the roads were so bad, and it wasted a whole day – and will waste another precious one on the way back!

I drove with Papa which was lovely, but we had a sticky start – 20 miles an hour over bumpy slushy road, through a countryside as bleak as the soul in despair! After what seemed an eternity Papa asked how long we had been going and I replied: 'about an hour'. 'Christ,' said Papa, 'five more of this' – and gloom and muttered bad language set in! After 2½ hours we reached the mountains and the countryside improved. Oh, I have to tell you – the whole 100 miles of the road was lined every 200 yards with Red Army men and girls, who sprang to proud salutes. They were magnificent looking, and this display went on long after darkness had fallen. On, on through bleak country peopled by a few grim-faced peasants. We passed the President's convoy – they stopped for some coffee and sandwiches – we persevered because we had heard about a rest house ahead – most necessary for more reasons than resting. On, on, bearing all with fortitude, patience and a bottle of very good brandy! Still no rest house, so we stopped and ate a very stale ham sandwich and drank a little soup plus a swig of brandy! And then off again. The call of nature was pretty desperate by now! I scanned the horizon: cars in front – press photographers behind!! Obviously no future in that! At last when hope had nearly died, the convoy stopped. We were at the rest house. Papa and I clambered out for what we thought would be a short pause. We were led into a small room – groaning with food and wine – and a smiling Molotov. From there on we never looked back and the frozen countryside melted and became quietly friendly. I even noticed that there were a few Cypress trees and that the Black Sea was quite blue. The Americans would not stop – they decided to hurry on. The Russians looked very disappointed, until Papa and I fell on the food! We had the most lovely lunch – just Molotov and Vyshinsky and Gusov and Papa and me and little Pavlov the interpreter, who is sweet. Oh, how we regretted our stale ham sandwich – it just took the edge off our appetites! Everything was friendly and informal – what charm they have, the Russians, when they smile. After about 1½ hours, we took to the road again. We still had another two hours to go, but these were enjoyable. Papa recited practically all 'Don Juan' and had about 30 minutes sleep – darkness fell, but our headlamps picked out our sentinels still lining the road. At long, long last at about a quarter to eight, we arrived.

Though the ablutions question is grim, it is warm and light, and Russian hospitality leaves little to be desired. Papa is very sweet and insists on me sharing his bathroom which I do – but if you were a spectator along the bedroom corridors here at about 7.30 in the morning, you would see 3 Field Marshals queueing for a bucket! And really some Field Marshals will not go into a bucket!...

74

6 February 1945   Yalta

Nearly 3 days have passed and I have not been able to write you a letter. I don't believe I have told you what this place looks like. It is quite fantastic! Not the Csar's palace, but some very great noble's 'little grey home in the West'. It looks a bit like a Scottish baronial hall inside and a Swiss Chalet plus Mosque outside! It was apparently a museum before the war, and as the Germans used it as their headquarters, was less knocked about than the other villas in the neighbourhood, which all show signs of looting. Everything, including furniture, had to be brought from Moscow to make the American villa habitable – including charming housemaids from Moscow hotels! The difficulties are enormous – but as usual they have all been overcome. . . .

As we stood on the terrace overlooking the sea – CIGS Alexander, Somervill, Portal, etc. – we saw an amazing sight. A great shoal of fishes were being attacked by air and sea. From the sea by a school of porpoises, from the air by hundreds of gulls – the poor silly fish just huddled together closer and the mass slaughter went on for nearly 3 hours.

I said to CIGS that they were surely idiotic not to disperse; but he said not at all, it is much better they should stick together. But Papa agreed with me, and said he felt that the CIGS's usual cool dispassionate judgement was, on this occasion, badly prejudiced, because of his weakness for birds! On my way to wash my hands for lunch I found Peter Portal feeding the goldfish in the conservatory with bluebottles he had caught in the library!

Today I motored with Kathleen [Harriman] and Anna [Boettiger] to Sebastopol. It was a 2½ hour drive over the same grand but gloomy country. The road is really very tortuous and in bad weather would be quickly impassable. Sebastopol is a terrible sight. I didn't see one house that had not been shattered – yet still the people live there. Strangely they did not look too poverty stricken or hungry. Our guide was a Russian sailor who showed us round the town as though there were no ruins at all! 'This' – he said with pride, 'is a very beautiful Church.' We looked at a scarred shell and nodded. 'Oh yes,' he said, 'Sebastopol is a beautiful city.' He took us to vanished monument after monument. 'This is the Sports Club – this square is lovely in Summer.' We gazed dumbfounded at a devastated area – a square wilderness of broken trees and shell holes. As we said goodbye, he said: 'You like Sebastopol?' For a moment I didn't answer – at once his face fell. 'No? You don't like it?' 'Of course, of course,' I said. 'It's just that it makes me so sad to see it like this.' But somehow it was the wrong thing to have said, he was disappointed. He saw Sebastopol like someone who really loves a person, still sees them, in spite of some terrible physical tragedy, unchanged, unbroken. But now he looked at Sebastopol with our eyes and said slowly: 'We will build it up again – in five years – you see. You will come back to Sebastopol, my

Sebastopol and I will show you round again?' We promised we would come back.

On our way round the town we came on a bedraggled queue of Rumanian prisoners. They were queuing for their lunch – something out of a bucket brought on a cart by a tired thin horse. One has seen similar queues of hopeless stunned humans on the films – but in reality it is too terrible.

Last night just before he went to sleep, Papa said: 'I do not suppose that at any moment in history has the agony of the world been so great or widespread. To-night the sun goes down on more suffering than ever before in the World.' Well I've seen a little of that agony these few days in Russia.

8 February 1945   Yalta

Papa is bearing up very well – despite the strain of getting through so much in really so short a time, and the accompanying patience and toil that a million complexities call for. Physically, however, this conference does not seem as hard as the one last year. They do not meet till 4 in the afternoon, when they have a whacking session of 4 to 5 hours and then they part, returning to their separate lairs. We dine quietly here – generally just Papa and Anthony [Eden] and me – which of course is heaven. The pouch arrives unfortunately at about midnight – which prevents him getting to bed much before two, though I do my best. He has been sleeping well though – without any little pink pills. Morning presents a certain problem as he wakes rather late, and there isn't time for breakfast and lunch and work and a little sleep before the 'do' at 4 – so now he has just orange juice when he is called and 'brunch' at 11.30 – then nothing till 9 o'clock! This seems a very long time, but he really is very sensible and says that what he likes best; so I feel the thing is to try it, and see how it works. . . .

9 February 1945   Villa Vorontzov

Last night there was a banquet at the Russian villa. The 3 'girls' [Anna, Kathy and I] were invited, and you can imagine we did not refuse! It was a lovely party. The 'Bear' as host was in terrific form and it was very friendly and gay, of course I'm prejudiced. Nothing can quite touch the Tehran birthday party – ever.

The girls were toasted, and Kathy surpassed herself by answering in Russian thanking them for all they had done to make everyone so comfortable. They were delighted. I sat next to twinkly-eyed Vyshinsky who had been at the 'picnic' lunch on the drive here. He is very nice and easy – although he can hardly speak a word of English. The food and drink proved too much for us long before half way through – and with a wink we both of us took to 'Narzair Minerale Vode'! and toyed delicately with our sucking pigs!

The head of the OGPU was there! With the aid of Mr Maisky (very friendly)

I recited to him my five Russian sentences – one of which is 'Can I have a hot water bottle please?' To which OGPU replied: 'I cannot believe that you need one! Surely there is enough fire in you!!' It looked as if there was a future to this conversation; but at this point, dinner was served and I went off to try my hot water bottle line on Mr Vyshinsky. It had a very different effect. I must have said it with great conviction. He said with all seriousness and not a little surprise: 'Why? are you ill?' Well, as my Russian lessons end at that point, I had to take to Dumb Crambo to make him see that it was a joke Ha? Ha?

Papa's eyes are sore – and are bothering him quite a bit – Charles [Moran] thinks he should see another eye-man when he gets back. He does not think it's serious but Papa thinks it is something more than just his eyelashes. Poor Papa!

I went for a long walk with Peter Portal yesterday. He is a gay and charming companion – and nearest to a 'buddy' we can gossip with on this trip. We are off to see a waterfall reported to be 1,000 feet high this afternoon. It is also reported to be a mere 7 miles walk – I know that would just be right for *you* – but *I* must go and make some arrangements for a jeep!

12 February 1945   ss *Franconia*

Well – it's over! Yesterday lunchtime saw the conclusion. Everyone in the highest spirits, and affectionate regretful goodbyes were said. Two days ago it looked as if we were here for a lifetime, and I had just settled into a pleasant routine, when suddenly the merry-go-round was off again! It had been decided we should leave the following day – easily, orderly and quietly. But on the way back from the American villa, Papa, having said goodbye to everyone, suddenly felt lonely I think. 'Why do we stay here? Why don't we go tonight – I see no reason to stay here a minute longer – we're off!' He sprang out of the car and whirling into the Private Office announced: 'I don't know about you – but I'm off! I leave in 50 minutes!' After a second's stunned silence, everyone was galvanized into activity. Trunks and large mysterious paper parcels given to us by the Russians – whoopee – filled the hall. Laundry arrived back clean but damp. Naturally 50 minutes gave us time to change our minds six more times. 'We will spend the night here after all and leave tomorrow lunchtime – We will fly – We will leave tonight and go by sea – We will go to Athens – Alexandria – Cairo – Constantinople – We will not go to any of them – We will stay on board and read the newspapers! Where is the pouch? Why hasn't it arrived?' Sawyers, tears in his eyes, surrounded by half-packed suitcases, beat his breast and said: 'They can't do this to me!' He put a sponge-bag in and then took it out. He carefully laid out the Lord Warden of the Cinque Ports suit, then changed it for the Royal Yacht Club suit. Papa, genial and sprightly like a boy out of school, his homework done, walked from room to room saying: 'Come on, come on!' Believe it or not, 1 hour and 20 minutes later, about 5.30, saw a cavalcade of cars groaning with bulging suitcases winding its way to

Sebastopol! And quick though we had been, we were last! The President left an hour before us – but on an orderly plan laid days ago. Stalin, like some genie, just disappeared. Three hours after the last handshake, Yalta was deserted, except for those who always have to tidy up after a party....

After the 1945 General Election my father was out of office. He decided to go to Italy, to Lake Como, for a holiday and I was released from my duties at Medmenham to accompany him as my mother could not go. As usual, I wrote to her.

3 September 1945   Lake Como
I wish you were here with us. I was so distressed to see you so unhappy and tired when we left, and so was he. We never see a lovely sight that he doesn't say: 'I wish your mother were here.' Wow! You know, I expect you will feel a little low and tired and oppressed by the million domesticities that will now sink down upon you, for a bit. Six years is a long time to live at such a high tempo, knowing as fully as you did all the moments of anxiety and worry, and decisions. You are bound to feel a reaction – as he does, and will for some time.

I'm quite anxious in case time lies heavy here. He has said he does not wish to see anybody but Alex [Field Marshal Alexander in whose house we were staying] and Admiral John Cunningham, who are coming in a few days – of course I think that is wonderful! But wonder how long he will really find Charles and me and a youthful ADC company at dinner. For the first time, for a long time, I felt nervous and selfconscious the first night at dinner. We sat at an enormous green glass table, with a cool impersonal yard or two of green glass between us, in an oval pale green room, with 4 white-coated 4th Hussar batmen attending to us. I felt like a goldfish in a bowl. I looked across the green stretch at a slightly perspiring ADC in an agony of nerves, in case something should go wrong, at Charles lost in a coma of philosophical meditation with himself about how many bugs the Italian water he was about to drink contained and whether they would prove fatal or not, and then to Papa looking pink in his white suit, and rather aggressively at some soup. 'Is this hot or cold?' he asked suddenly – 'Oh dear,' I thought. 'Very hot, sir,' replied the white-coated attendant. Papa drank his soup – I felt the next few weeks depended entirely on whether they could make consomme or not. They could! Very good. The tension in the goldfish bowl eased – all was well! As a matter of fact, I think all is very well.

Firstly the ADC [Captain Ozier] is a tremendous success. He is a big husky young man who has been through the entire war, and seen much action. I thought him about 30, but he is only 25 – Dunkirk to the Gothic line via Alamein, has physically matured him – but he is extremely youthful to talk to, intelligent, kind and considerate to Papa. They get on like a house on fire.

78

Charles and I sit back comfortably while the two boys fight the battles from Omdurman to Alamein!

Next the painting – the first picture was a success – a luminous lake and boats, backed by a beetling crag, with a miniature toy village caught in the sunlight at its foot.

Thirdly – of course the villa. It is a Hollywood palace with mirrors and mirrors – I never know whether I'm coming or going as I converge on myself from 100 angles – and my bathroom! It is cream and apricot marble. The bath is in the middle of the room like a throne – right in front of long French windows – so that one can see out over the lake to the mountains, and again more mirrors – so about six of me step into the apricot throne. It's fun – but I never feel I'm alone, and the first evening I was convulsed with giggles as a chorus of Sarahs completed her ablutions!

The weather is perfect, by no means too hot as yet – a cool breeze runs round the lake as though to order in the early morning – and then again in the late afternoon. The nights are cool and the crickets sing under the windows.

We should be very happy here – now at last one can sit in the sun without the thought of war sitting just beside one.

As for the Italians – I search their faces – they are all gay, brown and smiling, and seemingly quite untouched by the war. War to them is obviously like everything else in their lives, something physical – a physical catastrophe that happens, is unpleasant, is over, and forgotten, like an earthquake; not a moral or emotional upheaval to be pondered on, a bitter lesson from which something must be learnt. Oh no – the tooth has stopped aching – the sun shines again. Who won it? Who lost it? Who cares? That was last week – this is today. Look! Churchill – Churchill – Hurrah – Hurrah! Both the young and old know him. I was astonished at a bunch of children – the eldest not more than 12 or 13 – looked at us calmly and the eldest said, 'Churchill'. They can't do enough for us, they bring out chairs for us to sit on, towels to dry our hands with, and then retire about 20 yards and sit and watch for hours. Our ADC has the hearty contempt that all the soldiers who have fought them, or been long in Italy have for them. I think he thinks we are too polite with them. In front of a barrage of smiles, it is difficult to be other than cordial – but then suddenly the picture of Mussolini and his mistress in the market square flash into one's mind – and one remembers that there is no stability, no reserve in this crowd. They smile as the sun shines – and the sun shines brightly today.

He is going to start a new picture today. I really think he is settling down – he said last night: 'I've had a happy day.' I haven't heard that for I don't know how long!

The war was by now drawing rapidly to a close. There was little for any of us to do at Medmenham or, indeed, at any station. All of our eyes were fixed on demobilization – but my father's were alerted to the re-instatement of people who, after five, even six years of military life, must integrate themselves once more into domestic life. There could be no sudden release from rationing and coupons would remain part of our lives for several years. The beginnings of the Welfare State were in sight as Lord Beveridge came onto the scene, but there could be no sudden abandonment of the siege economy, nor an overflow of people unprepared for the return to normal life, any more than there could be a sudden return to the pre-war food supply or economy.

Your demobilization from the services was strictly regulated by the amount of time you had spent in them, but to keep the 'latecomers' amused educational and vocational training was introduced. Anyone who wanted to learn a trade could do so; anyone who had had a trade before enlistment could continue in it. When it came to my turn for an interview, I must say I didn't know what to do, but it was suggested that I might play a part in the entertainment of these waiting hours. It didn't particularly appeal to me, but then, among the 'driftees' of the end of the war, I met a charming officer, Captain William Duncalfe, later of the the Bristol BBC. He had written a play called *Squaring the Triangle*. I was to perform in this, and on my own part produced my long-time pre-war friend, *Gaslight*. These were to be happy and merry days again. We either put on plays at the station at Medmenham or at a theatre in Henley, where everybody turned up to give a cheer. And so these somewhat ebb-tide days were filled by 'educational and vocational' pastimes.

We were also commanded to attend certain lectures which were meant to instruct us on how we should behave in a peacetime world. I had an uncomfortable feeling that they were politically biased. The war had been won, officer types were conservative and people were looking for new answers. As far as I could see, everybody on the station was going to vote Socialist, and the officers, perhaps, Liberal. I mentioned this to Mary and she agreed. When next we were on leave together, we told my father of our feelings. He pooh-poohed the idea, but I am told that he did send someone down to listen to these compulsory lectures, and he began to try to adapt the magnificent machine that he had created to roll on from warmaking to peacemaking.

As I got into the charabanc which was to take us to the demobilization centre, I felt my heart singing like a bird; but then I looked across at some of the younger WAAFs, still ACW2s, and saw tears in their eyes. Were they thinking perhaps of lost loved ones, or was it that they would have to hand in their uniforms, of which they were so justifiably proud, to have them replaced with the rather dull 'civvies'? They would have to return to the more monotonous everyday life of kitchen sinks and bus queues. For some years of wartime everything had been done for them: they had been housed, warmed and fed, they had mingled happily and naturally with new companions from every walk of life and worked alongside them in a great joint effort. My elation dimmed. Perhaps it was not going to be easy for them.

6

'You Are My Heroine'

I was sitting one day in my little flat at 55 Park Lane when I realized memories would not pay the rent. A feeling of despondency was creeping into my bones and I was close to desolation when the telephone rang. A foreign voice rattled over the line: something about going to make a film. Despite being quite familiar from the theatre with living in a sort of fantasy world, perhaps my wartime training alerted some suspicions, let alone that English belief that we are the only real people in the world. However, this stranger began to explain that he was an Italian film director and that he wanted me in Italy to play a lead role in a film. Films had never appealed to me particularly; I had always preferred the instant action of the live stage and it was only a short time since we had been on opposite sides from Italy, so I enquired cautiously why he wanted me. Over the crackling wires in his near perfect but halting English came the reply: 'You are my heroine.' What woman could completely turn that down?

Mollified, if still cautious, I enquired further.

'I would want you,' he proclaimed, 'to play Elena in *Daniele Cortis*, which is a story of the triumph of duty over passion. It is by Fogazarro, a well-known Italian writer of the Victorian era. His stories are passionate, but moral.'

He further told me that Fogazarro had a belief that Nordic people held an icicle in their heart, that love could withstand the decreasing needs of passion, that idyllic friendship could ensue, that Elena was the Nordic type and that I was to be Elena. In all honesty, I thought, 'this Italian is having me on'. But I did manage to extract a promise of the script from him and when it duly arrived, I sent it to be translated and checked at the Foreign Office. It did indeed seem to be the story he had told me.

Without my knowing, my agent, the famous Al Parker, had given his wife Margaret Johnston a copy of a test that I had made for RKO under the kindly auspices of Ben Lyon, who was their representative in London at that time. Italy, seemingly wishing to reaffirm its fondness for the English, had little theatres at which Italian directors would roll the tests of foreign artists and, on passing by, one director had looked in, and seen my face, and declared, 'That is my Elena!'

But I decided on a further check. The Ozanne sisters, having finally concluded their business of finishing young English girls, had retired to Worthing. Alice still bossy, Lydie still melancholic and Marie bright-eyed and sparkling as ever. It was to Marie that I turned. Her Gallic enthusiasm positively leaped through the telephone when I told her of the proposal. I must do it she insisted, it was her great regret that she had never been able to take me to Italy.

'It is a land for women and your education will no longer, therefore, be incomplete.'

But what of the story, I asked.

'The story is beautiful and classic.'

But, I pointed out, we had not yet signed the peace treaty.

'I don't think the Italians took the war very seriously.'

But they had a dreadful war, I said.

'That was the fault of the Germans and of Mussolini. Who is financing the film?'

When I told her it was the Vatican, a touch of her Breton Protestantism crept into her voice.

'But,' she finally conceded, 'you will not come to any harm.' And when my father approved the project saying, 'Go ahead, it is part of the victor's job to help the defeated,' I hesitated no longer.

It was in a flurry of excitement that I dashed to telephone Mario Soldati, the Italian director, with the good news that if he still wanted me, I would like to do it. Get on the next available plane were my instructions. They had already started shooting every scene they could which did not include Elena. I hurled out my uniform and the wartime clobber from my suitcases and out went my Section Officer Oliver cap. I filled them with my new clothes and in a matter of hours, it seemed, was circling over Rome.

Soldati met me at the airport, a slim and intense figure, bearded and moustachioed – this of course at a time when beards were not popu-lar. His first words were, 'I have a headache.' He was subject to migraines, I was to discover. And where, I thought, is all this Italian charm?

'I see you are a good woman,' were his next words. 'You are my Elena.'

While the airport formalities were running their course, we went to drink a cup of espresso and sat in ruminative silence, eyeing each other, until I finally asked:

'What makes you think I am a good woman?'

After a brief pause, he replied, 'Your handbag.'

And silence fell again while I looked at my bag. It was small and neat, a little thing which obviously could not contain a pistol, for instance. In later years, I have taken to carrying a voluminous bag around with me – probably by now a bad woman. The next thing was a heart-rending sigh from Soldati, and I inquired politely about his headache.

'I have forgotten my headache. You will not be easy to photograph.'

It was certainly an unconventional welcome: disconcerting and not deeply encouraging. But Italy was to prove everything that Marie Ozanne had promised and Soldati was to become an important friend and mentor. Once during a close-up session in a minute studio, Soldati rolled up his sleeve to attend to some detail, revealing what was quite obviously the scar of a rather nasty bullet wound. 'Oh dear, Soldati,' I said, 'I am so sorry. Did we do it? Or,' with a little gleam, 'was it the Americans?'

'Neither,' he said proudly, 'my mistress did it!'

By the time he told me this, of course, I had discovered his reputation as a liberal and intellectual man – and how much he lived up to it. He once confessed somewhat solemnly that he had never really taken any active part in the war, other than that which civilians of all countries were subjected to. He used to confine himself to historical stories so as to be able to avoid the propaganda films. He made such classic subjects as *Eugénie Grandet* by Balzac – in which Allida Valli played the lead. He did not refuse to work at his trade, but was able to avoid involvement with the fascist regime. One of his personal gestures during the war was to walk every day three miles further than he needed, so as to avoid crossing the square where Mussolini lived.

Soldati escorted me from the airport to the Grand Hotel, an old-world luxury establishment that I was to grow very fond of – Lorenzo the hall porter and Ciano the telephonist, who was not confined behind the scenes, both radiated welcome. They were to become friends. I was taken to my suite, a magnificent apartment overlooking one of the famous fountains of Rome. I gazed at it, feeling bemused and slightly homesick.

Soldati instructed me that no expense was to be spared and that I should order what I wanted. He would be away for a few days reorganizing the shooting schedule, but would keep in touch. Bowing very low, so that his beard seemed almost to sweep the floor, he took his departure. I was later to learn the significance of the beard. When Soldati was flush, he cut it short; when he was on his uppers, he let it grow very long, thereby announcing to his friends that he did not wish to have any boring conversation about his financial condition.

Rome is the perfect city for a lone foreigner. The best of the population live high up on the rooftops of houses and churches and are made of stone, and need no introduction. The best? Well, that isn't quite true, and a little ungracious, for I have met several Romans who I have been very glad were not made of stone and who have certainly been worthwhile knowing and talking to. But on the whole, the enchantment of the city lies in its stones, the glory of it in its churches, flying saints, gesticulating apostles and quiet madonnas. Its warmth lies in its colours – coral, pink, honey and amber.

The people in its streets, for you cannot always walk with your head in the air, were in 1946 sad, shrewd and disillusioned; and they seemed little caring of anything but the immediate chance of a bargain. 'Benzine!' cried the little boys, with a downward gesture of their thumbs – unconsciously repeating the gesture of the Vestal Virgins centuries before. It did not, however, signify your death, merely that a gallon or two of benzine could be bought in a neighbouring side street for an exorbitant price. 'American cigarettes,' cried old women at every street corner (American they were not, but they copied the packets well). 'Change your sterling, change your dollars,' whispered an angular adolescent in your ear. Sixty feet up in the air, a bowed madonna contemplated her child, a gigantic apostle raised exhorting hands to the sky, and a winged figure of several tons of stone appeared to have just alighted on the cornice, breathless with news. The stone population whirled and flew and brooded: the human population scurried and schemed and sighed.

Well, it's a broad generalization, and I can no longer write carelessly of the human population, for I came on that visit to care for most of the people I worked with, and individuals have a way of upsetting generalizations.

The Italians were kind, courteous and dignified. The nicer ones felt bitterly mortified and were silent. Only the Communists jabbered. The rich Fascists? Well, they were just the same: still rich and still Fascist – which gave the Communists something to complain about.

There was almost too much spare time. The film belonged to too many people and it was impossible to contact them all at the same time and get a decision out of them. Still I plodded on. Every other day I abandoned it and every other day took heart again. An air of oppression seemed to hang over life in Rome. Wherever you went the walls and pavements and streets were marked with the hammer and sickle. One night in early October I went for a walk near the Forum through all the sunken ruins of Rome. In the moonlight and shadow it was mysterious and beautiful: and odd effects of the moonlight gave the ruins substance. I had been reading 'Graziella' by Lamartine. In describing Rome, he finishes by saying: '*Je ne sentais aucun besoin de mon isolement. Rome et mon âme me suffisaient.*' I was feeling just like that: very elated and completely happy.

One night I had to cross the large, empty space of the Piazza Venezia. There, like a big, black, hideous spider, drawn right in the middle of the square, was an enormous menacing hammer and sickle. A stone's throw away, overlooking the sign, was Mussolini's balcony. How can I describe how suddenly sinister and ominous the whole scene became? I had been walking in a dream world of sunken cities and gardens, but here was the world of fact – unhappiness, hunger and violence. It was said at the time that the Italians were not hungry under Mussolini. But there was oppression and there was ultimate disaster. His medieval palace looked cruel and forbidding. Everybody in Rome seemed resigned to war. They would believe nothing but that the restrictions imposed by the Allies were the precursor to more warfare. There were one or two Communist demonstrations, but they were not violent. The Romans seemed apathetic. It was often hard to know what they were really thinking. They did not appear hungry – I looked long and hard and I suppose under an olive complexion it might be possible to conceal galloping consumption – but the women and children looked well fed. Yet they talked of winter starvation, and every day strikes were threatened: all, I believe, because of the price of food. I ate in small restaurants, but even a simple meal for one person cost the equivalent of eight shillings. I didn't understand it: the shops were full of everything, butter, oil, sugar – things that the poor English had almost forgotten.

On one occasion later, during a break in filming, several of the unit were sitting in a teashop where there were masses of lovely creamy

Italian cakes. The others were gorging themselves quite happily, but I, thinking of my figure, which had to fit into some beautiful but tight costumes, refused a second cake. Soldati sighed and said, 'That is why England won the war. They could refuse cream cakes.'

It must have been five days before Soldati rescued me from my isolation at the Grand Hotel. I had read and re-read the script and, by this time, had summoned the courage, or the brashness, to inform him that the script was simply not good enough. His immediate response was that it had been good enough for the actress they had engaged during the time when I was trying to make up my mind whether to accept the part. I was appalled and asked Soldati whether this other actress had been sacked because of my arrival. He said this was so, making me feel worse, and I said, 'This is terrible. You can't do that sort of thing, didn't she mind?'

'No,' he replied, 'we paid her quite a large sum of money and sent her off to the hills with her lover. You see, Italians do not take acting quite so seriously as apparently you English do.' This is not a view anyone could take seriously later, after such actresses as Anna Magnani, Sophia Loren and others had made their name. But once Soldati had reassured me that my predecessor was happy in luxury, in the hills, and in the company of her paramour, I turned back to the script and asked Soldati whether he would care to spend the weekend with me – 'honi soit qui mal y pense'. It was perhaps not a suggestion one should ever make to an Italian and I saw a look of astonishment cross his face. My 'good woman' image was crumbling rapidly.

I hastened to reassure him and explained that, during the few days he had been away, I had found some English friends: Valerie Hayes, daughter of the manager of the Rome branch of Barclay's Bank and her fiancé, Captain Peter Moore, who had become Alexander Korda's man in Rome. Peter had advised me to have Valerie as my interpreter, companion and, happily, friend. So I was able to assure Soldati that he would be well chaperoned. He suggested Frigene, the nearest seashore to Rome, as a suitable place for a script conference.

Frigene is only about an hour's drive from Rome, so we squashed into a little Fiat and bumbled off there. The resort is a strip of about two miles of white sand backed by a narrow strip of windswept pines, all leaning at the traditional angle of Roman pines. We took long walks there and had a go at the characters of Daniele and Elena. In the evenings, Valerie faithfully recorded and typed. It was a most rewarding time which firmly cemented my friendship with Soldati. Since he has become even more renowned in Italy as a writer of distinction, it is very pleasing to recall one of the bouquets he offered me when he said at that time, 'I do not know yet whether you can act, but you have a good comprehension of the film world; possibly one day you will be a writer.'

The first two weeks back in Rome surpassed anything I had known in a hectic life. At any time during the first week I could have run straight home, but at the end of the second week I was happier as I had started to work properly. During the first days I was surrounded by kind but completely incomprehensible people. Only one or two spoke English or understood it, the rest was a confusion of bad French and hysterical-sounding Italian. Fortunately, Valerie Hayes, who had lived in Italy for much of her childhood, spoke fluent Italian. I asked the production company to have her assigned to me as interpreter, companion, secretary, guide and bodyguard – and from that moment, life began to straighten itself out.

I was sure that I had taken on a great challenge in Italy. If it were to succeed, I felt it would make an enormous difference to the type of parts which I might be offered later. I found it strange to work with complete strangers who spoke a language which for the first few days was incomprehensible chatter. I would gaze rapturously into the eyes of a fascinating young man, Vittorio Gassman, somewhat obscured by whiskers, and, in answer to some musical soft-spoken Italian, I would reply, in my bell-like and utterly English voice, 'I'm crazy about you too.' We were making the Italian and English versions at the same time, planning to dub the respective languages at the end of editing.

Quite soon after my arrival in Rome, I had gone to test for an English film, successfully. So after the first spell with Soldati, I was due to go to work for Victor Stoloff for five weeks and then return to the Italians for a further five. There was mad competition between the two companies, which was fortunate for me since both were considered to be employing the best technical crews in Italy and each wished to outdo the other. The Soldati crew were charming to work with. They would cry with you in the touching scenes and laugh with you whenever anything went wrong. I had to exercise my diplomatic side-step on such lines of dialogue as, 'In what spirit did you don your uniform?' There were any number of spirited answers to that one, but I answered, 'Like you, for my country.'

There was one tragedy. One of the few remaining bits of me that was as God ordained it – my hair – had to be lightened considerably and I became the colour of a marmalade cat. My face kept everybody busy. There was a lot of tut-tutting during the tests as strange little men flung themselves on the floor to gaze at me from different angles and then walked sadly away.

Rome seemed full of film people at that time. Alexander Korda's London Films were making *A Man About The House* in which my friend Margaret Johnston starred. When they came back from location in Ravello, it was like a reunion of Park Lane, Soho and The Ivy. It seemed then that the Italians were intending to make films one of their chief post-war exports. They had, of course, several trump cards: first of all the climate, and then the wonderful scenic backgrounds and historical monuments and ruins and towns that Hollywood, with all its ingenuity and money, could not really compete with. Mario Soldati shot nearly all his exteriors in real places (Cinecittà, of course, had been seriously damaged during the war). This was a delight for the artists, and I believe the audiences, and a thing rarely dreamed of in England or used in Hollywood at the time. When you gazed at a church, it really was St Peter, St John or St Paul instead of a plaster-cast mock-up or backcloth and when fountains were called for, it was a pleasure not to have to look at a bathful of water being shaken by an energetic stagehand.

The Italians had good cameramen and their photography seemed to me as good as the French. They were inclined to over make up the artists and I suspected the required acting style would be a little more on the ponderous side and that the speed of the film would be rather leisurely. I suspected that this might be a good thing. Hollywood had reached a zenith of slickness and rapid direction which were probably impossible to beat, but could be overdone; a more leisurely, straightforward approach to a story promised a welcome change. These were only first impressions from a week's work and the study of only one script. Soldati took infinite pains testing and re-testing a shot: and then, when I started, assured me that all the close-ups from the first two or three days' shooting could still be regarded as additional tests and would be reshot if necessary. My first tests were not too good: make-up too heavy and acting too slight. But the second showed all-round improvement and the stills seemed to please everybody.

The Italians never hesitated to commandeer a hotel lobby or suitable house as locations or dressing-rooms for artists. Once we had to go into a rather dismal palace. It had a magnificent wrought-iron spiral staircase with, on each landing, the doors to three rooms. The camera would launch itself into one room, the leading man into another and me into the third. The purpose of this operation was for me to walk up the spiral staircase, looking back after the departing figure of my delinquent husband, played by Gino Cervi, and saying farewell. I sat many hours in the little room while complicated camera angles were worked out. I was astonished to see there a faded and battered print of *The Stag at Bay* on a screen in the corner. I naturally peeped behind the screen, to discover a tin basin and other useful receptacles. I had noticed that there was a certain urgency that we should be out of this palace by five o'clock each day, which was rather different from the pace usually displayed on the film. Soldati would pay me visits to discuss the scene or the script. On one such visit, it occurred to me that there really was something strange about the place. He saw that I was paying no attention to what he was saying and asked me if I was wondering where we were.

'Yes,' I said.

His reply was this: 'You are in a brothel – we must be out at five o'clock *prontissimo*, when the girls return.'

During the waits, I wrote a poem for the girls – 'The Weary Heart':

> I could be happy if my heart could rest
> As lightly as my head upon your breast. . . .

When I finished my first session of working on *Daniele Cortis* for Soldati's company Universalia, I had done about a week's extensive shooting with them: eight in the morning to eight at night, sometimes ten, sometimes midnight, and, on the last day of all, till two in the morning. Although it was tiring, I was enjoying it and on the last two days I was beginning to feel that Elena – the character I was playing – was no longer a stranger. But temporary goodbyes had to be said. It was like the end of term, or being packed off to a new school, because the next day I had to confront an entirely new set of people, slightly prejudiced because they might feel that my allegiances and affections had already been given elsewhere, which of course they had.

I was quite confident that I could remove this impression in a few days, but by the end of the first day I had been stricken by a peculiar and unromantic complaint and I had to take to my bed for a fortnight. Six days were spent with the most exciting fever. Never having run a real temperature before, I was inordinately proud of the dizzy heights I attained and I kept my temperature chart (a ham even when ill) along with the other documents and photographs which formed the milestones and landmarks of this Italian adventure. Having been unable to eat much even before I was ill, and eating nothing during the first six days, I woke one morning with a frenzy for food. Positively kilometres of spaghetti slipped down my throat; and meringue chantilly which as a child I had always longed to eat. Somehow, owing to Cousin Mop forcing us to eat healthy bread and butter and to finish our health-giving mutton and cabbage first, I had never had the heart or stomach to eat such delights when they eventually appeared. But now they disappeared in their happy dozens: and no sooner finished, than after '*cinque minuti senza fa niente*' – five minutes doing nothing – I started wondering how long it was before the next meal. Despite my gorging, I was still too thin for the film. So it had to be further delayed – till I could put on weight.

My father had been informed of my illness – I had refused to go to the military hospital and the poor young military doctor threw up his hands in despair and said I would need various antibiotics to reduce my temperature. Hospitals and doctors always held for me a sense of claustrophobic fear – although without them I might well not have survived my early youth. But I was happy in my hotel surrounded by the affectionate and concerned Italian friends and a delightful doctor called Monteleone who also threw up his hands in despair and exclaimed, '*Troppo delicato.*' The young military doctor telephoned the embassy who informed my father who promptly despatched Mary and told the embassy, 'I am sending my daughter Mary to look after Sarah, as she is quite obviously not able to look after herself.'

When Mary arrived, her flushed cheeks and excitement outdid what was left of my fever. She told me in breathless sentences that she had fallen in love with the British Assistant Military Attaché at the embassy in Paris. He had been in hot pursuit of her and as, that particular weekend, he was coming over to England to see her, she had felt sad when she dutifully agreed to comply with my father's request. Her attaché, Christopher Soames, had met her in Paris and escorted her to the Italian-bound train at the other side of the city. Murmuring his understanding, he had ensconced her in a suitable compartment and stayed to talk to her. Suddenly the train jolted and made noises of departure. Mary said, 'Quickly, Christopher; the train is leaving, you must get out.' Christopher remained, smiling placidly. 'But I am coming with you,' he had said. I gathered that he had proposed to her in the Simplon tunnel, which I realized, when she had ended her tale, was the reason for *her* fever.

Christopher was enchanting and brought bunches of flowers to the invalid sister-in-law-to-be and to Mary of course. Mary counted that I always had more than her dozen roses. I had eighteen! She pouted, I consoled her and said, 'But I am older than you.' She accepted it a trifle easily, I thought, but the climax came with one of the bunches of flowers. Attached to mine was a poem:

> I have seen half-bred horses win classic races,
> I have seen men die with smiling faces,
> And now kidneys floating in empty spaces –
> So I have faith.

So now you know my unromantic complaint!

As my fever rapidly declined, Mary's increased. I wrote of this dutifully to my mother and father saying how wonderful I thought their marriage would be and that I was well and that I would look after Mary, but the powers that be removed any necessity for this, because Christopher had to return to duty in Paris.

After tearful goodbyes, Mary and I settled down to our respective convalescences. We had more fun together than I could remember having since nursery days or the last holiday we had spent together at Eastbourne in 1940. She discovered Rome in a few days and would come back and tell me about it. 'It is a coral and amber city,' she said, and when Soldati took her to see the river Tiber, with Churchill emotionalism but also sincerity, her blue eyes filled with tears and she recited the whole of 'Horatio' – well almost the whole of it – to the astonished, bewildered and finally captivated Soldati. There were tears in his eyes and voice when later he said to me, 'She revived for me in an instant the ancient Roman tradition which I had forgotten – indeed which perhaps I had never felt until that moment.'

Soldati was from Turin in northern Italy and explained that Rome had never held the magic or significance for him that perhaps it should have. During twenty long years, he said, he had bitterly resented and hated the overgrown, overblown, hollow symbol of power which Rome represented. 'But here, suddenly, at the edge of the Tiber in the late afternoon sun, an English girl revives for me the real tradition and glory of a far-off, forgotten, but once great Italy.' You can imagine my happy fury as I lay in bed, patiently, trustingly, while my younger sister stole my director from me. Mary seemed to know all Rome and from embassies to hall-porters, all doors swung open.

When Mary finally had to leave, Valerie and Peter Moore pushed her onto a train with a basket of food and wine sufficient to last her while she rumbled across Europe for two days. Peter was the perfect person to be London Films representative in Italy. He was a young man with chameleon-like qualities. He was very Irish and in Ireland the Irish would recognize him; but once from those shores, he had the ability to assume the nationality of almost any country he was in – certainly France and Italy at that time as he spoke the languages as fluently as a native. It is not possible to say how helpful he was. I was not a London Films artist at that time and he was under no obligation to help at all. But his continual good advice about such things as how to liberate your laundry, how to obtain at five minutes' notice the royal suite for a friend who just happened to be passing, or how to get a seat on a plane from which real VIPs had been turned away – in all these things he proved invaluable. Finally, he had one great and most endearing art: he knew how to order food, and delicious meal after delicious meal was placed before me. He was later to become Salvador Dali's trusted business manager.

Since to have a complete picture of my life in Italy it is important to know all, two days after convalescing and before finally starting work with Stoloff on his picture, *When In Rome*, I had an unfortunate row with the production company. For those two days, I remained in my room in injured silence (not so silent with my friends) until the matter, which as usual concerned publicity, was put right. Every emotion had to be gone through, indignation, hurt, tears, cajoleries, assurances; finally, flowers, forgiveness and forgetting. The only thing that was missing was background music by Puccini. It was all necessary, but a pity that it took a little while for confidence to be restored. Though our smiles were as amiable as any at a diplomatic dinner party, both sides walked with the wariness of cats on warm bricks.

I finished playing Iris in *When In Rome* at the end of November 1946. I had my thirty-second birthday out there on 7 October, which I would have ignored except for the fact that Vic Oliver married again on that day. All ended happily with the film and I really was sorry to say goodbye to the crew. Victor Stoloff, the director, could not have been nicer to me about the part, and Scalera, the producer, sent many agreeable compliments and dewdrops and hopes for further films with them.

Many years later at a party in New York, I was approached by a man I had never met. His introduction was strange: 'You don't know me, Miss Churchill, but I once did you the best turn that was ever done you.' This was intriguing. It transpired, however, that he had been Victor Stoloff's film editor on *When In Rome*. The part of Iris had finished up in its entirety on the cutting room floor. It takes time to discover that some-times it is of such drastic actions that good turns are made. I was obvi-ously very bad in it.

Unaware of this – and grateful for the compliments – I left to rejoin Soldati and his crew in Vicenza. All night, practically, I packed and the next morning Peter Moore, Valerie and I and an enormous quantity of luggage and three baskets of food and wine squeezed into an Alfa Romeo for the journey to Vicenza. We had been told it would be a six-hour journey on an autostrada in the Alfa Romeo. Well, it was twenty hours – ten of which were in fog at night. It was awful, but we managed to laugh most of the way – we had at least to keep the driver, Peter, awake. Finally we got so sleepy that I ordered a stop, for it really was too dangerous. We all fell dead asleep for about an hour, only to discover on waking that we were a mere fifteen minutes from our destination.

I proceeded to catch the most ghastly cold, and for four days would happily have died. I did not dare retreat to my bed since I had already held up both productions for so long. So I staggered through the four days looking swollen, and with hardly any voice. But nobody seemed to mind since the voices would be dubbed anyway. The Hotel Roma at Vicenza was cold and bleak and the hot water was uncertain. Since snow had fallen, it was impossible to film outside without severe penalties. I wore two vests, a long-sleeved cardigan, trousers and ski boots – all under my romantic 1880 costume, because I'd lost so much weight due to the Roman fever. Through my frozen brain I would occasionally remember what I had told my parents: that this was what I had chosen. So I really couldn't complain.

Vicenza was a land of autumn. It reminded me somewhat of Persia – slim silver trees, shallow blue-grey rivers, snow-covered mountains in the background. The story was meant to take place in spring or early autumn. But the snow kept falling, so the prop men kept laboriously brushing it away and hanging fake leaves on the trees. To be nice, the production company had given me the best room in the hotel – the largest, of course. I yearned for a small room, a humble room, where I could keep warm. But I didn't want to hurt their feelings. Having stood it for two weeks, though, I finally felt I could tell them that I would be happier in a smaller room. Years later, my mother was to visit Vicenza and stay at the same hotel; she was shown to the very large room and the manager, she told me, said: 'Your daughter, Sarah, occupied this room just after the war.' I hoped it was warmer!

When my filming was finished, I wrote to my father in a reflective mood:

Now that, at last, my part of the battle is over, I sit and wait results with, I suppose in a way, the exhausted calm of a man who, having made his defence, awaits the verdict. I – me personally – can do no more. For the last five months I have sighed, smiled, raged, sorrowed – for the camera – and it's all on celluloid in little cans and I can't get it back or erase it or alter it.

I went on – after a few domestic details – that I had been thinking seriously about *me*:

It seems I must always hurt the person who loves me. [I had ended an old love affair which my father suspected but about which we did not speak.] What have I done? Compromise as best I could – fight with one arm free only, constantly looking back over my shoulder – trying to reconcile two opposite aims – progressing little with the fight, and hurting and being of little use to the other side of my life. Which is right? Christian and kindly upbringing point to the first. It says, quite clearly, you must conquer and control and live for others. But what about 'To thine own self be true, thou canst not then be false to any man' – and – 'Often rebuked, yet always back returning – to those first feelings that were born with me' – and – 'I would be walking where my own nature leads me; it vexes me to choose another guide'. Have you ever felt imprisoned? Have you ever felt a cage of circumstance, even affection, hemming you in? Or have you always been, no matter how bitter the moment, free? Remember Chequers – when we knew it was all finished finally and legally with Vic? You called me across the room and whispered in my ear: 'Free!' I had no answer – for already I knew, already I was not. Men can be free – perhaps – but women never. 'Love is of man's life a part – Tis a woman's whole existence.'

Well, it is men who wish, and demand that it should be so! I am too often reproved for making it *only* a part. Well anyway, for the moment I am more or less free – but then again only at someone else's expense.

This letter is so hard for me to write – prising open an oyster is hard work – but distance somehow brings one closer than living in the next street – and I have tried to open my heart to you, so that perhaps you can understand a bit, all this – all this to the outside world, crazy endeavour, is serious, and even if there is nothing tangible in the way of success to show for it – I shall of course be very disappointed – nobody likes losing, or making a goose of themselves – but I can't ever feel I was wrong, for this life I have chosen has brought me in touch with human beings and with the human heart, and given me friends, and revealed to me, if not the remedy – the reason for so much in this world.

I posted this letter to my father, which was the proper answer to a telegram in which he had said: 'When are you coming home?' I had replied rather impudently: 'When I am ready. Your loving mule.' This was the first time that I had ever used this nickname which I had given to myself. The facts, however, supported the name and it was one which stuck to me. The film was over, the goodbyes had been said, the tears were shed. The promises of loving each other ever after and of writing frequently were over – I realized it was time for me to go back to London.

My father was to ask me, in later lengthy stays away from him on theatrical assignments, if I minded when a show broke up.

I said, 'Very much.'

And he said, 'So do I.'

The hardest break of all was Soldati. He was a most delightful companion and another one of my true mentors, and he had given me an inside view of the Italian character. When the film was over he came to England and I asked him down to Chartwell for lunch. Soldati was frankly alarmed at the prospect. My father went all out to make him feel at home. Soldati arrived, his beard now nicely short. He did not drink, because of an incipient ulcer, but he took the customary glass of champagne and in a few moments was happy and relaxed in my father's genial presence and soon they were rattling away merrily together. After the meal, cigars, brandy and coffee were offered. Soldati refused the brandy and, although he didn't smoke, accepted a torpedo-like Havana cigar, which he put in his pocket saying, 'A memento.' My father promptly gave him another one: 'Two mementoes are better than one.' Then he pressed him to have some brandy but Soldati refused. My father pressed him again, as persuasive and genial as a host can be.

'But surely a little brandy never did anyone any harm?'

Soldati finally relented: 'Well, sir, if you insist – just a tumblerful.'

We all looked desperately heavenwards, grasping ourselves to stop laughing, and the meeting ended in enormous cordiality.

Shortly after Soldati returned to Italy, my father had to deliver a speech to the Young Conservatives in the Albert Hall. He asked me if I would like to read his speech. Needless to say, a great privilege. When I got to the bit about Italy, I froze with horror. My father was still in his wartime bombastic mood – going on about the treachery of 'that jackal, Mussolini' and, incidentally, perhaps without meaning to, degrading the Italians for their weakness. I threw one of my very few tantrums at my father: 'They are a highly intelligent, febrile and industrious people. Who

96

else would think of denying themselves the repair of their own houses before building the Scala Opera House up first?'

I had had an opportunity of watching a rehearsal at La Scala while on my film assignment. It was freezing cold, the heating non-existent because of the efficiency of Allied bombing. The singers assembled on the dimly lit stage, wrapped in mufflers, overcoats and gloves. A skeleton orchestra shivered in the pit. The director, equally muffled, said: 'Whatever you do, please just take your cues, hum, but do not sing.'

They followed this direction, and the lovely melodic theme of the opera (the name of which I do not remember) filled the cold auditorium. It obviously also filled the hearts of the performers as, after about fifteen minutes, they started to sing full out, as if christening the newly-built Scala. The director jumped up and shouted, 'No! No! Keep it down! Keep it down!' and the conductor tapped ineffectually upon his desk. But they were away and no one could stop them. I was sad not to see the opening performance, but in a way I had.

I said to my father, 'I shall not be in the audience if you intend to say these things about the people you agreed I should go and work with and who have become my friends.' He didn't say anything and I left the room. I did go to the meeting, thinking that I would slip out of my seat when the Italian passage was to come up. When it did, it was in eulogistic terms and he turned his benign, cherubic and impish grin on me. I loved him. Generosity always triumphed with him.

I was now based back in London with the film tucked underneath my arm, so to speak, as proof positive of my work and sojourn in Italy. My agent Al Parker handed it to Alexander Korda, who screened it and immediately offered me a contract. He also arranged for a private viewing for my father.

The film was in Italian and the English dubbing had not yet been done. I was dubbed in Italian by a top Italian stage actress. So I wrote a synopsis of the story, as well as sorting out still pictures and background information. I sent a copy to each of my family, but the only person who really took trouble to read it was my father. He questioned me at dinner about it. A great romanticist in the classical style, he said he was looking forward to seeing it. So we all repaired to a little viewing cinema with Korda's special entourage.

I sat in the back row prepared to die: but the vivid memories and the added scope that this adventure had given to my life quickly relieved any embarrassment which most actors feel at seeing themselves, and I sat relaxed. At the end – it was a private viewing with only friends present – they all crowded round in delight.

Then they went to my father and said, 'But it is wonderful. *She* is wonderful.'

He turned, with his enigmatic smile, and said, 'Yes. And she makes money at it, too.'

Korda beamed and said that he was going to look for a suitable part for me to play.

On getting home, I ran to the telephone and called Soldati and told him the news. He had said that he did not think the film would set the Thames or the Tiber on fire but that we had no need to hang our heads. He was thrilled at the acknowledgement from Korda which I felt was so due to him. Later I went back to Rome under the auspices of Peter Moore and Diana Graves, cousin of Jenny Nicholson and daughter of Robert Graves, and tried to dub the film, not with any marked success. Dubbing was never to be popular with American or English films. The sub-titles were easier, but the speeches were so long. That was a serious fault in the film. If they had a sub-title, it had to begin at the nose and go right on down to the chin and shoulders.

Soldati was right. *Daniele Cortis* never set the Thames on fire, but we did win an Italian prize at the Festival in Lugano. So it had played its part and everyone concerned was happy.

7

Christmas in Marrakech

In 1947, after the delights of Italy, I accompanied my father on a real holiday. We spent Christmas and New Year in Marrakech, which was one of his favourite places for painting. Once again, my mother was unable to accompany us, so I tried to keep her in touch with our progress by frequent letters. I reproduce some of them here with no apologies since they give, I believe, an unusually accurate picture of holiday time spent with my father.

11 December 1947

It was the most perfect flight. We were transported as carefully as a crate of eggs and deposited gently on the pink airfield in about eight and a half hours. We flew across the Bay [of Biscay] and down the border of Spain and Portugal and only had to fly at 8,000' for about an hour. We had a most delicious luncheon – eggs in aspic, cold chicken and champagne – prepared for us by the Embassy. Papa thoughtfully wanted to spare them this trouble and had asked the manager of the Ritz Hotel to prepare lunch for us. Equally alert and thoughtful was Rufus Clarke, who called up to inquire: apart from the honour they no doubt felt at being given the order, just how much did they think of charging? £30 was the modest minimum. At this, Rufus took it upon himself to ask the chef at the Embassy to oblige!

Our day in Paris was enormous fun and well worthwhile. Anne and Esmond Rothermere gave us lunch. Diana and Duff [Cooper, the British Ambassador] had to go to a farewell press lunch – which they spared Papa from – and from which Diana bolted at the last minute!

The party in the evening was scintillating. '*La crème de la crème*' even *la crème fouettée* floated about in Christian Dior, Jacques Fath, Schiaparelli and Lanvin creations.

We dined with the Comte and Comtesse de Chambord first – the Comtesse is an amiable and large lady – who for this occasion was dressed in black and green horizontal stripes! The star of the ball of course was Odette [Churchill].

She wore a Schiaparelli dress of vermilion satin, hour glass and bustle which was caught with a bow just below the 'Topsy' as Papa remarked – and which made the men's eyes linger in the far distance long after she had passed! Diana [Cooper] of course looked lovely – pale aquamarine satin, covered with aquamarine tulle, her fair hair crowned with gardenias; she went through the whole evening unchanged – even at 5 o'clock in the morning. The star couple were Odette and Papa – Papa looked pink and smiling and shy and sweet. He stood irresolute in the middle of the ballroom aglow with his medals and stars – 'I would like to dance with you,' he said to Odette, 'but really I am not very good. Won't you sit down and talk to me for a moment?'...

Do not be unhappy about your decision – though it would be the crown of enjoyment to have you here. As you are not feeling very well, I'm sure you are wise: Paris was exhausting and followed by the flight, I would have been more worried about you than him, for he is the toughest of the lot of us and his powers of recuperation rapid. Only of course I am worried about the cold. It is much colder than last time. Bright sun but really cold after 4. Bill [Deakin] and I will really have to get him indoors by 4.30. The hotel is warmer than the villa, though – which is a good thing.

I hope everything goes all right. Of course I am a little anxious – I hope he is going to be happy and content. It is impossible to know yet.

16 December 1947

It is getting much warmer! It is quite different to when we arrived. We have settled down into a pleasantly monotonous routine which varies very little. So far he has not left the hotel, he paints from a high balcony of the new wing of the hotel – and as it has till now been cold, I am glad. But today a sortie is planned – just a small one – to the pink walls. He is inclined to work a little too late. Bill is an enormous help to him – but also a temptation to work on too late at night.

Bill planned to leave Dec. 22nd and meet his wife in Paris for Christmas but now great telegrams have been sent to persuade her to come out here for five days so that Bill can stay longer. The 'girls' and Sergeant Williams and Greenshields are all very good and devoted, and seem happy and thrilled with the place – as indeed they might be, for it is really a terrestrial paradise. The people in the hotel are very nice and do not stare or bother one – with an exception of one man who tried to take photographs of Papa. We ignored several attempts, then Sergeant Williams appeared from behind a palm tree and delivered a little lecture about the rules of a private hotel being respected and the man, crestfallen, packed up his Brownie camera and fled down an olive grove. Sergeant Williams retired majestically behind his palm tree again!

Colonel and Madame Hauteville are lunching tomorrow. The Colonel is the

Commander of the area. On our arrival he drew Bill aside and said: 'I want you to understand this is *not* a democratic area – this is a military area. If there is anything – or anyone – you do not like, just give me a telephone call – I will be right over!' The Glaoui himself met us – and we are shortly to eat a sheep's eye or two with him.

The 'Souks' are deserted of tourists, and the poor Arabs look forlorn sitting in their little shops surrounded by their bright but cheap wares. Though the hotel is full, I feel they are rich French from other parts of Morocco rather than France, who are used to the life and do not buy souvenirs. They must miss the 'sooveneer' hunting G.I.s of the War. So, accordingly, Miss Gilliat and Miss Sturdee [secretaries] were given a great welcome when Bill and I escorted them down to the Souks. They fell for a big Moroccan bag each and were delighted, and people hurried from all the neighbouring shops to see the now rare birds, 'tourists', buying.

It took us an hour to buy the bags, for we looked at everything else – and bags and belts and silks were sent from the other shops for our inspection; they were still nice to us when they saw we were not really buying anything. Miss Gilliat declared it was the most wonderful afternoon of her life – so it was really a successful afternoon.

I do hope your oranges and lemons got through the customs all right. Large quantities will not be easy to send now the plane has gone back but we are going to try and send small amounts regularly. There is a limit to the amount you may send out.

The British Consuls at Casablanca have been wonderful in organising whisky – for there is none here....

19 December 1947

I have been commanded by Papa to write to you all, a full description of the dinner we had with SE the Glaoui (not I understand Glowie!)

It really was a most superb and sumptuous evening. Bill and I and Papa all enjoyed ourselves enormously. The more so, because we were alone with him and his son (not the yellow knickerbocker motorcycle one). The evening therefore was quite informal and despite the Glaoui's bad French, really at times incomprehensible, not a bit stiff.

His son met us at the door and acted as interpreter, often springing to his feet during the course of the evening to serve both his Father and Papa in a most humble, filial, and Papa said, absolutely proper manner! It was certainly an evening conducted in the *ancien régime* style to put it mildly. The Glaoui and Papa basked in a positively navy-blue reactionary mood, while colossal negresses and eunuchs (?) (Papa says NO! not these) padded about, carrying to and fro great copper and earthenware bowls and plates of food.

We sat round a low table. The juniors on pouffes, and Papa and the Glaoui on a low sofa. They padded and propped Papa up with cushions till he was tightly wedged on his sofa, so he couldn't fall off – and dinner began.

We had been warned it would be strictly in Arab style, but still there were many things to learn.

At first a red copper intricately worked bowl was brought, also a large copper kettle. 'You are to wash your hands,' murmured Papa. I held out both, and warm rose water was poured over them. I was handed a small towel, the size of a sheet, to wipe them with. I noticed the Glaoui only washed one hand, the right. Then we started.

I wonder if I can remember all we ate, because eat is all we did! A sort of second wind came to us round about the sixth platter of food, and, by then, all shyness of eating with one's fingers having gone, we were plunging merrily ahead as to the manner born. However, we were to learn that all courses are not eaten with the fingers, and Papa committed one small social error by plunging his fingers into the centre of a great bowl of what looked like stewed and mashed apples and semolina, only to be handed a spoon! How could one know? The Glaoui gallantly waved away his spoon and plunged too! Later, somewhere round the tenth course, an ice cream turned up. I am sorry to say that though it was quite clear that this was one of the courses to be eaten with a spoon, Papa was enjoying himself so much that, muttering, 'I simply must', he plunged his fingers into the ice cream. The Glaoui and son luckily were highly amused.

Now, back to the menu. First, soup in bowls with spoon. Then I think a whole sheep, yes, a whole roast sheep. Fingers. We were definitely at this stage still a little restrained. I could hardly believe I was expected to claw quite viciously at any part of the animal I thought looked tempting. I gave a nervous tug, but nothing much happened. I then found that the son, in intervals of eating heartily himself, dislodged delicate morsels and left them lying about in my segment of the lamb.

I was very grateful. Presently the Glaoui himself passed me a trifle he had dislodged. Then I think, yes, then a thing that looked like an enormous mille-feuille appeared. We boldly dug our fingers in! It was indeed a kind of mille-feuille, but not sweet. It was a vegetable one, full of sage and strange sweet herbs, and dripping in butter and flaky pastries. Then, came the most wonderful almond paste pastry wheel, made in widening circles. Oh! 'how I wished I hadn't eaten so much'. This, for me, was *the* dish.

First it was easy to eat – you just broke off a piece quite neatly like a biscuit, and munched and crunched merrily. Delicious almond paste, slightly reminiscent of mince-pie, but crisper and more nutty. I made my side of the wheel look pretty silly. By this time I felt I was very nearly grease up to my elbows, so I discreetly had a good tidy up. My table napkin and Papa's began to look like a baby's bib after a disagreement as to where the rusk and milk should go. The Glaoui's napkin and that of his son remained snowy white. When I looked up the almond wheel had gone and there, to our amazement and slight misgivings, was a bowl containing pigeons in lemon sauce.

'Crikey!' said Papa.

After the briefest pause, we forged ahead dipping our bread in the yellow sauce, and plucking at the half-submerged pigeons. Then came another vegetable dish, sort of vegetable marrow surrounded with dry semolina! the one Papa inadvertently plunged his fingers into, only to discover it was a spoon course. But by now we had our second wind and nothing could daunt us. Papa looked up with a seraphic smile, and said sotto voce: 'This goes on for hours, you know.'

Now memory blurs a bit, I think a final meat course. But who knows? Some little time after, the ice cream turned up. Spoons *please* in future! Then tangerines heaped in a pyramid, but we said no. Then came the intricately-worked bowl again. I remembered. I held out one hand only, a little water, a little soap, a little water, the vast towel. The Glaoui this time however washed both his hands; I mean a real scrub! practically behind the ears! Then they cleared the table away, and I am sorry to say this revealed a little circle of food at my feet that had unfortunately fallen during the battle. The whole thing was very difficult but by then we had warmed and after Papa had plunged his fingers into the wrong bowl no one looked back!

Brandy, cigars, in another room. All the rooms were rather cold, for they had no doors, just great hangings like carpets, so that you can imagine yourself in a tent, if you want to. Luckily Papa kept his coat on the whole time.

We talked of this and that. The Glaoui nodded, and began to get a little somnolent.

'You're so right,' said Papa suddenly – 'quite right. Clothes for instance – very sensible. *Toutes voilées ou toutes nues*. Quite right!'

The Glaoui awoke with a start. '*Ce sont des topiques philosophiques,*' continued Papa. The Glaoui agreed vigorously!

Coffee good. Mint tea delicious. Papa drank two cups. He signed some of his books for him. They saw us to the door. It was a lovely evening, they saw we had really enjoyed ourselves, which was better than all our thanks could be. The Glaoui's Guard of Honour saluted.... We discovered that Sgt Williams had eaten the same, in the same fashion, in an adjoining room. He was delighted, and Miss Sturdee and Miss Gilliat could hardly believe their ears. An Arabian night, to be sure!

PS In point of fact – in retrospect we discovered we really didn't eat very much! It's just the confusion of dishes and manner of eating – if we were asked again, I would do much better. Wow, darling – I will write soon to you again. He is happy and well, loves his routine. Today we are off for the first picnic. Mrs Deakin has arrived safely....

26 December 1947

... Papa is really well – working terribly hard – but no longer so late. One or two of us, me included, have suffered from a peculiar migraine these last days – I think it is the strong air and bright sunlight. I sent for my medicine and since two days it has disappeared. Christmas Eve was a gala evening. Papa invited the girls and Sergeant Williams and Greenshields who generally sit in the opposite corner to join us for the evening! We all put on evening dress and Greenshields in a great flutter borrowed a black tie from Bill and we all met in the sitting room for a cocktail, and then we went down in force to the dining room at 10.30. A glittering scene met our eyes. In the short space of the afternoon, they had transformed the large dining room. A gigantic Christmas tree 25–30 feet high had been installed and decorated. The windows were hung with branches laden with oranges, and daubs of white paint on the window panes made it seem that a blizzard was blowing outside – clever idea.

Everyone was 'dolled up'. It was a very international atmosphere – Danes, Swiss, Portuguese, Spanish, American – the smattering of English us, French, and an Italian waiter. When midnight struck, they lowered the lights, and with one accord the International melee rose as a man to their feet just on the spur of the moment and looked to Papa. They raised their glasses, and clapped – and '*Vive* Churchill' and 'Bravo' echoed round the room. The band who had practised hard all afternoon English surprises for us, played 'It's a long way to Tipperary' as the Christmas pudding was brought in. Renewed clappings and murmurs, and Papa stood up very moved and bowed to them all, and received the Christmas pudding as he does a casket on being given the freedom of a city. Then he got up – I thought he was going – but no,

'Whirl me round the floor once Mule – I think I can manage it.'

This was too much for them – like a famous dance team we took the floor amidst a roar of applause – we were very good – it was a waltz. Then he danced during the evening with Miss Sturdee, Miss Gilliat and Mrs Deakin – and I was whirled off my feet by Sergeant Williams – who is pretty hot on a rumba (Scotland Yard training is most extensive). I was also whirled by Greenshields, who was too shy at first but ended up the strongest. Papa stayed till two!

One event I did *not* relate in letters home. At the party, I had noticed that my father had been attracted by a good-looking fair lady who had sat against the wall with a gentleman; but now that the festivities were in progress she was alone, profiled against the snow-screened window.

My father said, 'Why is she alone?'

'The gentleman had to go back to his family,' I said.

'How do you know that?'

'Don't gentlemen usually go home to their families?'

Immediately he rose to his feet and said, 'Dance me around the floor.'

He danced me around the floor and stopped at the forlorn but proud lady. Looking at her he said, 'You are the Christmas fairy, may I have a dance?'

My job was once again ended. I returned to my seat and he took the lady in his arms. I have no idea what he said, but I can imagine. He never liked to see a beautiful woman alone. When their turn at dancing was done, he left her at her place. Meanwhile, the detectives were wondering if she had been imported as a spy. We never discovered her name, but later received a telegram: 'YOU WILL NEVER KNOW MY NAME BUT I AM PROUD TO HAVE DANCED WITH WINSTON CHURCHILL'

When the party was over, we left the room accompanied by our detectives. We were seen upstairs and ensconced in our beds, dreaming of the happy evening. Some time during the night, I felt a tap on my shoulder.

Immediately all my senses were alert: 'Is my father all right?'

'Non, je suis votre protecteur.'

So I said what I hoped was a Churchillian phrase: 'So keep protecting us!'

The gallant Frenchman removed himself from my room and was later removed from his duty.

30 December 1947

Well of course he caught a cold – he was really very good but I feared it was inevitable. It is much much colder here this year – and we have none of us except him felt too terribly well. I have worried and worried – even in the mid-day the contrast between sun and shadow is very sharp. This morning however he is very much better – and has survived the whole thing without a degree of temperature – and went straight to bed the moment he caught it – and wasn't a bit difficult – because he knew you would worry. This morning I have a terrible sore throat too, we all are slightly *congestioné*. This is *not* a good Marrakech year – although the sun shines brightly, it is too cold and although everything is lovely, I have worried and will worry about this. He must and will now cut an hour off the afternoon – but it is sad we have caught this really exceptionally cold year. I have thought seriously about moving 500 miles further south to Agadir – where Villiers who has arrived says it is warmer – a sea breeze – but less exceptional change between Midday and Sundown – and Sunlight and Shadow – but of course it is a formidable *déménagement*, and we do not know if the hotel could accommodate us and of course he does not want to go. The Doctor has just been and says he has now the '*légère bronchite*'! '*Savez – c'est Marrakech*', he continued – it is an exceptional year:

105

'It is too cold and too hot – it is too perfect this year'!...

Next morning – not very good news from Agadir and Taroudant this morning – we will probably have to stick it out here. It sounds funny to say 'stick it out' in this lovely place and with this sunshine, but of course the anxiety of the cold has cast a gloom on us all. However, we read that you are all having terrible weather including blizzards so perhaps we are worrying unnecessarily, and all our spirits will perk up again in a few days.

Papa is depressed by events – he thinks it is very serious and hopes the Americans take decisive action in Greece, and not fall between two stools.

Mrs Deakin is upset about her Rumania. 1947 comes to an end on a disquieting moment – perhaps we shall all feel much better when our colds are gone!

8

Dust and Dreams

I had first met Antony Beauchamp before the war, when I went to be photographed by him. He also photographed my sister Mary, who was then a debutante. His pictures made us look dreamy and wonderful. His skill as a photographer was just beginning. At that meeting he made no great impression upon me other than that I needed good pictures for publicity purposes. Then the war came and Antony Beauchamp was chosen to be a war artist and photographer. War has to be pictorially portrayed.

He was sent to Burma to draw, depict and photograph the 14th Army. One of his assignments was to have the privilege to photograph General Wingate, the British Commander-in-Chief in that theatre of war. General Wingate, ever anxious to bring attention to what had become known even then as the Forgotten Army, had spruced himself up. Antony, with courage and even with a certain brashness, asked Wingate if he would be photographed as he normally appeared, in his jungle clothes. The picture should show what the men were going through and Antony suggested that we did not need spruced-up parade gentlemen in the field.

Wingate looked at this young man, who perhaps could seem effete, with his camera, and suddenly realized what it was all about. He said, 'Are you a war correspondent?'

'No. A war photographer,' Beauchamp replied.

'What arms do you carry?'

'My camera – and of course a revolver.'

Wingate posed, with his beard and jungle clothes, and his photograph was taken. 'I do not think', said Beauchamp, 'that the 14th Army will be forgotten.' Two or three months later, Wingate was shot down by the enemy. But the 14th Army has never been forgotten.

In a lighter vein, another cameraman on the scene in Burma at that time was Cecil Beaton. He did not wear uniform, and Antony once told me that Cecil used to go about in a pink safari suit, but we must beware of apocryphal stories. He certainly made the troops laugh and perhaps alleviated the monotony of death in the jungle. Though I have had many things to say about the press in my life, the war correspondents and the front-line journalists and photographers who recorded the fighting always deserve a special mention.

After the war, when I had finally made up my mind to try to return to the beautiful fantasy world of the theatre, I had to find my image once again. I went to the already famous photographer Angus McBean. He did a most beautiful picture of me, but I was not satisfied with the bland, unemotional and immature picture that I was sure represented me no longer. I rustled through my telephone book. Beauchamp. 'Well, I will have a go at him,' I thought, as I was still living in 55 Park Lane and his studio was just around the corner. I knocked on the door, he opened it, and I said, 'Would you photograph me, please? I understand that you photograph faces.' And I flourished the pictures that had been published in the pre-war *Bystander*.

Antony Beauchamp had returned from Burma to find that his mother had not only taken over his equipment which she had said she would look after for the duration of the war, but she had also established herself as a well-known society photographer: 'Vivienne of London'. He had to compete with his own mother in regaining his reputation. My first appointment with him was a disaster. He had been in the middle of photographing a princess – a beautiful dusky princess – Niloufer of Hyderabad. He was enamoured of her beauty and, I think, of her. He suddenly had to switch his focus to a rather more prosaic figure at his door.

'Sit down. Turn your face – this way – that way – look around – look down – *smile* . . .'

On the word 'smile' I rebelled. After forty minutes, I got up and left, without smiling.

I went back to my flat and, remembering that I had a date, I cast the cares of my face aside, got into a maroon velvet suit, combed my hair, and went next door to the Dorchester Hotel. I breezed through the swing doors and looked around the foyer. My date had not appeared. 'Well,' I thought, 'at least I can walk home.' And then my eye focused on a dark, smiling young man. He rose and said, 'Miss Churchill, I have done you a great injustice. I did not know you had animation in your face. May I photograph you again, and there will be no fee.' I had not recognized him as the photographer of a few hours ago. Amused, I accepted. From then onwards, Antony started to photograph me at all times, from every angle, in animation, relaxed, smiling and serious. One of the results of all this endeavour was to be the *Life* magazine cover of me, which was to have a profound effect on both our careers. As all magnets attract, I was attracted to Antony. This was a man who had his skill in his hand – and sensitivity in his sight. But I had a career to create.

The first step was to get back on the English stage and I was happy to be offered the part of Henrietta in *The Barretts of Wimpole Street*. Alec Clunes played Browning and Margaret Johnston Elizabeth. Henrietta is a small frothy part and was perfect for me as it had a great gaiety and bounce about it. All my professional friends came to see it and it did me a lot of good. Afterwards, since Korda could find no suitable role for me on his books, he lent me to J. Arthur Rank, who had seen me as Henrietta and had said 'I have a part for her.' It was a film of modest dimensions, called *All Over the Town*. Norman Woolland was my leading man and Bryan Forbes, then unknown, was the cheeky messenger boy. We shot the film mostly out of doors in Weymouth. It was a small-town story of a girl who takes over the local newspaper during the war and has to confront the former editor, played by Norman Woolland, when he returns.

At the end of this stint, Rank asked me if I would go and open one of his new cinema chains in Canada. They were magnificent theatres and I was much feted. *All Over the Town* was shown, among all the other current Rank productions. In between my commitments in Canada, I could not resist the temptation to drop down to New York. There I found the film was already showing in what were called 'Art Theatres', it was not on the major circuits. But the cover picture had appeared in *Life* – it was 20 May 1949 – and overnight I found myself a celebrity in the way only Americans can do it. I purred with delight.

I went happily back to Canada and finished my chores for Rank, and then returned home, where there were distinct rumblings of suitable parts being found for me. By accident I ran into Gertrude Lawrence, who was a friend of my brother's. Gertie was not only famous in England thanks to her work with Noël Coward, but also in America, where she eventually made her home. They blacked out the lights on Broadway and in the West End when she died – a rare tribute. She counselled me to go back to America.

'The iron is hot,' she said. 'And you must not hesitate to grab hold of it.'

'But what about an Equity card?'

She said she did not think that after this personal success I would have any difficulty with my status in America, however humble the film may seem. 'My personal advice to you,' Gertie said, 'is that there, I believe, your theatrical life will take firm root.'

I took her advice, with some misgivings, as I was not quite sure I was ready to leave England, but having secured a job, it was soon time for me to leave for America and summer stock. It was a hot gruelling summer and, although Antony and I were both in love, I still had many doubts after my failure with Vic. Antony pursued me on the telephone. Our bills were enormous. Looking through some of the letters I wrote then to my mother, I am forcefully reminded what a stormy time it was to be for me. Plunging into American summer stock was in itself a tremendous theatrical experience and a happy one. New England was beautiful even in the great drought of 1949 – it remained green, for there were so many trees. The noise of the crickets and katydids (bigger crickets) and tree toads (enormous crickets!) was sometimes quite deafening.

The touring was exhausting, but I loved it. There was no doubt of my real love for the theatre: the only true serenity I have ever known. I would feel it sometimes when I was waiting to go on, either at a performance or perhaps in rehearsal, or even sometimes just waiting about in an empty theatre. At one New England theatre they had two great doors (out of which you slid the scenery) open for coolness. The soft black night, smelling of dried grass and ringing with crickets, pushed its way into the theatre. The voices of the players, separated by a thin canvas of paint, were a thousand miles away. The stage manager stood like a sentinel watching the cue lights, shadows moved stealthily and quietly about and I felt, unreasonably perhaps but unquestionably, at home among the shadows of those canvas halls and the dust and the dreams that lie thickly in any theatre.

I wrote to my mother:

Yes, I wouldn't have missed this for anything – I'm so glad you wanted me to do this. Antony is on his way here – he hopes, and I hope too, that America will afford him greater opportunity of broadening the scope of his activities. Also, of course, he is coming to see me. I have written to Papa – and he will probably tell you – I feel I am very near now to taking the plunge. I will tell you the moment I decide. Until then, there is nothing I can say.

I wrote to Papa also of my probable stage plans – which if they come through will keep me here till the Spring at least! 'A wandering minstrel I!'

The tour proved a professional success; the Theatre Guild (roughly equivalent to the British Old Vic or Prospect Theatre Company) wanted to put out a road show of it to all the major cities of America and possibly to Toronto and Montreal. I had to consult Korda first and again American Equity would have to give their permission.

Equity proved favourably inclined; the Theatre Guild decided to put on the road show, and Antony and I, amid all of this, decided to take the plunge. I wrote again to my mother from Sea Island, Georgia, where we were taking a break on 14 October:

The long summer is over at last. I have collapsed here on a strip of wind-swept beach.

There is so much to tell you – I feel almost paralysed when I pick up the pen. Well, first things first. Antony and I have decided to get married. I hope and pray that I will make him happy. I hope and pray too that you will find him an addition to our family circle. Thank you darling Mama for your patience and forbearance through these difficult months while I had to sort out my mind and heart.

Only two things spoilt our wedding for me: the fact that I was not at home and my parents were not there; and one last agonizing moment when I spoke to my mother on the telephone and realized that she had not received – that none of my family had received – my cables. They had learnt of our marriage from the press.

Once I had decided, I wanted to do it quickly (as, in fact, my mother had suggested) so as to minimize the time in which stories could be dug up by the press. I couldn't let my parents know earlier, because I was not sure of my decision until the last minute. By the time true purpose emerged from my procrastination I was a total wreck and there were precisely forty-eight hours left before I had to get back on the tour.

We could have been married in New York, but I dreaded the prospect of City Hall again. Apart from Bernie Baruch and the Lawrences I had no close friends there, and Antony had none. Suddenly, when all the fussing and fretting inside me were done, we both felt that since we were alone there by the sea and sand with fresh air and flowering azaleas and palm trees, if it could be arranged we would much rather get married there. It was an eternal regret to us that our telegrams were beaten by the news, for we told no one until we had confirmed with the local Western Union that my parents would be in England to receive the news. Otherwise I believe they would have liked how it was done, and would have been moved by the kindness and delicacy of the strangers who took us under their wing and gave us a wedding that I felt was fit for Antony and beyond what I ever expected could happen to me.

The manager of the hotel at Sea Island was a young married man. He undertook all the legal preliminaries, which were simple enough but involved a complete day of motoring here and there and considerable mileage. He then introduced us to Mr and Mrs Alfred Jones who seemed to own the entire property of Sea Island.

They were a charming, happily married couple with four children who had lived all their married life in Sea Island. They had a lovely house about thirty yards from the sea shore.

The children and dogs all bounded in from the beach and Mr and Mrs Jones made us feel that it would give them great pleasure if we would be married in their drawing room rather than in some city hall or the Cloister Hotel, which was the only alternative. We chose 5.30 when the sun was just about to set and everything was in a golden light. Mrs Harned, the manager's young and beautiful wife, assigned herself to me and I had to find a wedding dress.

I had with me a dress I had never worn because it was two sizes too large. Off we went and found Mrs Allcott, a delightful old lady who lived deep in a wood. Out came the scissors and pins; she undertook a job on the dress which a professional would have paled at, and it was beautifully done. Then there was the question of a hat. I was worried because the dress, though pretty, was not really designed for a wedding.

The next morning, while I was having my hair shampooed, Mrs Harned walked in with some pink veiling and small pink roses and before my eyes created a romantic hat; she then made me some gloves out of the pink veiling. Perhaps I should describe the dress: a high-waisted skirt of pale colours – greens, pinks, beige – with a delicate stripe in it of green, and the top, pink satin with a circular neck almost off the shoulders. This was what I was worried about, but the pink veil of the hat cascaded down over one shoulder and softened it.

It was nearly time for the wedding and I dressed myself. I was shattered when I discovered my parents could not have got my messages, and it seemed as if everything was to go wrong once again. But I convinced myself they would not want me to feel that, so suddenly a great calm descended on me and the sun shone benignly on us.

Mrs Harned and an older, sweet Scottish woman arrived. I was buttoned into my dress and they escorted me down to a car and off we drove in very good time to the Joneses' house. Mrs Jones met us and showed me the drawing room which was filled with flowers – great white chrysanthemums – and then I was shown upstairs where I waited watching the sunlight sink slowly, and the waves of the Atlantic lapping the sand gently.

The ceremony was simple, but they had enlarged the legal text and it included much from the prayer book; the judge read it slowly and kindly. There was also an orchestra which played 'Here Comes the Bride' when I entered and the Wedding March afterwards. I certainly hadn't expected that.

Afterwards, we drank champagne outside till it was quite dark and all the while the small orchestra played softly. Then we sat down to a delicious dinner. It was all over by 9 p.m. and as we left they threw rice at us! Then we drove, not back to the hotel, but to a lovely house which the Harneds and the Joneses had arranged for us to have. We were dropped at the front door by the chauffeur who drove away at once; all the lights of the house were on, all the doors were open, we went in – no one! Flowers in each room – and drinks laid out on a tray. All our clothes had been packed and brought from the hotel. The drive had taken fifteen minutes and we thought we were miles away, but in the morning we discovered it was next door to the Joneses! They had purposely made the driver drive us around so that we would feel far away. In the morning they came again and packed us off on the aeroplane. Alas, I had to start rehearsing right away with a new company for the Theatre Guild tour.

On our way to New York, I tried to write some of my thoughts to my mother:

They will come now – but before, the words stuck because I could tell you nothing definite. It seemed as if I would never get my thoughts clear – or ever be able to face starting again a life with someone. Antony has been very patient. He has asked me nothing but has borne through, never wavering in his intention, or faltering in a buoyant confidence that whatever the past, he was the future. Since it was suddenly here that I felt calm and happy and decided, I wanted it to happen here. The ceremony meant a lot to both of us. Only 48 hours before we plunge back into our busy lives – but we will never forget them – we are very happy and very determined to make a real marriage and life together. All in due course we hope to be the founders of a new line – the Beauchamps. We will head our family tree.

Immediately after my marriage to Antony, we returned to New York, where plans were already under way for a tour of *Philadelphia Story* with the Theatre Guild, thanks again to the fairy wand of Gertrude Lawrence. I had played in Gertie's and Richard Aldrich's summer theatre in Westport, Connecticut, where, once again, she had urged me to stay in the USA and not to return home, as my feet were being successfully planted on that side of the Atlantic. It was an accolade for a moderately known foreign star to get a tour with the Theatre Guild. The tour itinerary was, roughly, Philadelphia, Toronto, then down to a rather staid Detroit and Pittsburgh. It was in Pittsburgh that I had a surprising telephone call. We were to have played Cleveland the next week. The telephone call was from friends of mine in Cleveland who had been looking forward to my visit, offering me all kinds of American hospitality. My delight at hearing them on the telephone froze when they said, 'We were so disappointed when we read that your show has been cancelled.'

I was stunned. I thought that at least the Theatre Guild would have informed the principals, myself and Jeffrey Lynn. We had not been doing too well with James Barry's *Philadelphia Story*. It is a frothy, delightful comedy, made famous by Katharine Hepburn's creation of the character of Tracy Lord. I had been somewhat dubious in taking over a part so obviously dovetailed to her astringent and whimsical personality. When we were selling out on the tour in Philadelphia itself, I had the pleasure of meeting James Barry, who had travelled down to see how it was all going. He was to give me one of the bouquets that I still cherish. He said he had written the play for Katie. He was more than half in love with her and felt she needed a vehicle to highlight her special qualities.

'To me,' he said, 'there could be no one else as Tracy Lord but her. Yet you have shown me a different side of a Tracy I have never dreamed of, and given her another dimension.' Katharine Hepburn had always been one of my 'heroines' and Jeff had been her regular leading man before the war and it had been hard for me not to copy her. I felt tears of pride pricking behind my eyes.

Not many weeks later, James Barry was to die as, alas, was the Theatre Guild tour of his play to die in Pittsburgh. In fact, everything died. The theatre itself, the old Nixon Theatre, was demolished several months later.

I went to find Jeff Lynn and told him the shattering news about our notice. He was equally amazed that we had not been informed. The attendances were poor as the play was very main line and rather la-di-da and did not go down well in these industrial cities. Sure enough, the next day the notice all actors dread went up on the board. Meanwhile, unbeknown to us, our fortunes had been followed by the West Coast producers, Lewis and Young (affectionately known in the business as 'screw us and run'). A mysterious voice in a telephone call from the West Coast said, 'We have read the sad news of the cancellation of your tour but we have been following you with interest. Come out to the Coast and we will arrange a tour for you to star in *Goodbye My Fancy*.'

Still smarting from the Theatre Guild blow, I replied, 'Goodbye my foot. If you want me, it's me, the cast and *Philadelphia Story*.'

The next day, between shows, I was told there was a gentleman waiting for me in the restaurant. I went down, shook hands inadvertently with the major domo, who smiled sweetly and discreetly pointed in the direction of Mr Lewis. Coming straight to the point he said, 'Mr Young and I accept your proposal, if you and Jeff Lynn could halve your individual salaries.' ($1500 down to $750 per week.)

I went to the telephone and called Jeff.

'Splendid,' he said. 'Of course. Anything to keep the show on the road.'

I went back to Mr Lewis and said, 'It's agreed. Well done and thank you.'

That night, I had the privilege of pinning up the notice of continuation, under new management, of the show to the West Coast and asking any members who would like to stay with us to sign below. The notice was signed by myself and Jeff. Everyone signed, except one understudy who had a sick mother in New York.

We whirled through the end of the week to an empty theatre, but with a song in our hearts. Then we had a week off – which was covered by the Theatre Guild. No actor in his right mind can blame any management for closing a show that is losing them money. All was forgiven and forgotten, and, at the end of the week, the Theatre Guild gave a cocktail party for me.

The company had left for Chicago, where they had to change trains to proceed to the West Coast. There was a four-hour wait there and I should have been able to join them in good time. But the engine of my train broke down and it was discovered that we had a 'hot box in the caboose'. I stared at the conductor uncomprehendingly and he did not enlighten me; but my mind was agitated as the delay in unheating the hot box was to make me miss my connection in Chicago. Then came the blizzard.

At first, I was quite unmoved by this storm of snow and said, 'Well, take me to the airport and I shall fly.' They stared at me as if I had just been let out of a lunatic asylum, and told me politely that when this sort of weather set in, it could last up to six days, which would mean that there were no flights out for four to six days. The airports were closed already.

'But I have to get there. What do you suggest – sleigh and reindeers?'

My agitation and distress must have been apparent, for I was told there was a slow freight train leaving just after midnight, on which there were several passenger carriages, a dining car and some sleeping accommodation.

'I will take it,' I said, and booked a compartment for myself, and then found that I had time on my hands. What to do in Chicago while waiting for a train? My eye fell on a theatre poster, announcing that an English company were appearing – the name of the play I have forgotten, but a magnificent actor was appearing in it: A.E. Matthews. I did not know him personally, nor for that matter any of the cast, but I turned up and bought a ticket. In the interval, I went backstage and introduced myself. They gave me a great welcome. It was like going home.

The journey half way across America usually took four days in good weather. As we were following the so-called fast train to Seattle, which had a snow-plough, we made remarkably good time coasting behind it. I occupied my time in writing long letters to my friends, and of course one to my mother.

I had previously travelled across the United States by car when I was married to Vic Oliver, but this journey was different, as we were going by the northern route close to the border with Canada. We were to play three days in Portland, Oregon, and two days in Seattle, Washington, before climbing on the golden ski-run down the West Coast to San Francisco.

Although it was a four-day journey, the slow train was to finish only two hours behind the express. What I didn't know then but was to learn in detail later was that the company were as worried as I was myself to know where I was. To keep them all calm, although we had been on the road for months, the stage manager planned to hold rehearsals and my understudy prepared to take my place. Jeff Lynn, always delightful and courteous, must have been a great help and comfort, too. They could not know that I was padding along behind them like a bloodhound, under the shield of their snow-plough.

When I knew that we were within an hour of arriving, I asked the steward of the restaurant car if there was any drinking water left. He said: 'I can find you some.' I told him it was not for drinking, but so that I could wash my hair. The carafes were rescued from the dining car and I washed my hair in cold water. Then I composed myself for the arrival. I thought the Lord Mayor must have arrived – there seemed to be so many people on the platform.

The stage manager greeted me and said, 'Everything is organized, but the show will not now be until one o'clock.'

'A.m. or p.m.?' I asked.

The press laughed. 'Oh! We've waited much longer,' they said. 'We once waited a whole week for Miss Katherine Cornell.'

Apparently the audience would go home and come back when they wanted to, and they would watch the sets being put up. It looked as though our show would be ready to go at about one o'clock that morning. I was dumbfounded, but it was explained that they had so little live theatre out there, especially at that time of year, they wouldn't miss it for the world. So on went the show. I embraced my understudy, who grinned bravely.

'Never mind,' I said. 'I may still break a leg.'

We did have a glorious, warm success in both Seattle and Portland that made all the effort worthwhile; and then we were there, almost immediately it seemed, in that fantastic city San Francisco. Although it appeared to us, the excited and somewhat harassed actors, that we must be late, we were not in fact behind our schedule for San Francisco; so we had time to find our various digs and habitats and to see the city itself.

There are two theatres side by side in San Francisco – the Geary and the Curran. The Curran does mostly opera and musicals, while the Geary does the legitimate theatre. The two theatres share a wall and dancers can peep through and watch actors, and actors can peep through and watch dancers. The main thing about San Francisco for me as a 'thespian' – an actor and a dancer – is that it is a cosmopolitan city and therefore has great audiences. Everybody loves to play San Francisco.

We were to play three weeks there before moving down the coast to the Biltmore Theatre in downtown Los Angeles. I was glad for the long stop because it was election time in England in February 1950. Antony and I hated to miss it all and it was impossible to know how it was going. I wrote to Diana and Mary: 'As far as the Americans are concerned, there are only four candidates standing – The Churchills!' Randolph; Christopher Soames, Mary's husband; Duncan Sandys, Diana's husband; and, of course, my father. Everyone would wring our hands and send his or her love and every good wish to my father. They seemed to love him in America even more than their own president – if possible.

I was grateful that we were staying in San Francisco for three weeks – I loved this city and we were doing well with wonderful enthusiastic audiences which makes playing easy and a pleasure. My plans were to get quickly back to England, after the end of the two weeks in Los Angeles. But the best laid plans can be disrupted by good fortune.

9

Facts Are Better

During the two years' hard training, five hours a day, at my dancing school, I fell in love with my dream hero, Fred Astaire. I went out and bought a glossy picture of him and on it I wrote, 'To Sarah, my favourite dancing partner, from ...' and there was his famous signature – stamped, of course. I stuck this picture up in my bedroom and gazed and gazed at it, whirling and whirling about the place in his arms. I think the tune of those days was, 'Won't you change partners and dance?'

My father had been impressed by my perseverance in this difficult vocation and one day he came up to my bedroom and saw Fred Astaire's picture. 'Humph,' he said. 'Facts are better than dreams.'

I flared and said back to him (I must have been all of seventeen at the time), 'How can you have a fact without a dream? Leonardo da Vinci dreamt of the aeroplane and he never saw or flew in one.'

My father humphed again and left the room.

Seventeen years later, we were both proved right. I *did* dance with Fred Astaire. And reality did prove better than the dream. I hope other dancers will forgive me – especially Nureyev – but we all have our dream heroes. To me, as a dancer trained in the classical style, there was only one other dancer in the world – Massine. But I still get the thrill of my adolescent days when I see Fred Astaire dancing.

When I got to Hollywood, Ginger Rogers did me a great courtesy. When she knew I was to be in his next film dancing with him, she sent me round the film clips of her dance routines with him, and said, 'Study them carefully. You will see that basically the steps are simple and he does not really vary them much. The only thing is to keep pace with him – and, as Coward would say, "Don't fall over the furniture!"'

Many years later Ginger had a triumphant show in England. I went to her last night and sent her round a card of welcome and congratulations.

To my amazement at the end of the show she said, 'Thank you, London, thank you, wonderful people, and now I would like to introduce to you an old friend – one of your own, Sarah Churchill.'

I was frozen to my seat. Shielding her eyes from the spot lights she said: 'Hi, Sarah ... Where are you?'

I stood up to the warm ovation, which she had initiated, and she said, 'Be sure to come and see me after the show.'

I was moved. When the curtain fell, I slipped out through the little secret entrance, across the now barren stage, and into her dressing room. What can I say? She is a gracious and talented lady.

After the West Coast success of *Philadelphia Story*, I decided to move from my more humble hotel to the world-renowned Mark Hopkins Hotel on San Francisco's Knob Hill. The cover of *Life* featuring myself had proved an 'open sesame' for Antony as well as for me and he had got some excellent commissions with the film studios doing portraits of their starlets. He flew up from Hollywood each weekend in time to see the last show on Saturday night and we would spend a relaxed Sunday together. Our joint successes, I felt, should be crowned by a suite at the Top of the Mark. Well, of course, not quite the top – the top is taken over by the famous revolving restaurant and cocktail lounge. I have vertigo, but somehow, you don't notice it up there, even in spite of a cocktail or two.

Since my arrival on the coast, agents had called unceasingly, which I found flattering, but bewildering. I had at this time no agent except Al Parker in London, who was too far away. My East Coast activities had been managed by Mr Hoyt, a charming gentleman, but it was mutually agreed that should things go well I would be better represented on the spot in Hollywood. I confided my thoughts about so many agents to Antony, who was equally bewildered. Anyway, perhaps Antony and I were enjoying ourselves and the sweet taste of life too much to bother about anything but the present.

One Sunday morning, however, the telephone rang and a soft, purring voice announced that she was Princess Alexis Thurn-Taxis and would like to take a cocktail with us. I did not wish to commit a gaffe, so I made agreeable social noises and also discreet enquiries. I discovered that it was a famous Austrian name, a name that I should have known, perhaps. Her husband was a director and she herself was one of Louis B. Mayer's top readers and a casting director. Antony and I mentally chewed over this information. Her professional name, presumably her maiden name, was Miss Lillie Messenger. Without more ado, we arranged an appointment for cocktails with her at the Top of the Mark. She turned out to be a most vivacious woman, tiny (I almost towered above her) and plumpish, with twinkling eyes. I immediately nicknamed her 'Lilliput', though when we met formally for cocktails I naturally addressed her as Princess. She laughed and said, 'Well, I am just Miss Lillie Messenger.' She said she would like to see if there was anything she could do for us in the few weeks of our stay there.

She said she had seen the late Saturday night show of *Philadelphia Story* and expressed surprise that I had no one to represent me. I told her about the somewhat disjointed methods of my representation, and of the swiftness with which the golden ski-ride of the West Coast had presented itself. The conversation was easy and delightful, and the third time around the revolving floor, I said to her. 'I think my decision on a representative will occur the first time anybody offers me a part in a film.'

'Ah!' she said. 'So, you are interested in films?'

'Oh, yes indeed – aren't we all?' I replied, thinking of the trouble I was having with the juvenile lead in *Philadelphia Story*. Realizing that we were approaching Hollywood, she was trying desperately to lose the puppy plumpness that was so essential to the part she played. She was not the only one, as a metamorphosis seemed to sweep through the entire cast, filling them with excitement at the prospect of realizing their dreams.

'What kind of film would you like to do?' asked Lillie.

So I told her that I had started as a dancer in the musical revue *Follow The Sun*, and that I should dearly love, after the long hard tour in the theatre, to whirl and find my dancing shoes again. I told her the dream fantasy of my youth about Fred Astaire. She was the sort of person to whom you could confide what might have been whimsy to other people; in fact, I suppose till that moment I had forgotten my seventeen-year-old dream.

When I finished this cheerful and inconsequential reminiscence of those early days, she said, 'Well, as a matter of fact, I am casting the new Fred Astaire musical and MGM are looking for an English girl.'

I swear the Top of the Mark changed gear and revolved a trifle faster.

Lillie said gently, 'Finish your job here and in Los Angeles and I will look into things.'

She left us slightly stunned. I was glad it was Sunday with no theatre performance as I would unquestionably have fallen into the same bemused state as the rest of the company.

Theatrically, Los Angeles was to prove a disappointment. The notices were bad – industrial city again, perhaps? Or had we just been spoilt by San Francisco? It was agreed that the tour should end there, and I decided to go East again. There were nice repeat dates for me to play back on my old stamping ground and I accepted them, not wishing to dilly-dally about Hollywood looking as if I were hanging around for a job.

Before I left, I had a call from Lillie Messenger. MGM were more than interested and would I make a test for them? Judy Garland was to be the star and her husband, Vincent Minelli, the director. I told her of Antony's and my plans to return East. An audition was quickly arranged. Vincent Minelli was a gentleman. He explained that this was not to test my acting ability, but to check my features photographically and assess how I would meld into the general scene. He gave out an aura of sympathy and his eyes never left your face while you were rehearsing – he reminded me very much of Soldati. He said, 'Do something you like, what you feel.' He explained that neither the script nor the casting was complete.

I cannot recall what I did. It was not from *Philadelphia Story*, but I feel it must have been some lyrical prose, of which there is such an abundance in the English language.

As soon as it was over, Antony and I left for New York, leaving matters in Lillie Messenger's capable hands. Back in the bustle of New York and my East Coast engagements, I did not have time to brood. It was in Buffalo that Antony, who was accompanying me on a shortish tour, burst into the restaurant where we were having a pre-performance dinner, and said, 'You've got it! You're in the next Fred Astaire film.'

As soon as I could complete my engagements, I was required back on the West Coast.

I was naturally excited and found it difficult to finish my engagements. Lillie had arranged a contract, which she naturally handled, as she was now my representative on the West Coast. It needed my signature, so Antony and I flew back to California.

We arrived at seven o'clock in the morning and were met by MGM officials. Then Antony, Lillie and I all bundled off to have breakfast. I was at the studios by three o'clock and was taken by the producer Arthur Freed to meet Fred Astaire for the first time.

I am not sure that I didn't wish I was altogether somewhere else. All sorts of jolly things came to my mind, such as, 'Through these portals you pass but once' – looking for the exit. Everybody was polite. They looked at me and I had no alternative but to look back at them. There seemed little to say. Strange bits of music-hall songs went through my head, such as 'I'm here – because I'm here -- because I'm here' roughly to the tune of 'Auld Lang Syne'. The silence was interminable and beginning to get uncomfortable.

Suddenly, Lillie said, 'Mr Astaire is very interested in horse racing.'

I looked at this lithe, genial, sprite-like man and said, 'So is my father.'

The ice was broken and the conversation rolled merrily on about horses, race-courses and, although I was not up-to-date on Fred Astaire's successful ventures into the scene, what I was able to tell him about my father's horses, Colonist 2 and Vienna, saved the day.

The meeting broke up on a relaxed note. On the way back to our hotel in the car, I said to Lillie Messenger (from now onwards 'Lilliput'):

'I do not believe that acting will be as difficult as what we have just been through.' Knowing that I could trust her discretion, I said with appropriate respect, 'I think that Arthur Freed and Fred Astaire could have stopped a conversation between George Bernard Shaw and Winston Churchill.'

She laughed. 'They're not exactly the talkative type.'

The merry-go-round was about to begin. The photos were taken, the interviews given and the usual publicity announcing my contract with MGM was duly printed. But in the meantime and after only a few days, we were to receive a letter from Bebe Daniels and Ben Lyon – an invitation to take their beach house in Santa Monica.

It was a palace of the old Hollywood days, about thirty-five minutes from the MGM studios and right on the sand with the Pacific breezes blowing in and the Pacific waters lapping the door. We moved in straight away, although we had not yet found a maid, but we couldn't wait to leave the hotel. We had fun opening all the windows and stripping the beds in case of damp and spiders. There were no spiders, but plenty of damp; I much prefer damp. Every room had an electric heater, so it wasn't hard to dry them out, and we rang up the market for groceries, which were delivered in twenty minutes, also whisky. In no time, we were toasting ourselves in our faded and slightly sea-stormed palace of former glories.

We spent a lazy first day there and the next day I hunted for a maid. I called in at the studio to hear the musical score and then sneaked off to have a secret dancing lesson so that I could prepare for my first rehearsal with Fred Astaire.

When I finally got the script, I discovered I had to sing. My heart sank. Although I can take liberties with my voice on the stage – like Gertrude Lawrence – I was no real singer. And the role was that of a professional singer. When I told Lilliput about this she said, 'Oh! That doesn't matter. You can be dubbed.' In other words someone else would sing for me. But I did not like this idea at all. If it had just been an incidental part of my role, I would not have minded, but to have as the centre of my part something that someone else would have to do for me was distressing.

There were several other problems with the film and I felt it would be inopportune to speak until they were settled. Meanwhile, I kept on my secret dancing classes with two French brothers, Nico and Pierre Charisse. Finally, I plucked up courage and said I would like the producers to see me dance. They were surprised, but an audition was arranged for ten o'clock the next morning.

Pierre and I arrived. He had danced professionally for twenty years and was a small, tough, wiry man, but he was nervous for me, and I was equally nervous for myself. We met at a café outside the studio and had a swig of brandy, then chewing some gum and looking as innocent as the dawn, we presented ourselves in the rehearsal hall. We ran through it first with the strange pianist, and my heart thumped so loudly I felt I couldn't breathe, though all the windows were open and it was still cool.

Suddenly the door opened and like executioners, in marched Arthur Freed the producer, Roger Eadons the associate producer, Nick Castle the dance director and Fred Astaire himself. They sat on a row of chairs like crows. Antony sneaked in casually and joined them.

'Don't be nervous,' said Fred, kindly.

Little Pierre drew himself up: 'We are not nervous. We are honoured you are here.'

Well, we did it. At the end they applauded, spontaneously it seemed, and Fred congratulated Pierre on the routine, and said to me, 'You *can* dance. You dance very well. But I could never lift you as he does.'

They all trooped out and we were left panting. Antony was delighted and said they really had been pleased; but I could not rejoice until, in the evening, I heard that they had agreed to change the part into that of a dancer, instead of a singer, and that I really was to dance with Fred Astaire.

I worked hard at my dancing, practising with Pierre Charisse nearly every day. I was happy doing it and carefully avoided getting myself involved in the various studio fracas. At the beginning of July I made a wardrobe test with Fred Astaire. We stood side by side solemnly while everyone discussed if we looked all right together. Fred was shy and apologized for the fact that he had no toupé on, saying, 'It makes me two inches taller.'

Meanwhile, I sagged at the knees and said I couldn't think that anything was necessary – 'Why I only come up to your chin.' Then we stepped round in a circle in an awkward way, as if neither of us had ever walked, let alone danced in our lives before. And that was the end of that day.

While the cameras were purring away, Fred told me with a weary smile that he had been worried about Judy Garland. 'She is so unreliable,' he said. She had looked radiant and wistful to me, but sure enough was out of the picture before long. She had one of her many upsets and left; which meant, alas, that her husband Vincent Minelli, with whom I had done my test, left as well. Judy Garland was replaced by June Allyson. Through it all I kept out of the arguments as far as possible, sat in my palace and thought how fantastic it was to be paid hugely for doing nothing.

I did in the end, however, manage to get on to the set, and *Royal Wedding* was finally made, though not without another major crisis when June Allyson discovered she was pregnant, so that all the major dance scenes had to be re-shot. The third and final choice of leading lady was Jane Powell, who learned both the singing and the dancing she was required to do with great rapidity. It must have been a great relief to Fred Astaire, for whatever other qualities the earlier choices may have had, Jane Powell was as efficient as a toothpick, and the poor girl must have felt she was dancing on very thin ice.

As it turned out, my first professional stay in Hollywood was not a long one. I realized that the glitter of the place was tarnishing, but there were many happy encounters in the brief time that I spent there and even I who call myself 'the late Miss Churchill' had made it in time to see what Hollywood was all about. No expense was ever spared and all creature comforts were looked to; but for me, the sharp difference between the activity of the theatre and the seemingly endless wait to start work was tiresome. I am an impatient person and if I am not active I would rather stay in bed.

I filled in my time by keeping up my dancing lessons with the Charisse brothers, who would be proud to be remembered not only for themselves but for the beautiful Cyd Charisse of the endless legs, then the wife of Nico the senior brother. I amused myself also by dancing anonymously with Pierre Charisse in their school demonstrations. I am not a gregarious person and was quite happy to sit idly by, enjoying the fact that I was in a Fred Astaire film.

Antony, however, was not letting the grass grow under his feet. After the success of his picture of me on the cover of *Life*, his portrait of the then still unknown English actress Audrey Hepburn had added to his reputation. When he discovered Audrey Hepburn in a chorus line in a London theatre, before our marriage, he told me he had found another face for his series of 'New Faces'. He said he went backstage and said he would like to photograph her, but she had replied that she was afraid she couldn't afford his fees. He said, 'I will photograph you for nothing. You can pay me later.'

Much later, when she was a big star and able to choose her still cameraman for a film she was making in Italy, she remembered and asked for Antony. She was always one of our favourite people, both as a person and an actress.

Antony was sent to scout out some Americans, yet unknown, and the studios were very co-operative – sending a succession of their beauties to him to be photographed.

He didn't set up a formal studio, but used the Californian landscape and sunlight to enhance what he thought were the main features of their physical attractions. He also used Bebe and Ben's house, which afforded many backdrops for different stars.

One of the most memorable events, even at that time, when she was totally unknown, was the visit of a shy little blonde girl who came in wearing, for some extraordinary reason, an enormous mackintosh. Her agent came in with her but said perhaps Antony would like to photograph her alone and he would wait outside in the car.

Antony raised a somewhat quizzical eyebrow to me, meaning, 'What the dickens am I to do with this one?'

I suggested the terrace, thinking the mackintosh coat was somewhat unsuitable for the Californian sea and sky. So, up they went on to the terrace and moments later Antony flew down the stairs in a great state of excitement and said, 'Fetch me a white rug quickly and I'll tell you all about it later.'

The forlorn little waif, when she saw the terrace with its plants and its view over the sparkling sea, had thrown off her mac and revealed herself in a bikini that must have taken about three minutes to knit. She spread her arms towards the sky and her whole personality changed. Antony, armed with the white rug, threw it over the cane sofa and asked her to lie down on it – which she did, with a seductive and kittenish but innocent air. Having exhausted the possibilities of the terrace, they moved to the beach. Then, the session over, she replaced her mackintosh and became the waif again. She thanked him politely, thanked me, and Antony saw her to the door and her faithful agent.

He came back bursting with excitement and said, 'Unquestionably I have photographed a star-to-be.'

He was right; she was Marilyn Monroe.

I have never been what is known as gregarious, though that does not mean I am anti-social. Hollywood was a round of parties, which I found alarming and sometimes boring, although people were kind. I tended to leave Antony to his field and stayed at home a lot, much alone, in my rented palace quite content, although idleness has never appealed to me. The entertainments I used to enjoy most were our own Sunday brunches, when we could return hospitality to people we had met. We got to know many people in this way: directors such as Preston Sturgis and Edmund Gould; actors Charles Laughton, Cedric Hardwicke; Paul Hesse, the famous photographer of Rheingold fame, who was to offer Antony half his business – an offer which he declined, mistakenly to my mind.

Here at these brunches I felt more relaxed and able to talk properly to each of my guests. Brunches were popular in Hollywood, as the guests could slip along casually any time from 12.30 and stay till 5 p.m., when they could go home to their early beds, to be fresh for their chores in the studio next day.

Three people who did not often leave their own havens were Garbo, Dietrich and Chaplin, but we were lucky enough to be invited to visit them. Garbo was already a virtual recluse, and Dietrich a famous home lover and fantastic cook. Chaplin at this moment, in the growing ferocity of the McCarthy period, was much in disfavour and sealed himself up in a fortress.

Marlene Dietrich I found a warm, ebullient and loving person. Having met us briefly at a party, she invited us to her house one Sunday. Presiding as a glamorous duenna in kitchen or dining room, she made everyone feel at home, including newcomers such as Antony and myself. She had an untypical set of people around her – more New York than most of the Hollywood parties. I formed a great admiration for her, thinking how well she had managed life at the pinnacle – and indeed all the way up to it – with ease and grace. Later, I worked with her daughter, Maria Riva, when I was on television in the *Hallmark Hall of Fame*. She was a beautiful girl. If it is difficult to live up to being a great man's daughter, it must be even more difficult to be a daughter of one of the most beautiful women in the world. Later, when misfortune struck me at Malibu, Marlene sent a message through a friend to say, 'Give Sarah my very best regards. Tell her I am thinking of her and to remember that this is all part of the business.'

A valuable friend was Harry Crocker, who wrote a mild and gentle column for a Hollywood paper. It was through him we stormed the Chaplin fortress. He was a long-time friend of Charlie Chaplin and had been in many films with him. But first, it was through Harry that we met Garbo in her hermitage. Already, what I consider her mania for solitude and fear of crowds was increasing. Once she went to a supermarket and, naturally, crowds gathered. She rushed into a telephone box and called Harry Crocker: 'Come and get me. Please.' He found her trembling, like a gazelle at bay, and took her home.

We had several delightful dinners with Greta Garbo, during which she was relaxed, happy and full of marvellous stories. Elaborate plans were made for us to go to a fancy-dress dance. Like a child, she loved planning and day-dreaming. Of course, we never went to the dance. Time and again she would be approached by leading directors to return to films, and scripts would be showered upon her by producers trying to winkle her out of her self-imposed retirement. Now and again she would toy happily with a story and get everybody worked up to a great pitch of excitement. 'I really think I have got her interested,' they would convince themselves. Suddenly the mood would change. The famous pout and Nordic melancholy would appear. 'I am sorry but I cannot do it.' The producer or director of the moment would hide his disappointment and Garbo would veil herself once more in mystery.

One night when we were having dinner with her, she said, 'There is a party. Let us go.'

'But we haven't been invited.'

'I have, and you are my guests.'

Fearful lest this moment of enthusiasm should wane, we fled the dinner table, scrambled into cars and actually got to the party. She rushed up to the host and hostess who proved to be Sam and Frances Goldwyn and introduced her guests. Needless to say they were delighted to see her. Not so some of the other stars, I thought! For the legendary 'shooting star' drew *all* attention; one leading star, in fact, left.

She grabbed my hand and said, 'Come quickly Sarah!'

Ignoring the solicitous waiters, she went behind the bar and said, 'What will you have to drink?'

Vodka was a popular drink in those days. She mixed my concoction professionally and then bent down to fix her own brew. She came up triumphant and smiling: 'Now we can go back to the party. I believe in always mixing one's own drinks at these affairs.'

This was not considered bad manners on her part, but then very little was, as her sorties into these parties were always celebrated moments. I wondered, perhaps wishfully, if she had put aside her shyness, although she was undoubtedly a great friend of the Goldwyns, to give the newcomers – Antony and myself – her special introduction.

We did not stay long at the Goldwyns' but were whirled away merrily, first to her house for a nightcap and then on to our own home. Antony, of course, was electrified and riveted by her.

'I have simply got to photograph her.'

A more complicated fortress to storm was Charles Chaplin's. He was by then happily married to Oona O'Neill, daughter of the author Eugene O'Neill, but I believe for mostly political reasons had sealed himself up in his house and we had to find a way to get Antony in. Harry Crocker was persona grata, and it was through Harry telling Chaplin that we were happy-go-lucky people who would not abuse his privacy, and also how much it meant to Antony, that a chink appeared in the armour. Antony was by now one of the up-and-coming photographers of the day, and perhaps Charlie remembered his visit to Chartwell and his meeting with my father. I certainly still remembered the enchanting performance he put on for the Churchill children. Perhaps just being English helped.

Harry got a tentative reply that Chaplin would be interested to meet us both, and Oona said to Harry, 'I doubt he'll finally agree. He may say yes, but he may back out.' She herself did not feel a bit averse to the idea, and I feel must have added gentle persuasion. Anyway, Charlie liked young people and was always willing to give a hand if he saw any hint of talent. One day, Harry came to us in great excitement and said an appointment had been arranged. Charlie had seen some of Antony's pictures which Harry had planted in his house. We were tremendously excited.

But, as Oona had warned, one day before, there came a polite but firm change of plan – he had to see his banker on that morning. I was disappointed for Antony, but he took it in his stride and sent the following cheeky telegram:

SIR HAROLD CROCKER MAID SARAH AND SQUIRE BEAUCHAMP WILL APPROACH CHAPLIN DRAWBRIDGE TOMORROW AT 3 PM WHERE WE SHALL REMAIN ENCAMPED UNTIL YOUR RETURN FROM THE 'BANKER'. I SHOULD NOT THINK OF DISAPPOINTING YOU BY LETTING YOU DOWN AND RUNNING OUT ON MY PROMISE TO TAKE YOUR PHOTOGRAPH!

Harry Crocker burst into laughter and said, 'I put my money on you.' Chaplin relented, the portcullis went up and the drawbridge came down. And we went in.

It was still with great trepidation, however, that Antony went to this meeting. Chaplin's courtesy could not have been more welcoming, and after giving us the then popular drink of Moscow Mule – vodka and ginger beer – he did a fantastic routine for us, which Harry joined in as he had often worked with him in the past. We were doubled up with laughter and relaxed. Oona and her children had come from upstairs and sat watching. Suddenly Charlie's mood changed and he said, 'Now to work.' Antony had been so nervous that, for once, he had taken along an assistant. The next routines which Chaplin did were more restrained – pausing professionally to allow Antony to get his pictures – but still just as hilarious.

Suddenly I noticed that the assistant's face had gone green. He spoke to Antony and Antony's face went green, so I turned another shade paler and was greener. 'What is the matter?' asked Chaplin. Antony turned to his assistant who was now trembling and asked the same question. The shutter speeds had been set incorrectly – Antony had not got a single shot on film. Charlie Chaplin was silent for a moment, obviously controlling his anger. Then, naturally and professionally, he said, 'Then we shall just have to do it again.'

When *Royal Wedding* was finished, edited, dubbed and released – it was called *Wedding Bells* in England – I began to feel that this part of Hollywood was to end for me. I went to Louis B. Mayer and asked him to release me from my lucrative seven-year contract. I saw the great old man alone and explained my position. I was well aware of the honour that he had done me in employing me, but pointed out to him that there were now three red-headed English ladies – Greer Garson, still in her prime, me at thirty-four, no longer a starlet, and the up-and-coming Deborah Kerr.

I asked, 'Actually, L.B., what do you have in mind for me?'

He pressed a button on his desk and asked for the planners and script writers. When they were all assembled he said, 'What do we have lined up for Miss Churchill?'

After some hesitation in their faces, they all answered as L.B.'s eyes were compelling: 'Nothing at the moment.'

He dismissed them and said it was with regret that he must accept I was right. He would release me from my contract. 'But stay around as you never know what may come up.'

It was a big decision and also a relief. What I didn't know at the time was that the great empire of MGM was already crumbling.

Lilliput was shocked at the decision I had taken on my own, but she was even more shocked later when she realized that she too was out of a job. She had been one of Mayer's right-hand women but now she was to learn what it was like on the other side of the desk. She was to remain a stalwart friend and still my agent and pushed hard for me in my desire to return to the threatre, as well as helping in the development of my television career.

Though I eventually returned to Hollywood to do some television work, I was sorry to be leaving at that very moment. Fred Astaire threw a lovely party to which it seemed 'everybody' was invited, and I headed east again, leaving Antony to photograph the enigmatic Garbo.

10

Hall of Fame

My first days in New York were busy and full. I was glad to be back. I had to begin to pick up my theatrical contacts again and I also had to look for a suitable place for Antony and myself to live.

After I had been back for two weeks, I realized that I had heard nothing from Antony; so I picked up the telephone to Greta Garbo and asked for him, saying, 'Miss Garbo?'

'Yes, Sarah.'

'*I* do not want to be alone.'

She laughed gaily and immediately handed the telephone to Antony. Crisply I inquired how long it usually took him to photograph a sitter.

'But she is different,' he replied.

'Yes, indeed,' I said, 'we cannot *all* be a legend in our lifetime.'

But Greta Garbo is a warm and generous person. She could not help but lure people to her and enchant them under her spell. In spite of her frequent declaration that she wanted 'to be alone', I suspect she is in fact a lonely person. She limits her friends and acquaintances, so it was a compliment to be in her company, for she is an intelligent and sensitive person. I could imagine her enjoying Antony's magnetic personality and playing her delaying game.

In answer to the obvious question, 'Was I jealous?', it never crossed my mind. I was more concerned that Antony should not be coaxed by the famous to forget the next step in his photographic career, which should undoubtedly now be on the East Coast of America. I was never jealous of any woman who crossed his professional path. To do so would have been as insane – and as tiring, since he must have photographed at least forty beauties in the early fifties – as if he had been jealous of my many good-looking leading men.

Things were going well for Antony – both behind the camera and in front of it. He had had several screen tests at MGM in widely different parts and they were treating him with great respect as if he were already a new Clark Gable. I was glad they were serious and taking trouble, because although he never sought that kind of stardom, or seriously dreamt of it, it was hard not to get excited. He remained calm and non-chalant during his tests and gave tips to the camera man as to how best to light him! There was, of course, absolutely no use pinning any faith on it, because the moguls one felt were quite unpredictable and could suddenly drop it all. With hindsight, it was as well that they did drop the idea, since the tests were not particularly successful.

Meanwhile, I was doing odd bits for television in New York. I did six minutes of *Romeo and Juliet* – a potted version of the balcony scene. I also did a half-hour dramatic programme in which I played a dual role: one a sinister veiled lady and the other a cockney slut in a long blonde wig. The disguises were to create an alibi for my husband to prove he didn't commit a murder, which of course he did. It was all very confused and complicated and I enjoyed every moment of it, especially the blonde wig and the cockney accent. This piece of immortal drama was later filmed in an expanded form with Marlene Dietrich starring. It was called *Witness for the Prosecution*.

Both these programmes went well for me and were received favourably. Unfortunately, I lost two other good roles – two of the best, I thought – by having to cancel when Antony and I thought we were returning to England: this proved a perennial problem. The rest of the programmes I did were fairly uninteresting interviews, but they filled a gap; and on one occasion, I was called in to replace Geraldine Fitzgerald at only a day's notice in a radio version of *Mill of the Floss*. After the comfort of the summer in Hollywood, I was once again living out of a suitcase and constantly moving from hotel to hotel – as all New York's hotels were very full and I hesitated to try anything more permanent until we knew our plans better.

There was a sneak preview of *Royal Wedding* in Los Angeles. Antony went and said it was thrilling – the audience went wild about it, and applauded all the way through, and cheered at the end. Of course, my part was really quite small; but it *was* romantic as I sat and sighed on a park bench with Fred Astaire, danced a few steps with him, *and* got him in the end. According to Antony, the film held together well, and the reaction cards (awful things passed round by the studio to ask the public how they liked the film and the stars) were good for me. It was like being at school again, with the general public marking you good, fair or poor.

At a New York party one night with the usual well-dressed elegant people, we met Marlene Dietrich again. I sat down next to her and she was her accustomed ebullient self. Antony had recently arrived back in New York flushed and triumphant with what I consider one of the most beautiful pictures of Garbo. He came over and joined us and Marlene said with her charming guttural accent, 'And what are you doing now?'

'I am photographing the ten most beautiful women in the world.'

'Ah, who have you decided upon?'

'Well, Ethel Barrymore.'

'Very good,' replied Marlene, 'but is she not a little old?'

'Does age have anything to do with beauty?'

'Who else?'

'Marilyn Monroe.'

'Ah yes, there is a great exuberance of talent there.'

'It would be a great honour, Miss Dietrich, if you would allow me to photograph you.'

'But you have not told me the other people.'

Antony, losing his head a little, said, 'I have just photographed Garbo.'

'Well, in that case you don't need me.'

The party seemed to come to an abrupt end – at least for Antony and me.

At the beginning of 1951, I started working in a play, *Grammercy Ghost*, which was to control my life for several months. It was an engaging idea about a girl who was left a ghost in a will. But it needed much attention to dialogue and a lot of tactful rewriting had to be done without upsetting the author. The excellent Robert Stirling was my co-star, and the rest of the cast was good. Our early reviews were fine, despite what I then thought was rather poor material, and we pressed on with our tour, checking the houses and the advances on the various box offices. We were heading for Broadway. It sometimes seemed no more than a distant glittering mirage.

When we were playing Boston, I met a white-haired man with a smiling, benign face. He introduced himself as Ed Cashman of Foote, Cone & Belding, a well-known and prosperous advertising agency. He asked me out for dinner after the show and it must have been Saturday, for I felt in no need to hurry. He explained that his firm were advertising agents for Hallmark Cards and that Mr Joyce Hall – Chairman and Founder – had been following my progress with interest. Joyce C. Hall was not unknown to me – he was known in the business as J.C. – as he had recently presented a showing of my father's paintings, which had proved an enormous success. I had played a part in this, as I had convinced my father and the family that the world should know this brilliant aspect of himself. There was a certain amount of murmuring in the family as empty gaps were to appear for a while on our family walls. But during a serious conversation with my father, I said to him that I believed art must travel and I was tired of the people who still thought of him as only a war leader. Some years after this successful exhibition Mr Hall was to make reproductions of a number of his paintings for Hallmark Cards.

Ed Cashman explained that Mr Hall was well aware of my influence in this matter of the exhibition and had followed my theatrical footsteps with interest. He now had a proposition to make: he wanted to hear my voice on radio to gauge how the large and very mixed American public would take to me. If it proved acceptable, he was thinking of branching out into television. He was selling many greeting cards, so he did not need the publicity, but he wanted at this stage, in the language of advertising, to 'upgrade his product'.

I felt a tingle of excitement and said that I would be more than happy to do the programmes. I did not know then that this was to be a most important new beginning. My subsequent career with Hallmark was to span over two years of consecutive employment, during which time my show was rapidly transferred from radio to TV; it snowballed in terms of both quality and length of production and was to be the first live two-hour show to be networked all over the USA. Television was still a new medium for performers and announcers alike. The Hallmark shows provided me with the perfect setting within which to grow, not only as an actress, but also as a behind-the-scenes person, for I was invited to enter into discussions concerning the show's scripts and planning and, afterwards, to join in the evaluation of its strengths and weaknesses. Because the programme was the first of its kind on television, we were all pioneers. It is difficult to know just how much the medium of television owes to J.C. Hall, not only in terms of his own *Hallmark Hall of Fame*, but also in regard to what seemed to be his unlimited financing.

The radio shows were well received and it was decided to plunge straight into television. First, however, it was necessary to find out how

my face would fit into the box. My voice was considered quite acceptable, now my face must go through a similar sort of test. My 'audition'
was, in fact, a series of fifteen-minute television programmes, the first of
which the newspapers correctly described as a 'dud'. I was to interview
the famous political figures of the day. Mrs Eleanor Roosevelt graciously
accepted to be my first guest, but it really proved, as a press cutting
says, 'a rather stiff upper-lipped occasion'. Though she was warm,
friendly and generous, neither of us could forget the strain and training
of our respective positions, one as the widow of an illustrious
President, and the other as the daughter of an illustrious Prime
Minister. Despite Eleanor's previous involvement in my 'security breach',
we both still seemed bound by wartime conventions and could hardly
find a topic we felt suitable to discuss in public.

I went to J.C. after the show and said that I was unhappy. I felt it
was not the right use of my father's name, or the possible use of connections with people I had known all my life. Although he was paying
me so handsomely, unless I could be employed as an actress, I would
find it difficult to continue in the show. There was a pause during which
my heart beat rather loudly. I remembered my decision to leave MGM
and the call of the theatre – was I taking too great a risk?

Finally he said, 'What form do you think the show should progress to?'

'What about a half-hour dramatic programme?'

J.C. thought for a minute and then said, yes, he thought it would be
possible. But first of all he believed we should finish the series of fifteen-
minute shows, as the preparation and planning for the new programme
would take some time.

I said that naturally we should finish the series, but asked whether it
would be possible for me to interview actors, film personalities and
writers who were closer to my own field. J.C. immediately agreed, as
this was an easy adjustment to make, and among the many delightful
people I was to interview were Alan J. Lerner, whom I had known in my
Hollywood days, Helen Hayes and Sam Goldwyn. Before I began, I had a
long talk with Lilli Palmer who had herself done a fifteen-minute interview show. Lilli was most eager to help and she introduced me to her
interviewer/script writer, whose job it was to conduct an initial interview
with the 'personality' in order to find out what they would like to talk
about, then draft a 'script' to be okayed by them. This enabled the final
interviewer – me – to angle the questions sensibly. I thought this an
excellent idea, which I subsequently adopted; it made both the inter-

viewer and the interviewee more relaxed and produced a more interesting show.

About three days before I was to interview Alan J. Lerner, I was staying with some friends on Long Island when I had a nasty fall from a horse, which left me with an open gash just above my right eye. I tried to squeeze it together and stick it with plaster, but after about two hours, I realized it needed stitching. My friend said she really was most concerned and wanted to ring up her special doctor. I was sure that this wasn't necessary and suggested that we should just drive to the nearest hospital where I could go into the casualty department. Fortunately, it was early in the morning and there were no other casualties around, so I was whisked in to see a doctor who was to give me some six to eight stitches and, while the doctor stitched away, the nurse took some particulars.

On hearing my name, he said, 'I thought I recognized you. We must do a good job on this. Aren't you on TV on Sunday?'

I said yes I did, but I could cut a fringe. While he was stitching, perhaps to keep my mind off this trivial but moderately unpleasant little operation, he said, 'I am going to tell you a story,' and went on to explain that many years before, when my father had been in America for a lecture tour, he was crossing Fifth Avenue near Central Park where the traffic is fast, to see his friend, Bernard Baruch. My father, always in a hurry, had stepped out into the road without looking, having presumably forgotten that Americans drive on the wrong side of the road. He was hit by a car doing about 30 mph and, perhaps fortunately, was hurled quite a few yards away, as otherwise he would have been run over. Not quite so fortunately, he landed on his shoulder and forehead, causing a deep incision between his eyebrows which was to be with him for the rest of his life, giving him the slightly frowning look. The car driver rushed up to him and my father said immediately, 'It was not your fault, but I would be obliged if you would take me to the nearest hospital as I am obviously in need of stitching up.'

A policeman came by to take the details and my father reiterated that it was not the driver's but his own fault and that he had not been looking where he was going. The policeman asked his name and when he said 'Winston Churchill' stared at him in amazement, and concluded that he must be suffering from concussion. The car driver offered to drive him to a hospital, which he did, after my father had once again insisted that there should be no charge brought.

'Oh, yes, I remember that accident,' I said to the doctor as he was stitching away.

'I was a young intern then and it was I who stitched up your father's forehead.'

I looked at him in amazement. 'Well, well,' I said. 'It's a small world. Now you have stitched up two hard-headed Churchills.'

After leaving the hospital, I felt elated and happy and suggested that we resume our riding excursion but, no sooner was I up on my horse than I felt very giddy and sick, obviously suffering from a slight concussion. I couldn't get off fast enough. However, all this cleared up and I made the show with no problem. The only minor difficulty was that I had to ask to sit the opposite way round from usual, which meant a slight rearrangement of the camera, so that my by now somewhat bruised eye would not show. Alan Lerner was greatly concerned about this and to cheer me up, when I asked if he would mind sitting round this way, he said, 'Not at all. This suits me fine; I have a glass eye in my left . . .'

I also got to know Helen Hayes quite well, having acted with her daughter, Mary MacArthur who, alas, was to die of polio some little while later. Miss Hayes was always to be my friend, for her daughter Mary had told her that I had been very kind to her, although I had not known of her predicament then. When Helen appeared on my programme, we decided we would find time to do some Shakespeare together, and I felt it a great honour to be with this first lady of the American theatre.

I think my last interview was with Sam Goldwyn, who I also knew from my Hollywood days. I felt that it was a triumphant climax to the show to have this great impresario of the film world and Hollywood to appear on television. He was easy, friendly and of course very interested in the set-ups, lights and cameras of our tiny studio. 'Most interesting,' he said, 'it looks so much bigger, even on your tiny screen.' But the moment the red light went on, Sam froze, having never been in front of a camera in his life before. It was difficult to get him to relax. When the programme was over, however, he went across to chat with Antony, by this time completely relaxed and beginning to enjoy himself.

I saw him out of the studio. There are double doors for soundproofing. As we stood in the compressed compartment in between, he said, 'Well, I don't think it went too badly.'

'Of course it didn't; it was wonderful.'

'With a little tightening up here and there it should be all right.'

'Mr Goldwyn, we are live! What is done cannot be undone.'

'In that case, we shall dismiss it from our minds.'

Antony was also working for Hallmark at this time both as a photo-graphic director and also a participant on the show. I had my own place on the set, with a sofa and chairs creating a general drawing-room atmosphere. When I had finished the interview, my guest and I would wander to Antony's 'studio' on the opposite side of the set, where they would talk about his work and he might ask if he could photograph them. It was a delightful concept and I should have been very happy but, as happens so frequently when husbands and wives work together, I did not enjoy the partnership and found it difficult to work with Antony. The Svengali traits in his nature came to the fore and he made me very uptight and, what was professionally very dangerous, he made me photo-graphically nervous.

It was during this period that the recognition of doubt began to creep into our marriage. However, I obstinately refused publicly to acknow-ledge having any doubts about my personal relationship with Antony. As I was doing a tremendous amount of work and frequently flying to and fro between America and England, it was not difficult to dismiss such uncomfortable thoughts from my mind. Even so, I think I probably inti-mated to my mother that I had misgivings about my marriage even at this stage, for in answer to a query from her, asking when I intended to return to England to settle down, I wrote: 'When shall we get some real pattern in our lives? I cannot say.'

All the while I was busy advancing my career in America, my mother was doing everything she could to see that my marriage had every possible opportunity for success. She demonstrated her concern for our future happiness by persuading the family trust to buy us a house at Ebury Street in Pimlico, which she then set about decorating and furnishing with loving care. She was hoping, no doubt, that we would one day return for good to live in this 'nest' that she had created for us. She did not allow her diligence to be tempered by the fact that she and my father had serious misgivings about my marriage to Antony; she just crushed her doubts and did everything she could to make us happy. Antony and I first saw the house when we were in England towards the end of 1951. We were flabbergasted by its beauty.

Our trip to England had been J.C.'s idea. He was a family man, he also believed in the alliance between England and America and that people should use their vote. There was a general election campaign in England at this time and, knowing how much I wanted to be there, J.C. had suggested that Antony and I should go to England and record a programme which would show American audiences what an English election was like. This was typical of Mr Hall's generosity and the way in which he did everything he could to increase my freedom, even during this time while the show was really still only in its 'trial' phase.

Antony and I were recording voters' views at the bar of the King's Head in Roehampton. I was recognized by a man who declared himself a socialist and told me in no uncertain terms what he thought of my father's politics. 'But don't think we don't like your old man,' he added. 'We love him. If he wanted a bed for the night, there isn't one of us who wouldn't turn out and sleep on the floor.'

When I got back to New York after spending Christmas with my family, I discovered that a new director had been appointed for the Hallmark programmes and that plans were being made for a series of half-hour dramatic shows. I was summoned into council. Foote, Cone & Belding had heard from J.C. that he felt very strongly about keeping me as hostess on the shows and that I might extend the role to that of narrator. The plan we developed was to produce weekly half-hour shows concentrating on 'Americana' – good dollops of dramatized history, since we were a family programme – and once a month to branch out into a European subject. I would introduce all the shows and take a dramatic role in most of them as well. I was delighted that J.C. was interested both in maintaining links between Europe and America and in allowing me to develop my personal ambitions in what was to prove a congenial show for everybody.

The new director, Albert McCleery, proved to be a remarkable person – and personality. His Scottish-Irish ancestry and my European-American ancestry were to clash sometimes. There were violent border wars brought on by our very different temperaments; but they never lasted for long. Though at times I felt it was a shotgun wedding, in the end it was to be a marriage of true minds. I came to respect and love him, for here again I had found a mentor who respected me.

Before joining Hallmark as director, Albert McCleery worked out an agreement with J.C.: 'If I do four out of five popular hits, then you must let me do a serious show.' Did I hear an echo of my own desires? Also he was on the record as saying, 'Close-ups reveal people's souls. Audiences like to look at exciting faces.' Did I hear another echo? Television with McCleery could undoubtedly turn into an exciting medium for the actor.

Albert had already become famous for his series called *Cameo Theater*, in which he used *only* close-ups of actors. He had quickly realized that with the decreasing appeal of the big screen, and the improving fortunes of the tiny screen, the public needed to be weaned so that they could enjoy the benefits of the younger medium. *Cameo Theater*, for the actors at least, was a riot. They might appear in beautiful wigs or hats and with the top of their bodies magnificently costumed. But as the camera went no further than the waist, and so as not to waste money, the lower half could be clad in blue jeans and tennis shoes, or whatever else happened to be convenient to the actor's wardrobe. I have a distinct memory of the hilarity caused by these shows among the performers. However, the personalities of the actors and of the parts they played certainly shone through, as McCleery wanted, in the big close-ups.

With Albert McCleery joining us, we were much strengthened and in January 1952 moved into our half-hour dramas. Antony, incidentally, did not work for Hallmark once we turned from interviews to drama. I invariably played the heroine and I seemed to spend an inordinate amount of time at the White House in the company of the president of the day, such as when I played Dolly Madison. This caused some hilarity in the cast which, of course, we tried to hide from Mr Hall.

There was an enchanting episode about one of the first American woman flyers called Harriet Quimby, in which I appeared on the airfield in a beautiful elegant long gown and a parasol, before changing into my flight outfit. Everyone in the cast enjoyed these pleasant excursions which, although largely accurate, were somewhat fantasized for the American family audience. The Harriet Quimby show produced one piece of newspaper nonsense that I was trying to avoid. Generally, the name of Churchill was causing less comment by now. But Harriet Quimby smoked cigars. I thought it all over very carefully and decided that I would merely pick the cigar up. I would go no further. But my caution was wasted as next day headlines proclaimed: 'Sarah Smokes Cigar!'

I was always the heroine, but my inner ham personality was dying to tear my hair and throw myself about in more extravagant roles. So identified did I become to American audiences as myself playing these heroines that, on making my first entrance in one show when I was playing Florence Nightingale, my stage father said, 'Good evening, Miss Churchill, how lovely you look.'

How any of us got through the twenty-eight minutes left of the show we will never know and the poor actor went into a state of shock and couldn't get over it. It was an actors' joke for many weeks; and a number of head waiters and taxi drivers addressed me as 'Miss Nightingale'.

But life was not all television. Dramatically staged readings had become very popular in the USA at that time. Emlyn Williams was doing a one-man feat with his readings from Dickens and Charles Laughton, Charles Boyer and Cedric Hardwicke were doing Shaw's *Don Juan in Hell*. I worked hard with a fellow actor, Edward Thommen, editing the famous exchange of letters between Ellen Terry and Bernard Shaw. It was to prove a most soul-satisfying exercise. The first reading was a success, with the audience's attention held the whole time, even though at three hours we were much too long. Only last trains that had to be caught and sheer physical exhaustion deterred some of them from staying to the end. I was thrilled, because at last I thought I had found something really worthwhile which I should be able to do in London. I felt I had made another journey of discovery. Although I was planning to stay and work in America, my heart was never far from London and I felt that the possibility of a West End staging of the Shaw–Terry letters might help to stabilize my home and theatrical life there. I had not, after all, appeared on the London stage since the war.

On 6 February 1952 news of King George VI's death shocked America. I wrote a letter to my mother at this time which I think describes both my feelings and those of the American people:

... I cannot tell you how great the shock of the King's death was here. It was amazing to see the detailed and affectionate recordings by the Press of the whole sad ten days. The papers suddenly seemed all English and there was no other news, and American friends seemed to grieve as if he were their friend and King; it really was remarkable. We heard Papa's moving tribute to him very clearly and of course followed every moment on television, which was impressive. How glad I am that Queen Elizabeth has Papa at her side for comfort and guidance – and the glory of the two are so right to start another 'Renaissance'.

Later on that month, my father came over to America, with my mother, to address a joint session of Congress. He had the unenviable task of asking America to collaborate and co-operate in financing the situation at hand. The British were not very popular in America at this time, as it seemed we were always asking for money. I had the privilege of being seconded from my duties with Hallmark in order to be with my mother on this occasion. As most people know, the President cannot attend Congress when there is a visiting potentate. President Truman, therefore, had to stay at home and Mrs Truman with her daughter, Margaret, accompanied my mother and me to hear my father's speech. We were dismayed at his entry as there was no applause or recognition, as is generally politely accorded, and the little old man stumped his way through in dead silence. Mrs Truman and Margaret sensed and shared our embarrassment; I suppose we should all have known better. My father had a very peculiar way of doing his own speech shorthand. He used 'headlines' on pieces of card, which he could refer to without taking his eyes off the audience.

He cleared his throat and put on his specs, saying, 'I have not come here to ask for money!'

There was mild applause as one or two fins flapped. He then completed his message simply: 'For myself!'

This remark received roars of laughter and a standing ovation before he was able to continue with his important speech. Needless to say, he was able to get all the money he wanted.

The occasional breaks from the Hallmark shows also presented an opportunity for Antony and myself to spend some time in our London home and to build some home ties. Although I had left the 'protecting wings', I was never far away in mind and spirit from my parents; Antony had not always been quite so lucky and there were many times when he had not been on intimate terms with his family. When we got to Ebury Street on one visit home, I suggested to Antony that his parents should come to see it and enjoy the little garden that we had. The garden had been sadly diminished in size by an air raid shelter which was intended to discourage any blockbusters. Unable to move it, we made a flower bed on its roof, and it stood solidly in the middle of the garden like a lady with a flowery hat about to open a bazaar. With Antony's parents, we enjoyed simple lunches together, and were able to improve to some extent the family scene.

Antony was as happy as a sandboy in London, but naturally wanted to improve the house. I told him that there would be plenty of time for this and that, meanwhile, we should ask my mother to join us on a holiday in Capri. When I first suggested this to my mother she, being Scottish and having to restrain various extravagances of Winston's, which her children seemed to have inherited, indicated that we really should find better things to do with our money. We pooh-poohed this and said that it was all arranged. It is indeed a lovely moment when a child can return to a parent not only the love and care which has been lavished upon him or her, but also the joy of financial independence. She said she would be delighted to accompany us, but she would have to bring her maid, whom she would of course pay for. We agreed, but naturally did not allow her to contribute in this way. It was a happy holiday.

I remember an anecdote from that visit. We were sitting in the famous, tiny piazza where you go to see your friends and the Bull of Capri, which is solemnly walked through the piazza, brushing close to the crowded tables, scented, perfumed and flower-bedecked.

My mother said to me, 'I thought you were afraid of cows.'

'Yes, but this is a bull, mama, hadn't you noticed?' I restrained her with a gentle hand, 'but don't look now!'

There was a rather more serious occasion on that holiday as well. As soon as it was known that we were on Capri, we came under considerable pressure to visit Edda Ciano, Mussolini's daughter. At first, my mother would have none of it lest it might seem we were consorting with the enemy. But finally I persuaded her that, after all, the war had been over for six years and a visit could do no harm, so we went, my mother and I, to take English tea. It was curious how little we found to say. Signora Ciano seemed an impassive figure to me; but anyone who has suffered the loss of a husband at the orders of her own father must live with an unimaginable grief. The difficulties of our conversation were only resolved when Signora Ciano mentioned that she was sending her daughter to school in England. At last we had a comfortably banal and neutral matter to discuss and talk flowed a little more easily.

The year of Queen Elizabeth's coronation, 1953, was to prove an exciting and varied one for me both in America and England. It started out in fine fashion when I was one of five nominated for the best television actress award – I don't recall who actually won the award. Also there were plans afoot to move the Hallmark shows from their production base in New York to Hollywood, and we were working hard on our production of *Hamlet*, the first live two-hour show to be networked across America.

Financing *Hamlet* was a bold move by Hallmark, typical of J.C.'s courage. NBC-TV had failed to attract the two sponsors they were hoping would pay for an hour each of Maurice Evans's two-hour version of the play. So Hallmark stepped in to finance the whole operation themselves at a cost of well over $100,000 – a huge outlay for a single programme in those days. The *Variety* story about our plans had one of those wonderful *Variety* headlines: 'Hallmark Backs Faith in Longhair TV With 100G for 2-Hr "Hamlet".'

Ed Cashman pointed out in the *Variety* story that Hallmark had got excellent results both from the regular *Hallmark Hall of Fame* TV programmes which I hosted and similar radio programmes hosted by Lionel Barrymore. They had also had a good response to the two television performances we had done of Gian Carlo Menotti's opera *Amahl and the Night Visitors*. Directed by Albert McCleery and George Schaefer, it was a version of the same production which Maurice Evans had taken on tour around GI camps during the war and to Broadway in 1945. It was Maurice's television debut, the first of many distinguished appearances, and he received well-deserved high praise. To my delight, Jack Gould in the *New York Times* wrote: 'As Ophelia, Sarah Churchill was unusually fine, playing the mad scene with a wistful delicacy and simplicity that was thoroughly rewarding.'

The production attracted a lot of attention, so much so that a few journalists were allowed on the set, dressed as extras, to get the flavour of the event. When we had done *Amahl and the Night Visitors*, I had persuaded J.C. that this almost religious story should not be interrupted by commercials, and he had agreed that only the introduction and conclusion should carry advertising. With *Hamlet*, however, we did have commercials at the beginning, middle and end. We didn't mind this at all since it gave us time for a breather in the middle – and remember it was a live production.

We did the show on a Sunday, it was 26 April, and a week later there was a wonderful assessment, not just a brief review, of the whole making of the production, in the *Chicago Sunday Tribune*. The article was a delight, but the headline said it best of all: 'Shakespeare Scores TV Hit With *Hamlet*'.

My regular work with Hallmark continued, although I was beginning to feel that I should make a change. Ed Cashman had told me that I could have the show for life if I wanted it. That sounded rather like a jail sentence to me, though it was a heart-warming compliment. I knew even then that I would never accept such an offer as it would completely sever my ties with England and hopes of theatrical success there; I would have become an American personality rather than an English actress. Also, I was going through a very difficult patch with Antony. Our marriage barely existed in anything more than name. I did agree to take a part in one of the series of TV dramas he was co-producing in England, based on the real-life experiences of the British police detective Bob Fabian of the Yard. But my appearance was really only a face-saver, and had no effect on bringing us back together.

In the middle of the year, I was forcefully reminded how far from home I was, and how much this was beginning to affect my professional plans. It was the day on which we were producing the last of the summer series of *Hallmark Hall of Fame*; I had planned an end-of-season party for the cast and company. During the show a gentleman from the British Embassy arrived at the studio and spoke to Albert McCleery. I thought Albert looked rather grey and understood why after the show. No one likes to be the bearer of bad tidings, and Albert had to pass on the message that my father had had a major stroke and that I must return to England immediately. Albert asked whether I thought we should cancel the party and I said certainly not. I wanted to keep this news private and knew that to cancel the party would only draw attention to my absence and flight home. My dresser helped me pack and I slipped away silently and was homeward-bound, while the party on the boat which we had chartered to go round Manhattan continued merrily.

My sister Mary was at the airport to greet me. We were surrounded by the press, who naturally had smelt something afoot, but we were able to explain my sudden arrival by informing them that I was home for a holiday, having finished my present contract with Hallmark, which was the truth. Mary and I were unable to talk with the press around us. Once we had reached the privacy of the car, she turned to me and answered the anxious question in my eyes.

'No darling, he's alive, but prepare yourself for a shock.'

My father had suffered a stroke on the left side which had left him almost totally paralysed. We drove on in a stony silence until Mary said, 'He'll still be able to paint, his right hand is all right.'

I think I said, 'I have a feeling he could paint with either hand.'

When we arrived home at Chartwell, the first thing I noticed were the ramps which had been placed over the steps for the wheelchair. Before I saw my father, I was briefed on what had happened. It had been at a reception at No. 10 Downing Street. He had sat down in a chair and suddenly found he could not get up again. He nodded towards Christopher Soames – recently appointed his Parliamentary Private Secretary – who, sensing something wrong, went to his side. My father asked him to excuse the company as diplomatically as possible, for he felt very ill. Christopher and Antony Montague-Browne, his private secretary, went to the guests and said the Prime Minister was extremely tired and wished to apologize but that he must go to bed. When all the guests had gone, the valet, Christopher and his detective got him up and took him to his bedroom. Lord Moran was immediately summoned and my father said that, next morning when a Cabinet meeting was due, he must be got downstairs to the Cabinet Room before his colleagues arrived. As he had instructed, he was already seated in the room next day when the Cabinet filed in. One or two of the Cabinet Ministers said later that he had been unusually quiet, but they had seen no signs of the stroke which Lord Moran diagnosed.

The Cabinet left. The car was brought round to the door and with the faithful escorts at his side, he was helped into the car and driven down to Chartwell. Lord Moran told my mother that he could not predict anything for sure, but that my father's stroke was a slow leak, he appeared to be sinking fast, and he could not say when it might stop. With Mary and Christopher at her side, she took this in her usual style and it was agreed I should be sent for immediately.

Mary asked me, 'Are you prepared now?' and I said, 'Yes, of course.'

The shock of seeing a great oak tree felled is as close as I can get to describing what I felt. My father was in a chair. I went over to him quickly and kissed him on his brow, then said, 'Darling, wow!' His eyes flashed brilliantly, but of course he could not answer and his face was naturally distorted on the left. With his right hand he managed to squeeze my hand. The weeks of his recovery went extremely quickly.

Obviously, the Queen was informed of the misfortunes and progress of her First Minister and she wanted to come and see him. My mother thanked her most warmly but said that if the Queen were to visit, people would think he was dying and he was not. He just needed time for recuperation. Somehow or other my mother and father were able to communicate. She informed him of the reply she had given to the Queen and he was able to communicate the message, 'Tell her I'll see her at the St Leger,' and, by golly, he did!

Inch by inch, the recovery grew steadier and the Sunday lunches began again. When guests arrived, he was carefully installed. One Sunday lunchtime, Antony, who was living in Ebury Street at the time filming the Fabian series, came down. We agreed that domestic problems should not disturb 'The Old Warrior'.

During lunch, Antony said suddenly, 'Sir, how is your left hand?'

My father raised it to about elbow height, where it was naturally in a trembling condition, and let it sink back to the table.

Antony said, 'Well, that's rather good, try cocking a snook at me.'

My father's eyes twinkled and he cocked a snook at Antony. The glasses were filled with champagne. We knew he was over the worst, and I felt free to return to America to continue my work.

I was genuinely excited to be going back to the USA. We had moved the production centre to Los Angeles and I had intended to spend a few days in New York to collect myself and a few things I had left there before going to the West Coast. But immediately on arrival, there was script trouble. I did not like the first script on offer at all, and as we were moving into an hour-long show for the first time *and* re-opening the Hallmark season, it was terribly important to have a good story. It meant turning right round there and flying out to the coast with a new writer and a story I had brought with me from England. The director agreed it was much better; so the poor writer had to sit up day and night to get the new script done. When I saw he was safely locked in his hotel bedroom with guards posted at the door (almost), I flew to Kansas City, to see J.C. Hall at home.

Before I went, I talked to one or two people about telling him that this really would be the last lap I could do with him. But they all advised me to wait until after the opening show and until we had seen that the new programme was on a firm footing. They thought that it would be quite a blow for J.C. It had been an expensive move for Hallmark to go from New York to the West Coast and the extra length of the show was very expensive. If it was known I was leaving, it would take the impetus out of the first show and affect all the planning of stories yet to be done for the series, as well as open up speculation about who would replace me.

So I agreed to wait for a month, by which time the programme should be settled, and I spent an evening with just J.C. and his wife and their son who was just back from service in Korea. We had a delightful time and I told him the story of our first show – which he liked – and then, next morning, flew back to Los Angeles to see if our writer had died. Luckily, he was very much alive, with a very workmanlike script, and we plunged into rehearsals.

The new series got off to a good start and I soon felt able to tackle J.C. about the future. It was not an easy conversation, because I did not want him to feel there was anything wrong either with his programmes or with what I considered his unlimited generosity. But J.C. was always a rather special man. He explained that he was thinking in any case of changing the format of the shows, of turning more to the occasional big specials rather than concentrating on the weekly shows. He hoped I would be involved. So, as with my leaving of MGM, it was to be a most amicable separation of the ways and, when my father agreed to give J.C. one of his paintings after my last show with Hallmark in February 1954, my happiness was complete.

11

No Time for Comedy

When I finally severed my regular connection with Hallmark I was thrown back on my own resources. But it was my own choice. I was to do several more 'specials' for Hallmark in years to come, but now I was looking for work, and I remembered an occasion which was an example of just how fickle the acting business can be. Some months after *Royal Wedding* was released, the film and I happened to coincide at a place called Burlington in Ontario. I was there to assist in judging the Miss Canada contest, and the film had arrived there on its way round the circuit. The coincidence was too much for the manager of the Burlington cinema and he contacted me, asking if I would make a personal appearance and say a few words from the stage. I was quite happy to agree and when I arrived in state at the cinema, escorted by the Burlington police chief, the marquee proclaimed: '*Royal Wedding* – starring Sarah Churchill'. Only a few hours later, after my judging duties were over, I drove past the cinema on my way back to the USA. The marquee lights had already been changed to read: 'starring Fred Astaire'. That may well have been the shortest span of stardom on record.

I remembered, too, a conversation with my father in which we agreed that life always seemed flat when a show finished. Then, just as I was working to get new shows on the road for myself, came the news, in April 1955, that my father had decided his show was over. At the age of eighty, he had decided it was time to relinquish the burden of being Prime Minister of England and retire to his beloved Chartwell. The Queen and Prince Philip went to a special dinner at 10 Downing Street – a rare privilege – and the news flashed around the world. In a letter to my mother soon after, I told her how movingly and superbly the resignation had been covered by the American newspapers. Even the normally somewhat inadequate Los Angeles papers rose to great heights, with the

On vacation with J.C. Hall of Hallmark at Grand Lake, Colorado.

LEFT Ophelia to Maurice Evans's Hamlet in the *Hallmark Hall of Fame* television series, April 1953.

RIGHT *The King and I*, Sacramento, 1956.

My painting, *Malibu Day*.

A well-staged photograph in the Los Angeles Hall of Justice.

Malibu Night, also by me.

On the way into court in Malibu.

LEFT With my family between shows of
Peter Pan. From left: Julia Lockwood
(Wendy), Arabella Churchill, my father,
me and my mother, with Emma and
Jeremy Soames in front.

LEFT BELOW Mending Pan's pipes,
closely observed by Julia Lockwood.

Henry and I just before our wedding.

Mary (*centre*) with Emma and Jeremy
Soames and some of my greyhounds.

With David Hemmings in the play *Fata Morgana*, Ashcroft Theatre.

BELOW With Lobo and his dog in Rome.

RIGHT With my father at the Guildhall; the statue is by Oscar Nemon.

A *Matter of Choice*
with Idris Evans.

Keep on dancing.

first three or four pages devoting every column to my father through several editions, and the New York papers were magnificent as well.

Individual Americans were very charming to me, too. For example, I remember that Frank McCarthy, who had been a distinguished colonel in the US Army and then become the youngest Assistant Secretary of State, sent me roses with a card saying, 'Affectionate regards on this proud and sentimental day'.

I had some very good friends in America then, people like Frank McCarthy and Lillie Messenger – still my agent – and Howard Holtzman, my then lawyer's nephew, all of whom helped me a lot in what was now a total separation from Antony. Also, I had some fascinating experiences beyond the theatre and television worlds. For instance, in March 1955, the Civil Defence Committee based in California asked me if I would like to become an honorary member. Apart from the honour, there was a particular purpose, since this membership would permit me to be one of a select band of witnesses of atomic bomb tests in the Nevada desert. I was fascinated to go. The committee wanted people with what they described as a 'sincere interest and knowledge' to view the tests. It seemed that people were so appalled by the atomic bomb that they preferred to do nothing and know nothing about it. The point of these tests was to prove to civilians that outside a certain radius – which was uncomfortably large – there was still a great deal of hope for survival. My principal interest was that I would be able to send an account of it all to my father. He had always believed in the value of eyewitness descriptions and one of the reasons he liked family with him on his big voyages was to make sure there would be some record of a personal nature.

The bomb was a fair-sized atomic one, and troops were in tanks as close as a quarter of a mile. Radio reporters in open slit trenches were within two miles and observers and TV cameras, where I was stationed, were seven miles away on a hill overlooking the Yucca Flats. We had no protection except very dark glasses, which we had to wear for three seconds only, just to shield us from the flash of the actual explosion, which they told us had the strength of fifty suns. If you did not wish to wear the glasses, you were supposed to turn your back and look at the ground or the hills behind, count three slowly, and such is the strength and speed of adjustment of the normal eye, you could then turn round and see the incredible rest. Most of the experienced people seemed to prefer this way; they said you did not miss a thing, that the removal of the glass mask took several precious seconds and you might lose the early growing of the fire-ball. They told you to roll up the cuffs of your coat so as to 'feel the heat'; also you were advised to sit on the ground or on a chair, as the blast could knock you off your feet.

From notes I made at the time, it went something like this: over the public address system they gave you 'H Hour' – which meant one hour to go – and excitement began to rise for it meant weather conditions were favourable. They warned you of the half-hour and that the weather was still good. You chose your chair or your piece of hard desert to squat on; the cameramen checked their focus and settled down. If you were a beginner such as I, a minor decision had to be made: whether to face the spectacle with my mask on, or turn my back. I gnawed a mental fingernail. Why, I inwardly muttered to myself, can I never do two things at once? An experienced man of one blast offered to guide me through, we would stand with our backs turned, he would count three and we would turn. I declined politely (as I wanted to do it alone), chose my chair and decided to face the bomb, plus mask. Dawn was coming up rapidly now. Sky was green and the morning star hung tranquilly and alone, all the others having disappeared. Silhouettes of cactus and strange short desert trees began to appear; down in the plain the 500 foot tower on which the bomb was poised was still invisible except for its two beacon lights. I looked at my watch – fourteen minutes to go.

They briefed us once again: 'Whether you face the explosion with mask, or turn your back without, the *instant* you see the flash count slowly, 1 – 2 – 3 and start to turn *slowly*, or remove *slowly* your mask. Eye discomfort is your guide. You will see the flash and feel the heat instantaneously, you will not feel the blast or hear the noise until seven seconds have passed – remain seated for at least ten seconds, the hills behind you will throw back both sound and shock.'

Thirteen minutes to go; I was thrilled. The cool sweetness of the desert air, the silence, the dawn – and the terrible flower waiting to explode in the plain below. The public address system crackled again: 'The final weather report is negative – the shot has been called off. Collect your equipment and report to the same bus that brought you out.' Even before the word 'negative' was completed, the tired, frustrated reporters were pulling out their film, folding their equipment and speeding to their bus.

The desert is cold at night, and the entire operation took ten hours: two-and-a-half hours in a bus that crawled in convoy; then five hours waiting, and then the homeward trek. Being with the press and radio and TV people made it fun, for they are never more humorous than on these exhausting, tough, exciting projects. As we sat in our darkened bus, disappointed, cold and tired, a weary southern voice drawled from the back: 'Wa don't they just admit it's er deurd.'

You laugh and fall asleep, or watch the sunrise and the jack rabbits hopping among the cactuses. You stumble out into brilliant early morning sun; scan bulletin boards for weather news; or get back to your hotel in Las Vegas, where you are greeted with the incessant chatter clatter of slot machines. People still at tables, or just starting the day session.

It was my first experience of Las Vegas and it really was non-stop, twenty-four-hours-a-day gambling from five cents to thousands of dollars. Slot machines; roulette; baccarat; crap. Hotels and motels seemed to be springing up at the rate of one a month at that time. Every star who could possibly perform in cabaret was playing there and all the big bands showed up there. There was not an inch without a neon light, not a cloakroom without a slot machine – it was incredible. The magnificence of the hotels, the deep plush carpets, the ceilings peppered with chandeliers: anything you wanted but the answer to the *why* of the deadly flower in the desert a hundred miles away. Sodom and Gomorrah? It could have been. I couldn't make up my mind.

I was able to get home to England to see my parents for a few days before starting on my summer theatre tour in *No Time for Comedy*. Once again, I was back on the road. I had had a long journey back from England, but on arrival I was plunged right into rehearsals. We only had five days to get the play ready and when you do this type of tour, you do everything for yourself; it really is too complicated to take a dresser. I was able to get some lovely clothes for my part and the play was gay and refreshing. We opened to a full house on the first Saturday at Matunuck 'Theatre-by-the-sea' in Rhode Island, and the audience obviously enjoyed it, though the cast were all nervous and for once in my life I was unsure of my lines, though luckily it didn't show. During the last three days before the opening, I had developed an abscess behind a wisdom tooth and was in great pain. Large doses of penicillin reduced it to only a soreness; but it didn't help me to learn my lines.

Matunuck Theatre-by-the-sea was a real barn complete with beams, and there was a little inn about a hundred yards away where everyone connected with the theatre lived. Any time after 5 p.m., the outside world from neighbouring towns began to come over. People would have dinner in the restaurant, then come and see the play; and then, afterwards, return to the restaurant where there was a small cabaret. It was very gay and during the day one could wander happily on the seashore. The air was velvet and for mid-June quite cool. It was very much community-living for the actors. You could go out, naturally, if you wanted to, but would have needed a car as the theatre was quite remote. So it was a bit like school; you all sat at long tables and there was no choice of food, which was of the meat loaf variety. I recall that my bedroom there was very sweet, but that the bath water was cold! However, an atmosphere of enthusiasm reigned over all.

Bob Carroll was my leading man. He was good in the play and was very nice. I felt he had grown both as an actor and a man in the four years since I had first known him. We had great fun both on and off duty. Bob and I spent a lot of time flying kites. It was a most amusing and soothing pastime. There by the sea the wind was strong and you could go walking with them, as you would with a dog. Only they were sky dogs! Telegraph wires had to be negotiated either by pulling the kites in low enough to fly under, or by hurling the end of your string – wrapped round a piece of wood – over the wires. Those kites became a sort of talisman for Bob and me. They were christened Ermintrude and Boxer – the first, mine, was one of the flat, flappy sort of kites; Bob's, as its name suggested, was a box kite. The company always knew where we were by those kites. We tried to work out a signal system with them as well – much complicated by the vagaries of the wind.

But soon it was time to pack ready for departure to the next theatre. I would always pack the theatre things at night and personal things in the morning. I still had not found a way of travelling light! And what with kites and painting equipment – I had started painting again – the odds and ends were growing. At 5.30 in the morning, I was awake with the birds and a grey dawn. My mental alarm clock called me, as we had to catch an early train into New York about three hours away and then go by train or fly to Syracuse to start the new week. I had to go ahead on this occasion as I had to rehearse with one new actor. But this tour was to prove much easier on me than some previous ones as we carried the three principals with us, so that the rehearsing could be kept to the minimum.

In Fayetteville, near Syracuse, in upstate New York, we had a very hot week, but the show did better than in Rhode Island now that the summer season had really got going and we got good notices. I also realized that this was the centre of the Jerome country; and I visited Pompey where Jennie's father, my extraordinary great-grandfather, was born. One evening I met Mr and Mrs William Travers Jerome III, whom my mother and father had entertained about two years previously at Chart- well. They were very charming to me, and then on the same night a deputation from the Jerome Chapter of the Daughters of the American Revolution invaded the theatre and claimed me as eligible to be a daughter through my Jerome blood. I was presented with a traditional silver spoon and roses after the last curtain and I must admit that for a moment I was quite confused and uncertain how to respond. Then I simply said, 'Thank you, I shall try to be a good daughter,' and everyone was delighted.

There was no painting and no kite-flying that week; it was far too hot. We were all looking forward to our next port of call: Marblehead, which is by the sea on Massachusetts bay. The Fayetteville theatre was in a big school and did not have the charm of Matunuck, but the audiences were receptive and, perhaps even more important, numerous. The company actually all stayed at Cazenovia nearby, because Fayette- ville lacked any good hotel. We were in a charming inn with old-fashioned housekeepers who spoiled us, and a nice manager and his wife who would leave 'on the house' sandwiches and beer for the players on our return. Furthermore, they gave us a wonderful rate, like the good old touring days. I remember that they charged us only $4 a night instead of $10. So we were a company of beaming contented actors.

When we left Fayetteville and arrived at Marblehead, Massachusetts, I lost my head because it was so beautiful, just like Devonshire and Corn- wall, except the houses were of wood slats instead of stone. I remember so well the sea lapping and buffetting the shore and how the smell of lobsters and humbler fish pervaded everything. There was no air cooling in the theatre, so I merrily dripped and swallowed my salt pills and gallons of water and rushed out when I could to catch the wanton breeze that flirted about the water's edge, but refused to come inland one inch. It was all quite lovely.

I lived in 'digs' as a paying guest, in a large house, the bottom half of which was an antique shop. More accurately, the bottom half of the house was for sale, and the top half, where I was, was already 'stickered' up. Everything was marked 'For Sale' – my bed, toothglass, chair, picture, book. Somehow, though, I felt a sense of permanence; it wasn't a roaring trade. So despite the fact that I laid my head on a bed that might be sold by the next sundown, or that I may have inadvertently sat on a chair and removed to myself the sale ticket, I felt that we all – chair, bed, tooth-glass – would still meet at nightfall.

The following week we played Boston. But since Boston is only fifteen miles from Marblehead, the company stayed on living there and we would hurry in to the city, salty and sunny for the performances. I did spend some days in Boston as well, doing odd jobs and meeting up with old friends. I got one chance to have a quick lunch with an old theatrical friend who was one of the few people who had really been able to help me with my acting: Edward Thommen, with whom I had done the reading of the Shaw–Terry letters, and director of the Poets Theatre in Boston. It was a very brave venture devoted to 'try-outs' and readings and the promulgation of the English language 'as she is spoke'.

I also took the chance of doing a little medical research. My mother had been suffering badly from neuritis and the Vincent Memorial Hospital, which is part of the Massachusetts General Hospital – a world-famous research laboratory for women's illnesses – is right there in Boston. So I took the liberty, hoping my mother wouldn't mind, of seeing the head specialist in neuritis, to glean some information as to what forms of treatment they used. To my delight, I was able to pass on some useful information on treatments and the names of some doctors in Boston for my mother's own doctors to consult.

The summer touring season in the United States is precise – mid-June to mid-September at the outside. That season, 1955, seemed to fly by and in no time at all we were getting to our last dates and I, as usual, was uncertain about my plans. Luckily, Albert McCleery had plans for me and I was due to do some big television films for him. But the summer had been fun, almost all the time. Robert Carroll had proved a most charming and considerate companion and an excellent and attractive actor. I believed that he stood every chance, providing luck stayed with him, of making himself into a top leading man – and I thought that if this happened, he would become a star.

Sadly, his father died near the end of our tour and so for all of us in the company summer fun was over. We rehearsed another actor in seventy hours so as to release Bob – we did not carry any understudies. This all happened in the midst of some amazing floods. Although we were untouched in Clinton, Connecticut, since we were effectively an island, the five towns nearest us were all evacuated. Also, there had been a drastic change of plan: instead of playing the Edgewater Beach Hotel, which had collapsed under a bad financial season, we had to make a 400-mile hop to Camden, Maine. With a new actor to rehearse and the near impossibility of getting there, we were frantic. But the theatre managers chartered two sea planes and flew in and got us. Robert rejoined us after these adventures, but everyone felt exhausted themselves and sad for him. It made for a quiet end to the season.

Almost exactly a year later, I had a very different end to a summer season. I arrived in Sacramento on 5 August and then spent the most uncomfortable, disagreeable three weeks of my professional life. I suppose I must admit that is not *quite* true, for I topped the box office record for the summer and the second week was bigger than the first. Everybody said it was the finest production in six years, so I surmounted a tough hurdle professionally. But the circumstances were so punishing and frustrating I hated every minute of it. 'It' was a production of *The King and I* in which I took the female lead, Anna. It all took place in a heavy unrelieved temperature of about ninety-five degrees. Sacramento, I decided, must be a hole in the ground.

It was a pity, for the houses, though I found them rather grotesque, were really quite charming. They were narrow four-storey, white wood houses, bursting in all directions with what appeared to be octagonal bay windows; heavily encrusted with curlicue carvings and surmounted by little porticos. I was reminded of those funny white twirly sea-shells, encrusted with bleached barnacles, plus their own eruptions, that you find on West Coast beaches. Well, the Sacramento houses looked like that; the streets were wide and the trees old and beautiful, with the tops of the crazy houses lost in them. Inside the house where I stayed, there was a clutter of bric-à-brac; neat, steep, winding circular stairs; tall, coolish box-like rooms with lacy curtains that never gave the promised flutter, because there was no breeze to stir the big leaves that hung like a heavy green curtain outside.

The performance under the auspices of the Sacramento Light Opera Association's 'Music Circus' – and a production secured for me by my old friends Lewis and Young – took place in a gay striped circus tent which seated some 1,600 people. We performed in the arena generally reserved for elephants, lions, seals and clowns and we made our entrance down the gangways through the audience. The holiday-makers, full of popcorn and Coca Cola, were hot in their long-sleeved shirts but, in spite of this, they were attentive and wildly appreciative. I believe they got a positively sadistic enjoyment from our energetic exertions as, in our voluminous hooped and petticoated skirts, we bounded up or down the gangways for our entrances or exits.

It was the first performance of *The King and I* since the death of my good friend and mentor Gertie Lawrence. It was a privilege for me to wear the same costumes which she had worn for the part she so wonderfully created. However they did make a hot privilege. There were no microphones, so, for two-and-a-half hours – Anna is a long part – I had to bellow. Being 'in the round', one had constantly to change one's position so that all sides of the tent could feel they were at 'the front of the action'. You could never let up or relax, for half the tent at any given moment must get the back of your head, so your pitch and enunciation had to be faultless if you were to be heard. Also, the circus was neatly placed at a major crossroads with traffic lights and, after 9 p.m., the heavy trucks carrying California's market produce rumbled their way through the town – with a screech and hiss of steam brakes as they stopped on the red light, and a roar and rev of throttle as they moved on the green.

Nevertheless, for all the perspiring and panting and exhaustion, a strange magic took place every performance. Theatre in the round, especially a pageant like *The King and I* with its lovely sentimental music, can be very beautiful and completely compelling. Eyes riveted on the little amber arena, which somehow really became the court of the King of Siam with the concubines in their coloured dresses prostrated on the floor and the head wife and the English schoolteacher reaching a moving understanding as, with gracious patience and eternal submission, she implores Anna to make the man she loves a great man. The fierce unyielding battle between Anna and the King; the growing hope that East and West, by tolerance and respect, could unite in a triumphal understanding; the shattering bitterness of its impossibility, when naked barbarism flashes out; the majestic tragedy of the end, as the old gives way to the new – it all pulls the audience along to the very end. And it did, every night in Sacramento, despite trucks and crickets and every physical inconvenience.

I did have one very happy interlude during my three weeks' run. It was a presidential election year and I had a very pleasant time with Randolph for half a day when he was in San Francisco. General Sarnoff, who owned RCA, sent his private DC3 for me and whisked me off to lunch with him and Randolph. We then visited the 'Cow Palace' and watched the convention which Randolph was covering as a journalist. Randolph was in good spirits. Sarnoff was taking a paternal interest in him; he obviously thought highly of Randolph and seemed to understand him well. When Sarnoff was a young wireless technician, he told me, he was fiddling about with a crystal set when he picked up the first SOS of the *Titanic*. A human dynamo himself, he recognized Randolph's energies and mistakes. Randolph was at his best and we had a happy afternoon. Then I was flown back to my circus.

One of the reviews I got for *The King and I* shows just how bouquets and brickbats get combined by critics. I think it also shows why actors and others are selective in what they allow to be quoted. This paragraph comes from the *Sacramento Union*:

Sarah Churchill, a blondish English lady who could charm the crumpets off your tea tray, has all the grace, womanliness, intelligence that Anna needs. Her stage voice has all the flexibility and sublety of a rapier. Yet if you must say that she can't sing very much you are only telling the truth.

While my professional life was busy, happy and rewarding, I'm afraid it was a different picture in my private life. My marriage with Antony was over in all but name. I remember from time to time trying to work out how things had gone wrong, and I recalled a happier time when, before we were married, we were on holiday with my parents in Monte Carlo. My father, who thoroughly enjoyed gambling – not for high stakes, but for higher than he told my mother – was pleased that there was an underground passage between the hotel and the Casino. It meant that he, like other hotel guests wishing to avoid gratuitous publicity, could come and go with little fuss. On this particular evening my mother had retired to bed, probably after some gentle admonition to Winston not to go and lose the rest of his pocket-money – he had been on a losing streak for a day or two. Antony was not highly regarded by my parents, despite hard work on both sides. But he did try, and in discussion with my father he claimed he had a system for winning at roulette. My father was properly sceptical; but who doesn't like to break a losing streak? So we three stumped off through the underground passage to the Casino's bright lights. Using Antony's system, my father proceeded to win all night. In fact, we were all three a number of francs better off at the end. Antony had quite fortuitously scaled a pinnacle: any young man who proposed a winning system at roulette could not, in my father's opinion, be all bad. I hope my father didn't use the system ever again.

Antony Beauchamp was a shining and brilliant person in my life. I am drawn to brilliance, but there is also a part of me that is drawn by stability.

Not surprising really, if one thinks of my carefully stabilized and happy childhood. But the magnetic brilliance of Antony's talent could not, it appeared, brighten the dark side of his emotional character. Across the sunlit path a shadow was to fall which I could not lift. It was when I was freelancing and, therefore, had more time between jobs, that I finally became aware of his emotional instability and it caused me great concern.

It is difficult to diagnose somebody's emotional make-up; so let me simply describe a few incidents during our life together. The first that comes to mind was when we were sitting in the Garden of Allah, at one time a famous haunt in Hollywood much frequented by writers. There was a pool; Antony loved to swim, but I was too lazy and used to sit in a deckchair reading a book. He took a running dive, the loud smack of the water made me look up and I saw him reach the bottom of the pool where he lay quite still. I went to the pool's edge and thought, 'That's funny, I'm sure he didn't hit his head!' I decided that something should be done and I was about to dive in and pull him up by the seat of his bathing trunks when suddenly he started floating to the surface, where he opened his eyes and looked at me:

'While I was down there I wondered what it would be like to have a ton of water on your head. I dreamt I died.'

'Were you happy?'

'I dreamt I'd be at peace forever.'

'Were you?'

'No.'

I was determined to pursue this. But Antony would only agree to talk about it later over dinner. We chose some restaurant on Sunset Strip. I waited until we were half-way through the meal, and then asked him to tell me about the dream which he had had at the bottom of the pool.

'I dreamt with great certainty that I died.'

Calculatedly cool, I said that I had certainly thought there was some-thing wrong. Antony wondered whether we could write a story about a man who dived to the bottom of a pool and disappeared.

I said, 'Disappearance meaning death, I suppose?'

He nodded, and I said, 'It is one of those very difficult subjects, because no one ever knows the answer until it is too late.'

He laughed, and we did not continue the conversation.

Some months later, he came home late one night. He had driven to the edge of a cliff somewhere near Pacific Palisades at the end of Sunset and said he had thought he would drive the car over the edge. I had a prickly sensation, then Antony broke into laughter and said, 'But I didn't because I thought what the world would miss without me.'

There was another incident when Antony was on an assignment for *Life* to photograph a bullfight. We drove to Tijuana, just over the border into Mexico, where there was a corrida – the only one I have ever seen. We did the whole thing properly from beginning to end. The night before, we met the bullfighters, who took us to see the bulls. The next day, Antony took some rather fine pictures while I busied myself by keeping his camera loaded. I nudged him at one point and suggested he should take some of the audience's faces. He did so: from the stony, gnarled faces of the grandparents with their placid enjoyment of brutality, down through the ages to the wide-eyed horror of the small children. I don't believe we should feed a taste for brutality, even when it is quite voluntary as in bullfights. I recall how just after the war, the British authorities had to stop showing films of the torture and agonies of the Nazi concentration camps because they found that, after the initial stinging shock, people became inured; or if they were too shocked, they deliberately closed their minds to 'Man's inhumanity to man'. Man's inhumanity to bull is, of course, slightly different, but the brutalizing is similar.

We had found a nice hotel in Tijuana built to a circular design, which they say has a definite soothing and therapeutic effect. It had a patio and a pool. It was very pretty and in our little globe we were quite peaceful for a few days. Antony had recently been disappointed by the rejection of a film script which he had worked hard on.

He said, 'I wish we could go on like this for ever. Why don't we run away?'

'I'm prepared to,' I said.

'Would you change your name?'

'I thought I had!'

'But you'll always be Sarah Churchill.'

'Yes, just as you'll always be Antony Beauchamp.'

Perhaps I had made a sad mistiming of a perfectly genuine remark. And, of course, it was thoughtless of me, because Antony had not always been Beauchamp. His family name was Entwistle, but he had changed this when he ran away from home intending to be a society photographer. Very few people in America knew that he had personally chosen the old-English-sounding name of Beauchamp. Antony decided we must go home. We got in the car and he drove fast and furiously back to Hollywood.

When we were next in England I decided to take counsel. I thought it might be difficult, because Antony tended to put more faith in pills than people and I recalled a cocktail party we had attended in New York. In the middle of it, Antony suddenly broke out in a sweat and said he had to get out. I went to my hostess to ask whether there was any special guest I should say goodbye to. She indicated General Slim who, when I explained the problem, simply asked whether Antony had been in Burma during the war. He said with a smile that he could have a strange effect on people who had served under his command. But then he asked quite seriously and discreetly whether Antony was showing signs of bad temper and I had to admit this was so. General Slim said he was sure it was malaria, he recognized all the symptoms and strongly recommended that Antony should visit the Hospital for Tropical Diseases when we were next in England. I thanked him and left to find Antony shaking, cold and sweating outside.

But Antony strongly resisted a visit to the hospital: even under the strain of what seemed certainly to be a form of malaria, he refused to go. So when I sought out a psychiatrist and he said: 'I never take married couples unless both the partners come,' I readily agreed to take part in case I could help. But it got us nowhere.

There was another so-called 'cure' at that time which was very fashionable. You were put to sleep for four days with intravenous feeding. Antony jumped at it voluntarily. He came out looking absolutely terrible and was little improved. However, it was at about the same time that he managed to arrange for the setting up of his TV series, *Fabian of the Yard*, and he perked up. I was happy for him and he was working with delightful people, and I thought perhaps this was what the doctor *really* ordered – work. I came over to England to play in one of the Fabian films. The psychiatrist had hinted to me that perhaps I was an aggravation to Antony. I searched my soul and wondered if this were true. Certainly he showed no signs of missing me when I was away. But the one week of filming with him finally convinced me that we were not, and never could be, working partners, and regretfully I had to admit that we were no longer marriage partners.

I was forty-three. I had once again to admit defeat. By now Antony's wild, insubstantial infidelities were well known to others and finally discovered by me. My friends urged me to seek another companion. In solemn desperation I embarked on a few flirtations, but they could not fill my sense of loneliness and defeat.

Finally, taking a break in my work schedule, I returned to England with the definite intention and purpose of informing him that it was no longer worth trying to put a face on our marriage and that I would like a divorce. I took a plane and booked myself into a service flat – I didn't, naturally, want to stay in a hotel. That night, before I had contacted Antony, according to my old friend Lorraine Merritt, who was visiting England and who decided to stay the night with me, I never sat down. I walked up and down the room singing, 'I'm getting buried in the morning ...'

At seven o'clock the next day, 8 August 1957, the phone rang and I heard my mother's crisp voice – we never beat about the bush in our family: 'Sarah, you should know – Antony Beauchamp has committed suicide.'

At this time, I had to do perhaps one of the most difficult of all things: refuse the help of a friend. I have been on the other side when I have desperately tried to help and comfort and I know it is impossible, you can only share one thing – silent desolation. I asked Lorraine to continue her journey in England and leave me to cope with the rest. She did so. I assured my parents that I was all right and able to deal with the situation, and that I would see them when it was all over. I went at the request of the police to make the formal identification and later Diana, of course, came with me to the funeral. She drove with Antony's brother Clive; I went with his parents.

After the funeral and the settlement of Antony's affairs, I went back to Hollywood.

12

Malibu Nightmare

I decided I must have a change of scenery and rented a rickety cabin in Malibu. It was built, like many such sea-cabins, with its front almost on the highway and its back on stilts down to the beach. It lay between the thunder of trucks on the Pacific Coast Highway and the steady pounding of the Pacific Ocean. The noise eventually created almost an artificial silence and a slightly hypnotic rhythm. To answer the phone, you had to put your head under the pillow. At night, I would look east and south around the curving Santa Monica Bay to Los Angeles with its carpet of lights twinkling through the haze. In the morning, I would wake at dawn to see the heavy pelicans zooming in low like bombers to land on their special rock a mile away.

My solitude caused many of my friends concern, but I had, after all, chosen it quite deliberately, and even if it was to contribute to disaster for me, it was a creative period in which I wrote a lot of poetry and painted many pictures. Howard Holtzman was a poet and we used to enjoy each other's company by reading our works modestly to each other over the telephone at night.

I was rehearsing for a television performance of *The Makropoulos Secret* at that time. My early stage training always stood me in good stead for these live shows, because I had little difficulty in learning my own lines cast-iron, and would usually know the whole script by the time of the performance. Once I was sure that my lines and myself were one, I would act out the more difficult parts alone in my cabin, happily shielded by the roar of the road and the roar of the ocean. Then I would indulge in a certain amount of drink and – the famous trap – a few barbiturates to deaden the even greater roar of my voluntary isolation.

One night a couple of days before the show, when I was talking to Howard Holtzman, somebody must have cut in on the line and probably asked me questions, but I went merrily babbling on. Tapping of telephones was quite usual then – it was the height of the McCarthy witch-hunt – but it did not occur to me that operators listened in on conversations: 'where ignorance is bliss, 'tis folly to be wise.' Suddenly, two patrolling policemen were at my door saying that I was disturbing the peace. This was ridiculous. Even if I had been shouting, it would not have been possible to create any disturbance. It did not occur to me that anyone might have been tapping my telephone. However, I asked them in and let them look around the house; I was, of course, immediately sobered up by this intrusion. They appeared convinced that I was not creating a disturbance and they got ready to leave. My good manners were to trip me up: I showed them to the door. Six feet outside protecting territory, I became vulnerable to arrest because now I was in a public place. I noticed that they had a tommy gun in the car and now, foolishly convinced they were my friends, I asked them to show me their gun, and said, 'Do you really need these weapons, you might scare the pelicans?'

The conversation both inside and outside my sea-cabin must have taken nearly an hour. One of the officers looked behind him as we were speaking and saw his lieutenant coming along to investigate. One of them said, 'Sorry kid, you've had it now,' and pushed me into the patrol car. I struggled and kicked and certainly 'made a nuisance of myself in a public place'. Now they had got me. They took me to a small police station. It was about two o'clock in the morning and they asked me a lot of questions, to all of which I gave, I thought, merry answers. Not thinking myself a captive, I had at least, I thought, a captive audience. I felt sure they had no right to detain me, and should have taken me straight in to a Los Angeles County police headquarters. The reason for the delay was to show itself clearly when we did finally arrive in Los Angeles. It was a long journey, and I must record that they slapped me around. I naturally did not take this quietly. I was put into a straitjacket and forcibly assisted to the car by three police officers – there had been as many as six to eight of them in the small interrogation room, where I distinctly remember saying, 'You're a bloody lot of Fascists! You can hardly beat the infiltration of Communists into the United States by this kind of treatment!'

It was to be a long journey. I looked at my uniformed companions and asked the one sitting beside me whether he was married. He said, 'No,' so I then asked him whether he had a sister. He said, 'Yes,' so I asked him whether he could possibly do me a favour by combing my hair. He looked into the mirror at the other two officers. I had a feeling he was not happy about my predicament. I was right: he produced a dubious comb and by the time he had finished combing my hair, I had managed to slip, somehow, out of the straitjacket. Then I asked that, when we got to Los Angeles, they should please *not* assist me from the car; everyone has the right to prove themselves sober.

As I got out of the car, however, a policewoman came up and, I am convinced, deliberately tripped me – so the battle recommenced! As I was pulled about, lifted and dragged around, photographers took several pictures. Inside, the TV cameras were lined up and the pictures duly went around the world. Now I knew why there had been a delay: to allow the gentlemen of the press time to get ready.

I was taken downstairs where mug shots and fingerprints were taken. Then I was led to a private cell. Private! It was exactly like the ones in films with bars across one wall so that I was visible to everyone. I was allowed to make one telephone call, which by then seemed surprisingly civilized. I phoned Burbank Studios, although I had to go through the operator as I did not have the telephone number. I managed to speak to one of the producers and said: 'I'm afraid I'm to be a little late for rehearsal. I'm in jail, could you do something about it?'

I was led back to my cell and within half an hour, to my considerable relief, a bondsman appeared to put up my fifty-dollar bail. He also had a car and I asked him to take me to the studios, where the cast rallied around me asking what on earth had happened. I said I did not want to talk about it then and that we should get on with the show. Albert McCleery was in New York and sent me an enormous bouquet of flowers with the message: 'Churchills may lose battles, but they win wars – Love, Albert.'

I stayed that night in a hotel at Burbank and after the rehearsal I swept into the restaurant and promptly ordered a drink – in public! The next day when I got to the studio, the corridors were lined with press people. I refused to speak to them until after the show. When the show was over they asked me what happened and I replied, 'I can't speak about the case – it is *sub judice*.'

Then they asked whether I was going to be pleading guilty and I used Mr Asquith's reply: 'Wait and see.'

I was handed a note at the studio door that said my brother Randolph had flown in from New York. When I saw him, he said that I must plead guilty. I could not upset America, or Anglo-American relations. He said it would only be a nine days' wonder and asked me whether he should write my speech for me. I asked him what he would say. He drew himself up and said, 'I cast myself upon the mercy of the court.'

I enquired politely whether he was becoming a ghost writer or an actor.

Through the four days that I had to think about it, I was touched by the Americans' kindness in letters piled up at my door as high as my wicket gate; the letters ranged from ones of support and protestations of my innocence to one from a child who said: 'Dear Sarah, I thought policemen were meant to help you. I enjoy your programme. Love ...'

I felt assured of their love for me; how could I do less than assure them, as the grand-daughter of Jenny Jerome, that I loved them too? Four days later I appeared in court. I had written my own speech and I pleaded guilty. There was an audible groan from the press. The judge made what I thought was a rather pompous speech, then said that he was treating me like anyone else who would appear before him on a similar charge and fined me $50. I don't suppose, however, that Malibu Justice court always had quite so many cameramen packed into it. Little did Randolph know that this was not to be a mere 'nine days' wonder'. It was to be a ten-year trauma for me and it was to leave an everlasting scar.

Afterwards I drove away with my friends, and, of course, Lilliput. When we got near my little cabin by the sea I said to stop, because I was going to return to my house. They were dumbfounded and said, 'But you can't possibly!'

I said, 'Oh yes I can, and furthermore, I'm going to do so!'

Lilliput was extremely upset in her motherly way, but I persuaded her that I knew what I was doing. I spent the night there alone with relief surging over me: soon it would all be yesterday, or so I thought.

In the morning, I heard a noise in the front room. I sprang from my bed – I was still fully clothed – and found two patrolmen puffing cigars and looking around the room. I said, in my best barrack-room voice, 'What the hell do you think you're doing here?'

They stammered a bit and said, 'We never imagined you'd be here.

I said that I wasn't surprised to find them there, even though my own court proceedings had been pretty clear about what was a public or a private domain. I also asked them to remove their cigars from their faces when they were speaking to me. I then went into top-gear – and I believe Sarah Bernhardt would have been proud of me: luckily, I have forgotten exactly what I said, but from six inches *inside* my territory I prayed for every old-English word I could think of and swore at them like a trooper. They left, hurriedly.

I called Lilliput and said I thought the use of my sea-cabin had come to a conclusion and that I *would* like to come and stay with her. She was delighted and said I could have their private guest room which had a communicating door to their house, but also a private entrance if I didn't want to be disturbed.

Lilliput greeted me with her usual warmth. Standing in the room with her was someone she introduced as a doctor, who said; 'If I can be of any service to you . . .'

I cut in, asking just what he was suggesting. He said soothingly, 'Well, why don't you have a few days' rest, I know of a lovely clinic.'

I looked at him very straight and said firmly that I had already had a previous invitation; I would stay there with Miss Messenger. I turned and made my way to my own apartment. I had serious matters to attend to and busied myself on the phone. I called a girl who had done some work for me and entrusted her with the difficult task of answering all the letters. I spent two or three days dictating varying formats, and it was to take her some three weeks to finish the typing. But that could be done, I explained, after I had gone, and I signed innumerable blank pages. I also asked her if she would pack up and leave the little sea-cabin tidy.

Having attended to business, I then decided to attend to myself. I sent out a distress signal to my good friend Helmut Dantine, with whom I had appeared in a play at the Pasadena Playhouse called *Tonight at Samarkand*. He turned up promptly and I said that I needed his help; I felt the time had come for my flight to Europe. He meticulously worked out a schedule and arranged for people to meet me at every stop: Chicago, New York, Paris, Nice. For we had agreed I should not stop in England as I had received a charming telegram from Wendy Reeves at La Pausa in the south of France, where my father and mother were staying: 'LASSIE COME HOME, I AM WITH YOU H... OR HIGH WATER, LOVE WENDY GIRL.'

It was an invitation which I was ready to accept.

Helmut was as good as his word; he found a friend of his to look after me in Chicago; I had many of my own friends in New York and at Paris, where I had to change planes, Antony Beauchamp's brother, Clive Entwistle, met me and we had dinner together in a little room. He was described in the French newspapers, correctly, as my brother-in-law and

'Sarah's *chevalier galant*', so as to dispel any rumours of romance. But aren't the French always gallant when a lady is in distress?

Clive saw me safely on to the plane to Nice. He was allowed through to the steps. This in no way affronted me – the suggestion that I might not be capable! – I saw it rather as a further extension of Gallic courtesy. Once on board I fell asleep, knowing that I was on the home stretch. I had not realized that the press were still trailing me. One of them took a picture of me on the plane while I was sleeping. Fortunately, it was lovely and peaceful; all the strain had gone from my face.

At Nice airport I was met by Anthony Montague-Browne, who drove me to La Pausa. We had all the usual chit-chat about how they all were; they were well, and so was I. It was marvellous: for a talkative family, no questions were asked, but neither was any false chatter kept up; it could all wait until tomorrow.

Tomorrow – rested and calm, with the people who really cared about me – we discussed my future. Wendy was adamant that I was in no way a drunkard or an alcoholic. Thumping her fist on the table, she said she had been married to an alcoholic for twelve years, and that I showed no signs of such a disaster. 'If you love her and believe in her, she will find her own source for the distress,' said Wendy, who then suggested that I should go to the Bircher–Benner Clinic in Zurich which was entirely diagnostic and dietetic. Wendy was convinced that I was in a state of shock and that I did not need anything but time to myself. My father nodded his assent. My mother, as careful mothers always do, thought someone should go with me. But Wendy, once a top model and quite a formidable person in her own way, said she thought perhaps too many people had been around me to offer their advice, or their praise, or their consolation.

My father looked at me and asked me what I thought. I replied that I believed it was only for me to solve the predicament I had landed myself in. Air travel and money were all arranged for me and thanks to my family's concern I felt a ray of hope in my despair.

Diana told me later that, on the news of my Malibu disaster, she went to see Papa. He had every newspaper cutting spread out on the floor, and like a chubby teddy bear, was on his hands and knees, placing in order the various factors of the case. When Diana came into the room he turned and looked at her and said, 'She could win this case!'

Diana replied, 'I don't think she will – or wants to.'

When I arrived in Zurich, I checked in to the Waldhaus Dolder Hotel, about a ten-minute walk from the Bircher-Benner Clinic on slippery roads, iced over by the cold weather. I immediately found the bracing air reviving. But as I slipped and slid my way down the road, marvelling at the crystallized effect of frost on bare branch, still with my recollections of childish diseases, I was nervous. My doctor did not appear to be so.

Dr Liechti was then a woman of some forty years, perhaps a year or so younger than me. She told me the procedure was very simple: I had to turn up for my various tests and then we would meet to discuss the results. She said she knew by my record I would co-operate, and that they would like me, in the first week or so, to have at least one meal a day at the clinic. This led to my indoctrination to vegetarian food and an introduction to an extraordinary mish-mash called 'muesli'. I waited for her to say, 'Of course, there is no drinking,' but she didn't. I was grateful for her diplomatic omission. Instead she said briskly, 'We would like you to walk. We understand you had, as a child, a tubercular problem – nothing like clean air.' I still waited for chains and guards, but there were none. I walked back up the icy slopes to the Waldhaus Dolder. I was happy and at peace.

I ploughed through all the familiar physical and medical tests and Dr Liechti said there was nothing much wrong with me. Would I now like to see a psychiatrist? Enlivened by my muesli diet, I asked why, if there was nothing wrong with me. Dr Liechti patiently explained that the clinic was a diagnostic place and that they had to know what was normal before they could say what was abnormal. So I went to the psychiatrist. It was the only time I felt any strain. Did I love my father more than my mother, they wanted to know. Did I have any racial prejudices and why was I there? I pointed out that they should know why Dr Liechti wanted me to take all the usual tests: in case I turned out normal. But I took the tests, including the famous Rorschach ink-blot tests. For, I hope, an imaginative person, I must have been a dull patient. When the probing started into my feelings about my father and mother, that went too far. I immediately decided all foreigners were now enemies, and asked myself, 'What am I doing talking to the enemy?'

When I saw her next morning, Dr Liechti laughed with her usual equanimity and said, 'Well, you certainly passed that test!'

Next, she said, they had an important test for me to take concerning my heart. She spoke nearly perfect English, but there was still a slight lack of absolutely idiomatic usage when she said, 'Can you come to the clinic in the morning – without movement?'

I took this very seriously, because they were nice people and I am always interested in a challenge. So I got up one hour earlier than necessary and moved with extreme caution down the slippery slope to the clinic. I was strapped up to have my heart beat tested, and there came a look of amazement on all their faces: I was not registering, I didn't appear to have any blood pressure. I told them that I had been asked to come 'without movement'!

'But we can't register anything,' they replied. 'Run round the room!'

So I obediently trotted round the room until, finally, some signal appeared on the screen, and I was informed that my heart was perfectly all right. I was glad.

I was having luncheon at the clinic one day when I noticed an attractive man of about my own age who kept on looking at me as we toyed with our nut-cutlets. At length I asked him if he wanted to say something and he replied, 'I am Cesare Pio.'

'Oh? I am Sarah Beauchamp.'

'I know who you are.'

Immediately, my heart missed a beat: my fear of the press and the police awoke. I left the table, and the next day, when I saw my doctor, I asked, 'Who is Cesare Pio?'

She flicked through some papers, saying he was not her patient. I insisted, 'Well, he has addressed me in the dining room, could he be a newspaper man?'

She burst out laughing and said, 'Now I know what is wrong, you don't trust the newspapers.'

Dr Liechti assured me he was not a pressman, although she obviously could not disclose his particular reason for seeking help there. She also told me I must remember that in Switzerland there were no gossip columns.

The next day, munching another nut-cutlet, I turned to Cesare and smiled, and apologized saying I was afraid I had been rude to him the day before because I thought he might have been from the press. At this, the relationship became happy: I had made another lifelong friend. The friendship was firmly sealed at the beginning by the fact that Cesare had a splendid car. I looked at it longingly, murmuring about how boring it could be at the clinic. He agreed, and we were off!

We were not under any sort of restraint at the clinic. We could go to any nearby restaurant and say simply that we were attending the Bircher–Benner Clinic and our muesli and nut-cutlet would be served up on a silver salver! Many harsh things have been said about the Swiss, about dull financiers and chocolate and cuckoo clocks, and how they are internationally famous for having no sense of humour. But when I saw my nut-cutlet on a silver salver, I decided that the Swiss might not after all be so bereft of humour.

Cesare Pio and I, however, did get a little further afield. After checking our treatment hours, which fortunately were in the morning for both of us, we carefully explored the area by maps, and then we made our plans for excursions. Perhaps the most memorable one was our ascent of the Jungfrau.

When the time came for Cesare to return to Milan, I said that I would be staying for a while at the Waldhaus Dolder, for although I felt much restored, I still dreaded the outside world. After he had gone, I continued with my adventuring, but on a more plebeian basis. There was a funicular which conveniently stopped at the Waldhaus Dolder. I would take it down into Zurich and make my way to the railway station, where I would sit in the little beer garden, by now with a little glass of fondue wine and my pencil and notebook, and I would watch the people boarding and leaving the trains. I wrote half a novel, which may yet still come to life, and many poems and some songs at that time. Sometimes I would take the train that runs along the shore of the lake of Zurich and when I got to the end I would simply turn around and come back.

I obviously could not stay too long at the clinic. For one thing, it was worryingly expensive; I was wonderfully subsidized by my parents, but had on several occasions to write and ask them for yet more. I was not making any money professionally and had a number of debts to be cleared from my most recent spell in the United States. I was beginning to get slightly itchy feet and Dr Liechti was encouraging me to spend some time away from the clinic, perhaps in Rome for a few days – Helmut Dantine was making a film there – or in Venice, where Helmut's wife, Niki, was about to work on another. I had some hopes at that time of setting up a film of our own. Dr Liechti I'm sure recognized that I would feel better about everything once I had begun to stretch my professional wings once again.

Diana and Mary both visited me in Zurich bringing me much news and comfort; but the cost just seemed to continue mounting. The amounts seem almost trivial in these inflationary times, but some hundreds of pounds was a great deal of money then. Finally, despite frequent changes of plan about visiting different parts of Italy, it was the call of happy family duty which stirred me from the clinic. The Churchill Hall at the Technion in Haifa was to be dedicated; my father by now was too old to attend in person, so it was I who was chosen to represent him and the family. It was an enormous privilege. It was also a difficult challenge to face direct from Zurich and the protecting arms of the clinic.

Well, I did it and it was a wonderful shot in the arm for me. It was only a four-day visit and therefore only possible to skim over the surface of that remarkable country. But I was determined that I would take any opportunity in the future to visit Israel again. I was, perhaps naturally, fairly self-conscious about how I was coping with the challenge of this trip, but was confident that I was doing well. Consequently, I was furious with one English newspaper which reported that I had mislaid my ticket, that I was flustered, and that I was last to board the plane. I was particularly annoyed because I had really taken trouble to be not only on time, but early, and I only posed for photographs out of courtesy. When one of the cameramen asked me to pose doing up a bag, I swallowed a natural desire to say no and determined not to be bad-tempered. It was a lesson to me that I really had a reputation now – a reputation that was to dog my footsteps.

I took my consolation on my way back to Zurich for final tests by stopping off in Rome, where I had a wonderful day with my old friend Mario Soldati. Somewhat surprisingly to me, he was second-director on the epic film *Ben Hur*, which was shooting in Rome then. We spent most of the time talking nostalgically of our times together and looking to the immediate future when we were certain to make a film together in London. Like so many happy schemes in the movie business, that film never materialized. I continued to Venice, where I went shopping and sightseeing with Niki Dantine during a break in her filming, and so back to the clinic and Dr Liechti.

Cesare Pio suddenly reappeared one day to ask how I was getting on. I said I thought I must be doing well: nobody seemed to be interested in me any more, so perhaps it was time to go home. We had lunch together and sat on a little verandah, where he asked to hear what I had been writing. The book was too long, so I asked him whether he would mind a few poems. He said he would like to hear them and after I had read them, he asked if he could have them so that he could get them printed for me. One in particular interested him and he had it specially calligraphed. I naturally asked Cesare how he was doing and was appalled to hear he was learning to fly an aeroplane – at his age.

He said, 'It is *because* of my age that I must do something to prove to myself that I am not afraid.'

He bought his own plane, learned to fly, passed his test and got his pilot's licence. Then he flew solo – and then, thank God, he gave it up.

13

Peter Pan to Holloway

When I returned to England I was quickly reminded how important is the love of one's friends. I had been in a Swiss clinic for a number of months, but it was still the same year of my disaster in Malibu. My professional career was non-existent. But within minutes it seemed I was able to plunge into worthwhile professional activities. With the quiet help and prompting of good friends like Patrick Desmond, the producer and director, I soon had more offers than I could possibly manage to fulfil. I was being welcomed home with work.

The first production I joined was Terence Rattigan's *Variations on a Theme* which was playing in repertory at Worthing. Terence Rattigan in my opinion never wrote a bad play and always wrote remarkable parts for actors to get their teeth into – even small-part actors. Also Worthing was a good repertory company just then, including Gerald Flood and Susannah York among its younger members. So all seemed well set for my return to the stage. There was, however, a problem which I explained to my cousin Sylvia Henley. She accompanied my parents on the drive over from Chartwell for the first night. While they were resting in a nearby hotel I took Sylvia into my confidence. I was nervous because my first appearance in the play required me to rush on stage, head straight for the drinks table and pour myself a large brandy. As most people know, stage whisky and brandy is usually made from cold tea. But I was frightened that my first piece of 'business' would simply provoke a roar of laughter from the audience. Sylvia said she would take care of the situation and, sure enough, the moment I raised the 'brandy' to my lips she started the applause which is often given to the leading actor or actress on their first appearance. It was immaculate timing on her part. At the end of the first act her ringing voice could be heard exclaiming, 'Splendid! Splendid!' and after the second act she came back during the interval to assure me in person that the whole play was going well. Sylvia Henley was always my cheer leader.

Towards the end of the year, I made the mistake of trying to do two things at once. I managed both with some success; but the long-term consequences of perhaps over-reaching myself were to prove catastrophic. The first was that I accepted the part in the film *Serious Charge* of the neurotic spinster who, rebuffed by a vicar, takes sides with a youth who is charging the vicar with criminal assault. The film was directed by my friend Terence Young and also starred Anthony Quayle and Andrew Ray with the youthful Cliff Richard in, I believe, his first straight acting role. I thought that my part in the original screenplay was rather stodgy. When I explained this to Terence he readily obliged me by arranging for a fairly torrid scene to be written in for me and Andrew; this satisfied my theatrical ham instincts.

While we were shooting *Serious Charge*, I became heavily involved in my second 'thing' which was taking the title role in the annually produced children's classic *Peter Pan* by J.M. Barrie. I don't recall that the film shooting and actual performances of *Peter Pan* overlapped, but I do remember that rehearsals had to be rearranged around me to some extent. Despite the fact that Terence used to call me 'one-take Churchill' and claimed that he shot my scenes during rehearsal. I did get into trouble occasionally for being late for *Peter Pan* rehearsals. However, Patrick Desmond was producer-director that year, so I was often indulged.

I find it interesting, looking back over who has played Peter through the years, to note how often the part has been given to an actress in her forties, as I was; especially since the character is a boy who never grows up. But then, to me, the whole of *Peter Pan* is a fantasy; I don't have a lot of time for the Freudian and other ideas which have been read into it. I believe it is all a simple representation of happy family life: the children never leave the nursery.

One of the most challenging aspects of the play is that one has to learn how to 'fly' – or at least how to be flown. I had the same 'flyer' throughout the run of the play. He seemed morbidly interested in my weight, not unlike the old-fashioned hangman. But my safety depended at all times on his knowledge and ability, so I certainly didn't mind him knowing such intimate information – especially since I lost at least ten pounds during the production. When we first started work with the flying rig and hooks and wires, my instinct from my dance training was to jump; but my flyer quickly insisted that I didn't try to help him at all, otherwise he might be thrown off balance at the other end of the wire and there would be no knowing where we would both end up.

I remember on one occasion on tour when we had achieved complete confidence in each other, I, with my vertigo virtually overcome, was nonchalantly standing on a ledge thirty or forty feet up in the flies waiting for my cue. I looked down to wave to my flyer who just as nonchalantly waved back – with *both* hands. I almost had a heart attack, then realized I hadn't fallen: he had twisted my wire around one of his feet. I only had one disaster on the wire, and that was when Mr Kirby (the man who invented the rig) appeared at the theatre to fly me in person on his company's equipment. Since he was not completely familiar with the set, instead of flying me through the nursery window, he flew me slap into a scenery wall.

When the play opened, there were several performances which were almost Churchill family benefits. My mother took twelve seats on one occasion; Diana took a party just before Christmas; both my parents came one night. They were glorious occasions, though it is more nerve-racking to perform in front of your family and friends than the other unknown members of the audience. Randolph crossed swords with Patrick Desmond one night when he wanted to see me before the show. Patrick made the rule that we should never see family, or anyone, before the show since it was too disruptive. Noël Coward simply booked his seats from New York and then graced the theatre by his presence on the opening night.

After the London run, we took *Peter Pan* on tour around the provinces. I believe that it has never been surpassed as far as plays for children are concerned and the cast was certainly having enormous fun. My co-conspirators then were principally John Justin, who played Hook, and Julia Lockwood, who played Wendy and was to become a great friend. Julia had played the part to her mother Margaret Lockwood's Peter the previous year as well and, at first, she regarded me with the typically wary approach of the child who believes you are encroaching upon her mother's preserve. She was still only sixteen at the time. When we came down for our first dress rehearsal, and I was in the traditional Peter Pan garb, she suddenly smiled as if she recognized someone, and said how nice I looked and what a lovely tunic I was wearing. I said, 'But it is your mother's.' She gasped, and our friendship was able to begin. It is part of the tradition of the production that Peter Pans, as we are mostly much the same shape and size, generally wear the previous actress's costume, while during the long strenuous weeks of rehearsal another is made which they then put back into the wardrobe.

Once we got on tour, I recall all sorts of minor mishaps and confusions – such as having to replace Lost Boys or Pirates at a moment's notice, let alone keeping the many children in the cast in some sort of good order. It was not only on the junior members of the cast that the strain began to tell. We were playing in Liverpool, which is a fine theatrical city, and which brought back many memories for me – this was where Randolph fought and lost an election in Wavertree in 1935. I knew the Adelphi Hotel and the theatre, but we were actually staying at the Lord Nelson, a hotel which I did not know. I have an instinct for losing my way, but as one usually went back home with the other principals, it didn't matter as we all left the theatre together, so I never had to bother with keeping track of where I was going. One night, after the opening, we had all been greatly fêted, and we got back to the Lord Nelson where I had Margaret Lockwood's former room. The others wisely went to bed, but I stayed on in the bar. The people there couldn't have been nicer, and certainly I'm sure no ill-intent was meant, but in that old-fashioned word, they 'plied' me with too much to drink. After a while, feeling a little heady, I decided to go for a walk. I started on one of my midnight prowls, wandering around, looking at Liverpool, which is a fascinating city, and I ended up completely lost. It seemed there was no taxi of which I could avail myself. So I found my way to the Adelphi. But they did not turn out to be helpful. They took one look at my slightly distracted air and, instead of calling me a taxi – for there was no question that they knew who I was and where I was playing – they called the police. So, once again, I was in deep water.

They were sympathetic at the police station, as I explained that I really had to be at the matinée later in the day. The matron or wardress came with cups of tea, and when the superintendent arrived, he invited me up to his office. In fact, everything was done to reassure me that this was only a minor thing; but, as usual, I must plead guilty. I went back down to my cell. The producer, Patrick Desmond, the stage-manager, Pip Flood-Murphy, and the cast were all informed that I was behind bars, and I asked Patrick to assure everyone that I would make the show on time.

To get to the court in Liverpool you have to go down some stairs through an uncomfortable corridor lined with detention cells and then up some more steps into the dock. I was escorted, for some reason I shall never know, by four policeman, one of whom, I am absolutely sure to this day, tripped me up. So I fell. That is why I was carried into court by four policemen. They stood with me in the dock, and the magistrate started to ask me questions. I said I would answer no questions until he ordered these men out of the dock. 'Tell them to take their hands off me,' I insisted, 'I am not a criminal!' He promptly did so, and the large, comfortable police lady appeared instead. What they thought I was going to do, I have no idea, as my only intention was to get back to the theatre as quickly as possible. The magistrate then asked me if I had any-thing to say. When I said I did, he asked me whether I would say it from where I was or whether I would like to cross the court. This was obviously to give me the chance to make some explanation and defence of my minor misconduct. I seized on the chance of crossing the court to prove to them that I was fit and able. I walked into the dock and they handed me the Bible on which to swear and the card with the oath printed on it.

Again feeling nervous aggression rising in me, I said, 'I can't possibly swear if you hold it upside down!'

Immediately the clerk became flustered but he turned it the right way up. I then explained the circumstances: that I was wandering around Liverpool, which held many memories for me, and that I was looking for a 'habitat'. Now, this caused great merriment, being such a funny word to use, instead of saying, 'I was looking for my hotel.' Thus I managed to prove that I was capable, but I also proved that I had been tipsy. After this momentous speech which was being duly internationally recorded, I was fined the summary £2 and told I could go.

Patrick Desmond and Pip rushed forward and said, 'You can slip out through the back door.'

I said, 'I've never slipped out of anything in my life. I shall go out the same way as I came in!'

So, in my spotted-leopard coat, a detail which my mother never forgot, I swished out and down the main street – the theatre was not very far away – and saw a 'local'. I immediately went in, sat down and had a Guinness to restore my fractured nerves and also I suppose in some spirit of defiance, which I felt had to be dealt with before I got to the theatre. After all, it was to children that I was playing. We arrived at the theatre with the usual trail of cameras clicking us, and Patrick Desmond, my life-long and devoted friend, became quite upset because he was referred to in the subsequent newspaper pictures and stories as 'Sarah Churchill and friend' and not as 'the producer, Patrick Desmond'.

I went to the theatre and was greeted warmly by the cast; I did my practice flights as usual and the curtain went up on time. The reporters were there and wrote about how amazing it was that having been fined for being drunk, I could still fly with the greatest of ease through the air and land, tip-toe, on the mantelpiece.

The play proceeded, and when I left the stage that night, I heard that my mother, greatly concerned, had rung up and asked why it had been necessary to carry her daughter into court when, an hour later, she was flying on a wire. There didn't seem to be a suitable answer and, anyway, it was already over and done with and too late.

I decided that evening that the publicity for both me and the show would be very adverse, and Angus McCloud, who was for many years the organizer and arranger of *Peter Pan* made special arrangements, at my request, for me to stay the night in the theatre, and not go back to the hotel, nor indeed to venture out into the streets where I might be jostled by interested people. It was possible that all of them would be friendly; but at that moment, I did not feel in the mood to be jostled. So I sat in state in my dressing room. One of the stage cots was brought up and made into a bed, and I ordered food from, I think, the Adelphi – I always rather like to rub a line in. I ordered an enormous amount of food and ate my dinner there, rather like a classical prisoner awaiting execution the next morning. Special precautions had to be put on because, although there was a night porter, additional fire precautions had to be taken since I was not involved with theatre management. We spent a lovely night together, the night watchman, the extra fireman, Pip Flood-Murphy who stayed to keep me company, and myself. It is a most extra-ordinary experience – and a very rare one, I hope – to wander round in the middle of the night and see the stage, so barren, so strange, so familiar, in that ghostly atmosphere, with one working light hanging from the ceiling.

In the morning, I had a bath – there are generally baths in big theatres – and took my exercise up on the roof. The cast came in, and on we went with the next two shows. On Saturday, after the second and final show, I went and caught the midnight train to London, escorted by the ever-faithful Patrick and Pip. We were not bothered: by now the news of my arrest and court appearance had died down.

When *Peter Pan* finished, I decided to use some of the riches I had earned from it on taking a flat in Dolphin Square, overlooking the Thames. I had contemplated buying a boat and had gone so far as to write accordingly to my parents in the South of France, no doubt startling them with the prospect of their daughter joining them direct from the waves. In the end, I was content to watch other people's boats and the barges ploughing steadily up and down the river. Julia Lockwood also took a small flat in Dolphin Square. Her mother Margaret was not at first enthusiastic about our friendship; she was very doubtful about the influence I might have on the still young Julia. This difference was later resolved and my personal and professional admiration of Margaret Lockwood as a woman and as an actress remains firm.

These were indeed lively times for me. It was then that I got to know April Ashley. I had met her for lunch in Paris before her operation and she joined us in Dolphin Square after undergoing her sex-change in Casablanca – the only place in those days where this emotionally and physically delicate operation was available. We tried to support and protect April against the press and sometimes from her own more exuberant follies. I also recall it was during this time when, after an unusually lengthy party, I had found myself waking in a nursing home under the care of a young psychiatrist who has subsequently proved to be one of my great mentors and pillars of support.

Even when I wasn't getting into trouble myself, the newspapers were always ready to support the idea that I was. There was the occasion when a sad lady was admitted to, I think, the Westminster Hospital suffering from what may have been too much drink or drugs. She said she was Sarah Churchill – a 'fact' which was duly printed in one newspaper despite the actual fact that I was in the West of England preparing to play Rosalind in As You Like It at Croydon. I'm glad to say that the review of the play – in a different newspaper – said I played my part 'with an appealing note of husky languishing' and that it was 'an affecting performance'. My parents attended a matinée during our second week.

Unfortunately, however, things were beginning to build up against me. I was already on probation after a series of mishaps ending in court – as one quite sympathetic magistrate said, 'If you insist on being disorderly, do try to do it in a different district.' But it was not my instinct then to wander far afield. Dolphin Square was my chosen retreat and I would choose to take my midnight prowls mostly up and down along the river. I would walk along the Embankment often in blue jeans, sometimes barefoot; I don't know whether I was being 'avant-garde' or 'derrière-garde'. I certainly didn't know then that I was being watched. Immediately opposite my door was a famous club. As soon as one of the doormen saw me come out for a walk, he would call the local police station and say, 'She's out again.' An unmarked car – not obviously a police car – would draw almost silently beside me; I would be pulled in and off we would go to the station, where I would protest loudly and then end up once again at Bow Street magistrates' court. I recall one occasion near Victoria Station when I had been asked to leave a milk bar with the delightful name of 'Moo-Cow'; I was incensed when I heard the young constable who was looking after me say to his superior on the telephone, 'We've got her again.'

I became first annoyed and then outraged at this sort of procedure, but these arrests became too cumulative for anyone not to notice. And so, in July 1961, after some particular incident, no worse than the first, I was remanded for ten days to Holloway Prison for a medical report.

The headline of course was 'Jail for Sarah', and down I went to a detention cell below the court. Before long, I was herded with the other prisoners into a Black Maria in which you have to sit down, in your own private little lock-up cell, with hardly room for your knees. I cannot think why they thought I would be violent. However, I presumed it was routine. Apart from vertigo, I also have claustrophobia, which is why I never like people too close to me, and I always leave all the doors open. I must say that if it had not been for the conversations of the girls who were my fellow-travellers, I think I might have lost my mind.

We arrived at the grim fortress of Holloway Prison and were unleashed from our mobile private cells. I looked at the girls and felt rather giggly. One or two of them asked me why I was there. I said, 'Don't ask me now, I have a feeling we'll have time to talk about it later.'

We were shown into a room – now the pushing stops for, once they've got you inside, they don't have to shove you. We stood in a line and a nice woman in uniform said, 'Any of you who've been here before, stand forward.'

The whole line stood forward, except me. She passed over this gap in the line without comment and then told us all that, if we obeyed, life would not be unpleasant, but that it was her duty and the duty of her colleagues to see we conformed to the discipline of the place.

Next came washing and delousing. We were shepherded into a steamy wooden bath hut, where all our clothes were taken from us and we all had a good scrub under the eyes of a number of 'trusties' – other prisoners who by their good behaviour had won special status and wore red armbands to prove it. Then I sat in a cubicle waiting for the doctor to come round and pronounce me clean and free of infestation. The walls of the cubicle were covered in graffiti, so I had plenty to occupy me while I waited: 'Watch out for —— ' and '—— is a —— cow' and so on, all signed with initials. I was inspected and passed. As I was led off to the hospital section, I recognized some of my travelling companions from the Black Maria. But they all seemed destined for the prison proper and I began to feel very lonely. Next I was asked whether I would like a private cell in tones which might have been employed if they were showing me to a room at the Ritz. My first instinct was to opt for a dormitory full of rumbustious fellow-inmates; but then I thought I might do better in a single cell. It proved to be a perfectly adequate place, with a high hospital bed, and I was given a red flannel nightgown.

I think the most awful thing was the clanging of the doors and the noise of keys in locks – I imagine it must be the same for anyone who has ever been in prison for whatever reason. I didn't like the small, high window either, or the bars. But I sought to compose myself and within an hour there was a rattle in the lock and a banging of the door and a great bunch of flowers arrived and telegrams from well-wishers and a whole mass of cigarettes. Even though I rarely smoke, the cigarettes were to prove useful as I discovered they were virtually the principal monetary system in the prison. I was allowed to keep the flowers and cigarettes, but the telegrams were taken away again and, when I asked for paper and pencil, I was told I couldn't have them, yet.

Like, I suppose, so many prisoners, I decided to settle down. I was warm and comfortable, but I wished they'd turn the light out – there is always this light and the little peephole in the door for the warders to see what you're getting up to. I had a delightful nurse who came in and surreptitiously slipped me an acid drop. I am not much given to sweets, but in itself her gesture was a comfort.

I was to make good friends with some of the girls in Holloway. Pregnant women in the hospital section were allowed a special ten-minute walk in addition to the fifteen-minute break when all the hospital doors were opened. Once a day the inner doors to the main prison were closed and the inmates of the hospital were allowed to mingle. During one of these periods, one tremendous girl came up to me with a piece of paper and said she had written a poem about my father. I was delighted and asked if I could have it. Passing bits of paper between prisoners was not allowed, so I asked her if she would read it to me. I wish I had the poem to this day, it was very moving.

Looking at her large stomach, I asked why she was in there and she explained that she had been moved into the hospital section to have her baby, adding, 'Of course, I'm butch, you know.'

'If you're butch, why are you having a baby?' I asked.

'Oh,' she said, 'We roll them!'

She and her friend would pick up a man, take him back to their room and then steal whatever money he had. She said it was her revenge on men. I couldn't quite understand what 'revenge' she got out of it, when the consequence was getting pregnant. I asked her whether she had got much money, but she said no, her friend had taken it all when she was arrested. I then discovered she was in prison not for 'rolling' men, but because she was a truck thief. She would loiter near transport cafés – the ones the long-distance drivers used – and she would check the empty trucks parked outside. They were generally locked, but she would go on till she found one that wasn't. She was an expert driver, and would simply drive the lorry till the fuel ran out.

I asked, 'Is it fun?'

'It's the best time of my life.'

She simply loved driving lorries, and I must say she became a friend.

I was able to follow her escapades later as she had told me of a certain pub in Brighton where she and other Holloway alumni used to gather. I went down there once and, sure enough, there she was.

I asked her what she was up to and she said cheerfully, 'Oh, I've just stolen another lorry.'

'Why can't somebody *give* you a lorry?'

'But it wouldn't be the same.'

In other words, the fun of stealing was compulsive. It was lucky she was a good driver and never ran anybody over. I asked what had happened to the baby, and she quite cheerfully told me that she had had it and that it had been very nice too, but of course it had been adopted.

Some of the girls were determined to be rebellious, particularly in little things. For example, if you were sitting in one of the common areas when the governor went past, the rules required you to stand up. Several of the girls didn't want to. I suppose my earlier service training made me realize that obeying such rules really did very little personal damage, but I wasn't particularly successful in conveying this philosophy to the younger inmates.

The trusties had got it all worked out. I had a long talk with one who used to bring round cocoa. When I asked her how long she had been in she said she thought it unlikely she would ever get out, but being a trusty meant she could have almost anything she wanted – except freedom. I realized that she had made the prison her home and only really felt secure there. I asked her whether I could get anything for her when I got out. She said she would like two yards of material because she had just one more curtain to complete for her cell.

I only had one unpleasant experience in Holloway. It was when a girl suddenly barged into my room during one of the open periods. She confronted me angrily and started pouring out abuse until, finally, I got annoyed and demanded what right she had to shout at me. Surprised, she stopped and said, 'I want a cigarette.'

I told her that if she had said 'please', she would probably have got one, but instead, if she didn't get out, I'd throw her out.

A more amusing incident was when a girl popped in and said, 'Are you a lesbian?'

'No.'

She said, 'Well you will be if you stay here long enough,' and popped out again.

That of course was the lighter side. There was, however, in the next cell, a poor unfortunate lesbian who had been convicted of murdering her girlfriend. I learnt a little about her from one of the prison doctors who told me that although the woman had been convicted for life, she was a highly intelligent person who would almost certainly be transferred to an open prison. He said he was sure she would not be violent. It had been what the French call a *crime passionel* – she had caught her girlfriend being unfaithful with another girl.

The doctor who had explained about my neighbour was to become a very great friend of mine and, indeed, was subsequently to become my own GP – a position of thankless responsibility which the poor man still holds at the time of writing. Alan Gordon is a most splendid man, a South African who was able to deal with the tough customers in the prison hospital in the same language that they used with him; he gave as good as he got. He was also a great favourite with the nurses, a gentle, knowledgeable and humane man. He was not my doctor in Holloway since I was under a psychiatrist; but Alan would pause each day on his round to check that all was well with me.

The psychiatrist, who put me through a battery of tests which were quite familiar from my Zurich clinic days, was also, I thought, a fine man. During one of our sessions, the conversation turned to Ruth Ellis, the last woman to be hanged in Britain. He said that he and his colleagues had done everything they could to persuade her to appeal against her sentence; but she had been determined to die. If ever there was a suicide, he said, it was her. My case, luckily, was less problematic. But I do recall very vividly his words at our last meeting: 'Now, I have made out my report on you, and you go out tomorrow. You are a very persuasive lady, but I implore you: don't open your mouth in court.'

I promised I'd keep my mouth shut, but only after I heard from him that he was recommending that I should be taken off probation – which I found nerve-racking. He was also going to suggest that I should go for a while as a voluntary patient to the Maudsley Hospital. I said that was fine so long as I would be permitted to go there under my own steam and not under police escort. I was prepared to go anywhere in my own time and on my own feet. I said goodbye to him and to the nurse who had been so kind to me and got ready to go back before the magistrate.

When I went out into the bright morning, I almost rebelled. There outside was a large black limousine. As the other prisoners called out wishing me goodbye and good luck, I looked in this enormous car where I saw two uniformed policemen – driver and escort – in the front and a uniformed policewoman in the back, to sit by my side. I don't know what things suddenly spur me on, but, remembering my promise not to open my mouth in court, I thought, 'you're going to hear a piece from me now,' and proceeded to enquire why it was necessary to go to the expense of providing a limousine to take me to court when a Black Maria had been considered good enough to bring me to prison. Was I some sort of international crook? Furthermore, what were the press going to make of my arriving at court in a huge car surrounded by police officers in uniform?

My tirade must have been effective because I think the policewoman came close to tears. She turned to her male companions and said I was perfectly right and that drawing such attention to me would be quite unfair. Then she turned to me and asked if it would help for her to take off her hat and tie, open the top button of her shirt, and sit with me in the car as a friend might. It was a great help.

So I arrived at Bow Street to hear the verdict. When I got into the court, I stood and there was a long speech from the magistrate who said it seemed I had passed all the tests. He noted that I had promised to take more care of myself, and commented that I was much more liable to damage myself than other people. I was fined a few pounds as usual, but dismissed from any more serious charge on the condition that I would 'seek further help' at the Maudsley Hospital. Did I have anything to say? I had been told to remain silent – I couldn't say anything. My sister Diana was in court, she came rushing up to me, but I said I was determined to walk out alone. I naturally thanked Diana warmly for being in court to support me; but out, alone, I walked.

Waiting just around the corner was Alan Gordon. His broad, beautiful, South African smile greeted me and he said, 'Thank God, we're through at last. Would you like to have a small brandy?'

There is one extraordinary thing I have found out about myself: when it isn't there, I don't miss it; but when it is, I do like it. I said, 'Yes.'

So off we drove to his flat where, over the chink of glasses, I pointed out that we must not forget that I had to report on time at four o'clock to the Maudsley.

Promptly, if somewhat merrily, at four o'clock I was there.

14

Third Honeymoon

Bellfire Susie is not, as far as I'm aware, a name that appears in the *Guinness Book of Records*, but it is still well remembered by followers of form at Wimbledon Stadium. Bellfire Susie was the name of the greyhound bitch Alan Gordon and I jointly owned and kennelled at Wimbledon. I was not involved in greyhound racing for many years, but I remember with great affection the time spent planning, speculating, worrying, rejoicing and having to find quantities of money to keep the whole thing going. Alan had suggested the involvement as a sort of therapy after I finished my not specially happy stint with the Maudsley – the hospital was marvellous, but there was some disagreeable publicity when one of the people there discussed my case with a newspaper.

Greyhound racing was enormous fun. We owned a number of dogs as well as bitches from time to time. It seemed to me, however, that it was a sport which was especially open to fiddling and nobbling and various sorts of villainy. I don't suppose I would have made it a lifelong interest, but I enjoyed it while it lasted and made many friends in consequence. It was certainly a good deal less expensive to own a racing greyhound than a racehorse.

It was at about this time, towards the end of 1961, that Mrs Katie Jones came into my life, first to be my maid, and later to be a great friend. She has been with me for a very long time. One day at Dolphin Square, I went into the kitchen and saw her with tears in her eyes. Was there something wrong? She said she had been looking at herself in the mirror and thought she could have done better for herself. I suppose in many ways, she could. In her youth, she must have resembled Marlene Dietrich because she has such high cheekbones and dark, wide-spread eyes. I said we would have to see what we could do about improving things, and I told her that I had made a plan. I had already decided I must go away to

Spain to have a long holiday and sort myself out. If I found a decent place when I got there, I asked Katie if she could make arrangements with her family and perhaps come out and keep me company.

I had decided on advice from other people to head for the Costa del Sol which was warm and inexpensive – if still, in those days, a trifle primitive. I found a villa quite quickly at Marbella and settled down easily. It was only a few yards from the sea, a large, rambling affair all on one level, and I felt small and rather ridiculous, but never lonely. I was adopted almost immediately by a stray dog who looked at me as though I was an intruder, for his home was on a battered deckchair on my newly acquired terrace. I looked at him and he looked at me – I don't know what one should say in dog language, but after giving each other the 'once over', he went back to the deckchair and I went to the bedroom I had chosen.

The next day, I made a sortie to learn the geography. I was only about half a mile outside the then small fishing village of Marbella. The mountains along the Costa del Sol do not press you into the sea; there was a good stretch of green pasture land where you could walk easily in a gentle incline to the foothills. To get to the village itself, you could either make your way by a short-cut through a ploughed field, or walk along the beach where the fishermen's nets were stretched out to dry. Marbella is half-way between Gibraltar and Malaga, about fifty miles from Gibraltar. On a clear day, which was rarer than the name of the coast suggests, you could see the twin peaks of the straits of Gibraltar. It was essential to have a car, and I acquired a little Seat – the Spanish version of the Fiat.

There were, apart from two rather grand hotels, a couple of bistro-bars, but the 'only place to go' in the evenings was a restaurant and bar with a club-like atmosphere started by an enterprising Englishman and called the Jacaranda. I had not been in Marbella more than a few days when I discovered that April Ashley was also taking a villa nearby. We made plenty of friends, among them a charming man whom everybody called 'Lord Audley'. It was the custom, since there were very strict money exchange regulations, to go into Gibraltar once a week, where we could collect the permitted amount of English sterling: £50 a head, if you had £50! It was a courtesy, when you took a car, to say the night before, loudly and clearly in the bar of the Jacaranda, 'Anybody want to go to Gibraltar?' So you filled your car and went into Gibraltar. On one occasion Lord Audley appeared and asked if my car wasn't full, could he come with me the next day. For once it was empty, so we arranged to meet in the market square and pushed off together. In the main street of Gibraltar, we separated to do our shopping.

Liptons was a *must* for groceries then, as supermarkets had not yet appeared; Saccone and Speed for your Scotch and gin, because although Spain has many admirable qualities, I couldn't drink their Scotch, or, except in dire circumstances, their fundador brandy. You were allowed to transport so many bottles per head back into Spain, which you declared as you crossed over the border. About once a month, the Spanish border guards would say, 'Too much whisky, Señora Sarah,' and confiscate one bottle. But they would never fine you once they were absolutely convinced you were in no way smuggling or defrauding or generally being disagreeable to their laws.

On the occasion that Lord Audley and I went to Gibraltar, we met at a little restaurant for lunch, carrying our separate parcels of shopping. I saw him looking rather glum and naturally money sprang to my mind. I asked him if he had spent all his money and said I could afford to pay for lunch. He told me it was much worse than that: he had to tell me something. I suggested we should have a drink first.

But he said, 'I'd rather tell you before we have a drink ... I am not Lord Audley – I'm only his manservant. My name is Alec.'

He explained that the real Lord Audley had suffered a stroke and was partially paralysed and that, as his valet, it was his job to travel ahead to arrange matters. Alec said, 'He's such a wonderful man, that I've almost come to feel I am him.'

At the beginning, when Alec arrived, everyone assumed he was Lord Audley and he never got round to changing the impression. What he could do now, he said, was to introduce me to his master when he arrived in a few days' time. I said that I had to go back to England to get Katie, my housekeeper, who was coming out to keep me company. Since she had never flown before, I felt I should go and get her. Meanwhile I asked Alec if he would keep a friendly eye on April. I hoped we should all meet again when I got back. Alec said he was sure we would and said he knew that the real Lord Audley would want to meet me.

So back I went to England and collected Katie with a quick turn-about. It was her first flight, but having been in the RAF during the war, I thought I could ask the pilot to do a tour of Gibraltar for her. The plane flew round the great rock. Katie, a trifle giddy, said she didn't believe it. When we touched down, there was Alec with the car. We rumbled our way through to Marbella and cruised our way to my villa Santa Cecilia. I told Katie she wouldn't have to do much dusting at the villa. You just had to open the windows and the breezes blew it all away. I asked Alec whether Lord Audley had arrived yet, but he said they had been delayed and were driving up. I discovered later that Henry had a beautiful benefactress, a guardian angel who was taking care of him; they were both arriving in her Rolls Royce.

Katie and I set up home quite quickly. Trumpa, as I had named my dog, still slept in the deckchair, so I considered ourselves fairly well protected: me at the front door, Katie at the back door and Trumpa in the middle. One day, after I had done my usual trek over the ploughed field to do the mid-week shopping, I parked my car outside one of the small bistros and, giving the keys to the parking attendant as usual, went to my usual table where I ordered my usual rum and coke. After anyone had had more than what they considered your quota of drinks, they would not give you your car keys back, so you would have to walk home. The next day you would be able to pay a small fine or forfeit to retrieve your car from the local police station. There was never any fuss. A very civilized arrangement, I thought.

Alec was sitting with another man at a table not far away. He came over to me and said, 'I would like to introduce you to *the* Lord Audley.'

Here perhaps I should give a sketch of Henry Audley. We were only a few months apart in age and both flaming redheads. We had both been on the London stage at about the same period in our youth, and how we managed to miss each other between the Kew Theatre and the Embassy Theatre, I do not know. But if you believe in destiny, destiny was determined that we were not to meet for many years.

Henry was a highly sensitive and artistic person. He actually did paint, though this was not his principal artistic expression. He was essentially a designer and was the founder and moving spirit of Audley Glass along with his French engraver, Jean Peyre. Quite recently, I discovered that he wrote some good poetry, and even had a book called *And Beacons Burn Again* published before the war. The most surprising thing was how, in many ways, our style of poetry was very similar.

Henry's sensitive nature had inclined him towards pacifism, an inclination which greatly distressed his father. His father was a dying man at the outbreak of the war; Henry gave in to his wishes and joined the Worcester Regiment where he progressed to become a major and was decorated with the MBE. Much of his war service was in India and the

Far East and much of his work was in Army Welfare – experience which was to prove useful later in his life.

Henry was extremely good looking, over six feet tall, and in his earlier years something of a playboy and a dilettante. He was fond of fast cars and had one appalling accident which may well have affected his later health. There came a day, when Henry was living in Paris after the war, when he decided it was time to make a change. It was a dramatic change. He jumped into his car and sped south to a retreat where Catholic monks were running what amounted to one of the first experimental 'open' prisons. Henry was always inclined to humanitarian work. Under the guidance of the monks, he studied to become a Roman Catholic for two years.

There, one day, the senior priest at the open prison asked Henry to take charge of his job while he had a short sabbatical. Henry was alarmed and said, 'I don't know that I'm experienced enough for that.'

The priest simply said, 'Let me decide that. I think you're just the person and, besides, your French is almost perfect.'

So up the hill went Henry to look after various shades of criminal.

He told me that one jolly thug approached him and said, 'We'll see that you come to no harm. We won't run away from you.' For which Henry was extremely grateful. He had had the awful feeling that he would lose *all* the prisoners.

It was a successful experiment. But soon afterwards, Henry decided to go back into the world again. He could not find it in himself to become a Roman Catholic, or a monk, or to join any form of holy orders. He had inherited his title by now and determined to devote himself to one person in life. This led him to marry June de Trafford. This was not to be a success. Henry found himself plunged back into the glittering but, for him now, rather vacant society world. The marriage did not last, and Henry and June parted. Then came a terrible blow: Henry had a massive stroke in his sleep and when he awoke he was, as well as partially paralysed, completely blind. He was extremely ill for several months, though the blindness was only a temporary disability.

When I was introduced to him that day by Alec, it was instantaneous – that amazing thing that only happens in novels, it was definitely love at first sight. I can find no other cliché more apt. I went with him to where he was staying at the Marbella Club Hotel to have lunch. Marbella was still fairly primitive in its resources, but there were two fine hotels, the Guadamina, famous for its golf course, just outside the town and the Marbella Club where Alec had made sure that Henry's room was near the front so that he would not have far to go from the car. There were no steps for him to negotiate, but there were dangers such as slippery marble floors and sunken baths. Luckily, he progressed quickly and we were never out of each other's sight. How it was that nobody ever got a whiff of this galloping romance I do not know, because there was only one street in Marbella.

Sometimes when you do not try to cover things up, people just accept them. When Henry saw my little villa Santa Cecilia, he liked it as much as I and we moved in together very quickly. We startled one of my English secretary friends by carrying a double mattress into the house. 'You ought to have done it at night,' she protested. But that would have attracted much more attention and, after all, it was only a mattress. And thereupon our courtship was cemented and from there we would play a little game.

I have found in life that if you do not embarrass people and make it easy for them to understand, they do not question you. When my maid would arrive at the villa in the morning after a long walk from the town, she would come to the back door and ring the bell. Whereupon Henry, already dressed and getting more agile every day, would proceed past Trumpa to the front door, outside which he would stand. I would let the maid in and engage her in spirited conversation for a few minutes about the day's menu and activities. Henry would then ring the front door bell and my maid would say, 'Ah, it is the Milord inglés,' and would rush to the door to let Henry in with great pomp and ceremony. As it was quite obvious that he could not have walked from the town, and as there was no taxi in sight, she would play up beautifully and apparently not notice that he must have flown in from Marbella.

Henry was an enchanting and attractive man and we were welcomed at many places and parties. But I always stressed that when he felt tired, he was not to move or go anywhere and that the time was our own. In our own time, we were completely convinced that we were going to marry – and marry quickly with no delay. I suppose now that at the back of our minds we knew time would not always be on our side.

On one of our expeditions to Gibraltar, towards the end of March 1962, we sat down in a restaurant to write letters. I wrote to everybody that I could think of: my brother and sisters, my mother and father and some friends. The gentleman who ran the Jacaranda was often on the hot line to the *Daily Mail* in London, and since we did not want our business known and in the press before we could get home, I put all the letters in a big brown envelope and addressed it to Anthony Montague-

Browne, my father's private secretary in London. He told me later that he got the shock of his life when he opened it at Hyde Park Gate where the family was living then. All these letters, obviously from me, fell on his desk and he thought, 'Oh goodness. I think she's gone and done it.' After all my many hazards, he thought I had finally taken the plunge and that these were the letters saying goodbye and all the other things one says in a suicide note. He told me that he sat there for a long time. Finally, he opened the one addressed to him – and heaved a sigh of relief since it merely announced our happy news and asked him to deliver the rest of the letters to the family, so they could all be informed at the same time.

There was great family rejoicing when we got to London. Randolph promptly looked up Henry in *Who's Who*, found that he was the twenty-third Baron and the fourth oldest dynasty in England, and was greatly impressed, saying, 'Well, *that* puts the Marlboroughs in their place.'

Everybody was delighted – 'Sarah's come home at last' – and we had a lovely time. We went to Chartwell for a weekend and had long sessions with my parents. But we decided we would get married in Gibraltar. My mother gave us a painting of Marrakech which she and I had chosen together as a wedding present, and we flew off with Diana accompanying us to our wedding in Gibraltar. The whole wedding was beautifully handled. The registry office in those days was up two long flights of steep stairs which would have been very hard for Henry and it was a rather pokey little room when you got to it. It was the Registrar himself who suggested that we hold the ceremony in the Rock Hotel. So we did, in the ballroom. Diana and Katie were my matrons of honour and I had borrowed a suitable dress and hat from my niece Celia since there was no time to collect together a conventional trousseau.

It was a wonderfully happy occasion. We stayed on at the Rock Hotel for a couple of days – long enough to take Katie over on a day trip to Tangiers before seeing her off back to look after our villa in Marbella. Then we were off ourselves on what Henry, in a letter to some friends, described as 'the first step on an enchanted honeymoon journey'. It was so exhilarating that it took me ten days before I was able to find time to write properly to my mother. Happily, I still have copies of both Henry's and my letters to refresh my memory.

In the first place, as I reported to my mother, we were met off the boat at Tangiers and flowery salutations for my parents were presented. There were some press photos and we were swept off to the best – also, we discovered, the only fully working – hotel suite in Tangiers. Hardly had we tottered past one of the telephones in our suite than the President of the Tourist Offices was on the line wishing to make a presentation to us. We got into our rooms at 12.30 p.m. and within a couple of hours a determined, stocky, bespectacled President of Tourism was shown in. As Henry reported:

He proceeded to make a longish speech of welcome clutching two rather important red cases wrapped in cellophane. When finally we were allowed to clutch them in our warm hands we tried to rip off the cellophane. That took time. Eventually, expecting at the very least 'something in Gold', we found that our gifts were two cigarette boxes-cum-match boxes in crimson plastic. We *raved* about their beauty and usefulness. After half an hour of this, the President was 'in a hurry' – so we were able to dash for a quick arrangement.

I should explain that an 'arrangement' for Henry and me was, quite simply, a drink.

The next day we visited the Governor of Tangiers and the day after that we set off for Fez in a smart little red sports car. Although the journey took almost twice as long as we had been led to expect, at last we were really alone together. It was very hot indeed. More than anything else which saved us on that journey was a Thermos ice container we had been given as a wedding present. We rapidly decided we could not move anywhere without it. Henry even claimed that I was planning a series of velvet and brocade covers in all the colours I could find so that I could carry it as a handbag.

After recovering for a day in Fez and simply gaping at the scenery visible from our hotel, we ventured into the old city under the care of a local guide. Since Henry could not really walk far, he was given a fine upstanding brown mule to ride. I was given a smaller white one and our guide, whom we promptly christened Uncle Ben, had a minute donkey, so small that his feet seemed to touch the ground and made it look as though the donkey had six legs. We travelled like a royal procession, much fêted. At one point, our entourage actually provoked a ragged cheer as we went along.

A letter of Henry's reminded me of a hilarious incident: 'One day, during lunch in the old city, Uncle Ben got completely carried away trying to explain the local deodorizing arrangements. He jumped up from our table, sprinkling orange water into his *djellabah*, then put a charcoal burner with sandalwood *under* his skirt.' We well understood the importance of such hygiene, but why did he have to show us at lunch?

After some happy days in Fez, we set off again for Marrakech. It was another long drive, some six hundred kilometres, and once again in great heat. It was Henry's first visit, which was a joy in itself. But as well, for me, it brought back many happy memories of time spent there with my parents. We visited the valley where we used to go for picnics and where my father would paint; we went for drinks with Madame de Breteuil at the Villa Taylor where conferences had taken place during the war; and at the Hotel de Mamounia it seemed that all the staff waited only for the time when they could look after my parents once again.

At long last, and many days later than we had originally intended, we began to make our way back to Spain and to Marbella. In all, I must have driven at least four thousand miles in North Africa, safely and happily. But there was one point when we took an inland road and went through the hills. We came to a very deep ravine where the bridge was a thing – it seemed to me – made of string and planks and gaps. It was a very dark night. I got out and looked at the 'bridge' while Henry asked, 'What's the matter?'

'Look at that bridge, we can't possibly go over that.'

He simply burst out laughing and said, 'Don't be ridiculous, it's probably one of the safest bridges in the whole of Morocco. It's a Bailey Bridge, put up by the British Army.'

Sure enough, it proved to be so; but I was very nervous because, at this point, Henry said, 'Move over!' and he took the wheel of the car. I walked in front so that the swinging motion of the bridge did not affect me so much and I prayed every moment to get to the other side. Henry swayed his way across the bridge and we got safely over. It was hard to keep him out of the driving seat after that.

We returned to a new villa, the Villa Aurora. It was on a small estate owned by a Swedish lady a little further outside Marbella than my old villa, Santa Cecilia. It was approached along an avenue of trees whose top branches seemed to lean over to talk and touch and created almost a green tunnel. It gave us a sense of security and privacy which we valued enormously. We were happy there and for long periods did little more than sit quietly talking and enjoying each other's company. Henry would go to swim regularly at the Marbella Club or the Guadamina Hotel since swimming was good for his particular condition. April Ashley, married by now – if not for very long – was still on the scene and lived quite nearby. It was a tight little seashell of a world. I could hardly believe that at my age I could love again as I did, and I could barely spare a moment away from Henry. We decided to stay in Spain for Christmas; London still held strange ghosts for us both.

Christmas 1962 proved to be rather busy for us. We found a suitable substitute for a Christmas tree which we decorated together and on Christmas Eve most of our local friends called in to see us between eight and midnight. Christmas Day we kept for ourselves and then had a small dinner party the following evening. The really busy time was a few days later when we organized an Anglo-Spanish children's party at our villa. It started promptly at five o'clock and Henry and I had expected that the call would have been for baby-carriages at about 7.30. But it was still in full swing at 9.30, which was very gratifying, and as I recall, nobody hit anybody else. There were a few tears from some of the smaller Spanish children who were a bit dubious about Father Christmas. We had had a proper Father Christmas kit flown out from England – he is not a character familiar in Spain – and we persuaded a bilingual Spanish friend to get dressed up. The reactions of the children were fascinating.

My present for Henry that Christmas was a black poodle puppy. We called him Piecrust Hannibal.

15

Sad Tidings

There was a hut in the garden of Villa Aurora. Henry and I decided it could make a very good workplace and with the help of one or two of the Spanish gardeners, it quickly became habitable. It also quickly became known as 'Henry's Cell'. Looking through some old papers in a trunk of Henry's, we had come across the unfinished manuscript of a play. I rather enjoyed what I read and encouraged Henry to finish it. He was strengthened in this intention when Patrick Desmond visited us, read it, and pronounced himself interested. He actually said he thought Henry should 'get on with it'; so the Cell was put to regular use and from time to time we would hire one of the shifting population of English secretaries to type up neat versions of his drafts. The play had been called *The Tired Twilight*, but I persuaded Henry that a more commercial title would be *From This Hill* and it was with this title in mind that we started planning a production in England.

The play did not call for a big cast – four principals and three smaller parts – which was just as well since we had no big financial backer. In fact, it was almost a family affair with me taking the female lead, Patrick Desmond producing and Jean Peyre doing the original sketch for the set designs. Basil Sydney, Frances Cuka and Jeremy Hawk were the other principals and the smaller parts were taken by Derek Smee, Timothy Parkes and Jon Finch.

We did a small tour before taking the production to the Ashcroft Theatre in Croydon. The reviews were mixed. In many respects it didn't make a very good stage play: I think maybe it could make a good radio play. But we all enjoyed ourselves and I don't believe Henry would have been able to sustain the physical demands of a major tour or a long run. My mother came to the first night at the Ashcroft on 1 April. Since it

198

was her seventy-eighth birthday, we had a marvellous opportunity to give her a party after the show.

We had returned to Marbella after our excursions with *From This Hill* when we heard the frightening news that my father had broken his hip on holiday at Monte Carlo. Back we went to England. My father was now in his eighty-eighth year, but still retained his capacity for recovery. When we knew he was on the familiar road to good health, we decided to return to Spain.

Henry was very anxious for me to get a second-hand car and drive back through France, which he knew very well, as he wished to show me the places that he knew and loved. Then we would go on to Madrid, down to Granada and Malaga and so on, until we reached Marbella. One place which should have been a high point of the trip was Granada. It turned out to be a very exhausting drive and many times I prayed for a helicopter to come. I could see that the car had been a misjudgement on my part; it was not the comfortable little Seat with the bucket seat, but quite a large car which swayed tremendously. I know Henry found it a strain. But, gallant as ever, he would leap out of the car when we got to our various destinations – he would never shirk his duties – and he would insist on carrying the suitcases, although I implored him not to do so. We got to Granada. Henry was exhausted and I left him to rest while I went down to get my hair done in the hotel salon.

When I came back he said, 'Oh, Cricket, you look so pretty, I must go and change, too.'

'Oh, don't bother to change. Why don't we just sit out on the balcony and have dinner here?'

'No, we're going out.'

He came out looking absolutely splendid in a white linen suit and we went downstairs. The stairs were marble and very wide, and there was no banister within easy reach. In such situations I always tried, very discreetly, to walk in front of him slightly. Suddenly he stumbled. I was able to prevent his falling, but it was a shock to both of us.

'Just sit on the stairs and wait a minute, I think we'd better call it off for this evening.'

But Henry didn't want to call off the plans for that evening. We got a taxi, and at first the driver showed us what he thought were the most remarkable things in Granada – the local jail, the post office and the railway station. After this we pleaded with him to take us to the famous caves where the gypsies lived. When he did, we were not really all that impressed: they were a little too touristy and there was an overwhelming smell of disinfectant. The taxi man, perhaps sensing the disappointment which we tried to hide, took us to a charming restaurant which proved to be quite a family affair and the evening ended with great singing, dancing and merriment.

When we got back to the hotel I went to the bathroom to clean my teeth and called out something to Henry who didn't answer. I popped my head round the door saying, 'Did you hear me?'

Henry had not – nor would he ever. I thought then that he had suffered a heart attack, but it was quite obvious he was not with us any more.

I called for the hotel doctor, who came up very promptly and shoved an enormous needle right into his heart. Although in a state of shock, I was still very much in control – the emotional collapse comes later – and I asked him what he had put in that injection, whether it was adrenalin or morphia, or half and half. He took this amiss – who was I to question him? – and asked me where I had come by this information. I explained that I happened to have a doctor friend who was sometimes called out on similar emergencies, and if he did not know the patient, he would not be sure whether to boost them or sedate them.

The doctor said rather abruptly, 'Well, your husband is dead, I have done what I could for him.'

The first thing to do then was to call the British Consul. It seemed that the nearest British Consul was in Seville, and that it would not be possible to get hold of him at this hour, two or three o'clock in the morning. So I asked the hotel to alert the local Vice-Consul, and very shortly three people turned up. The three Vice-Consuls were two brothers and a sister. They were very aged, and obviously had not been called upon to do any consular work for many years. They stood dumbfounded at the task that had been handed to them so late in life. But you cannot die in a foreign country without someone being informed.

I asked them, 'Could you please inform my family of what has happened?'

I imagined by their age that their apartment consisted of beautiful photographs of Queen Alexandra. I began to feel increasing concern as to whether they could handle the matter.

'It's in the London telephone book, Western 1617; please inform them of the disaster that has happened to me.'

Perhaps in their way they relieved me of some of the shock. They all mumbled and nodded their heads. Presumably they realized at last that they were there to confirm that the death, as the doctor had said, was through natural causes, and identify me, and take the proper steps.

The valet and the chambermaid arrived in our room, not knowing at that moment what had happened.

I said, 'The doctor says he's dead, but please let's see if we can bring him back to life again.'

If they were superstitious, they didn't flinch. 'What do you want us to do, Señora?'

'Let's massage him.'

This was before the kiss of life was well known.

'Take the arms and legs and we'll do what we can.' We gave up after half an hour when it became clear that we could not bring him back to life. They wanted to close the window but I said, 'No, open it, the spirit has gone.'

This they understood, and we left the windows open.

At dawn, I went to the hall porter and gave him my room key. I told him that my family had been informed and that all was in order. Then I said I was taking a taxi to look at the scenery near Granada. As there would apparently be a delay in getting the Consul from Seville, it seemed better to be away from the hotel for the day. I wanted to be with the warm people who know about the simple things, birth, life and death, and I wanted to see the sights that Henry would have shown me. I went with the taxi man and he showed me all sorts of places. We found a few bistros; he always entered them first and said, 'The lady has suffered a loss.'

So the long hours went by. When I came back to the hotel I was told that my luggage had been moved to the next room as they thought I wouldn't like to be in our original room. But I couldn't resist the temptation to look into the room. The door was off its hinges to permit the undertakers to do their work, so I went next door to my new room.

I discovered that the trio of aged Vice-Consuls had not been able to inform my mother and father. It was the police who eventually called Diana, and I learned that she had taken a plane to Granada. She spent the hours flying, and I spent the hours waiting and walking in the beautiful landscape that surrounds that city. On my return, the doctor who had been affronted by my simple medical question turned up again and asked me where I had been all day. I said I had been out in the countryside and that I had yet to recognize death as a purely medical thing, which I cannot suppose did anything further to endear me to him. He said he ought to give me a sedative. But I replied that I didn't think it would be necessary. I asked him to please leave me alone until my sister arrived.

'Will you be all right?'

'I promise you I will, I will call if I need your assistance, and thank you.'

And I didn't mean it sarcastically. He went his way partially mollified. I think he believed that I was not his enemy any more than he was mine, but there are strange barriers between life, death and the mortuary.

I left my door open and then heard an American woman's voice. By now everybody must have been told what had happened. She came in and asked whether I had eaten anything that day. I said I hadn't but that everyone seemed to be busy trying to get me to sleep so that I wouldn't remember anything. She urged me to eat something, as there was still some time before Diana was expected to arrive.

'What would you like?'

'Bananas.'

She laughed – the best sound that I had heard for a long while – and asked room service to send up a bunch. While I ate, she told me that she had been a widow for seven years and said, 'I have to warn you – it does not get any better.'

She kept me company until, at last, Diana arrived. For the distraught person she was meant to be, Diana walked into the room with calm assurance, an assurance which she immediately transferred to me as we embraced. There was no longer any need for a sedative, and I soon fell into a deep exhausted sleep. Tomorrow would take care of itself.

But tomorrow, new problems emerged. Where was Henry to be buried? Spain is predominantly a Catholic country and there was no Protestant graveyard. I had decided not to fly him home, as really he had no home in England. We had managed to get in touch with his sister, his only relative in England, who had said, heartbrokenly, 'He is in your hands, do what you think is right.'

Diana and I looked at each other.

I said, 'He was on his way to the sun.'

She said, 'Remember we are the daughters of a soldier: "where we fall, there we rest."'

Diana discussed the matter with the Consul from Seville, who turned out to be an old friend of hers. He said that he thought the only suitable place for burial would be Malaga. He would make the necessary arrangements in Granada for the release of the body, and motor with us to

Malaga where we would be able to bury Henry at the British Naval Cemetery.

There was still to be a waiting period. I asked Diana to inform the doctor that I would like to make my farewell to Henry. He was opposed to this, and said that he was in the mortuary, and that they had not yet had time to do any 'cosmetic work' on him. I said this didn't matter. Diana relayed to me that the doctor was highly opposed to a visit, but I was determined. The doctor gave in, now that officialdom and a relation had taken over. Diana stressed that we would be grateful if there was as little publicity as possible, and he kindly said he would escort us himself through the back entrance. I am always suspicious of back entrances, they are always the ones that are watched the most. However, I was grateful to him and thankful that we were now on resigned and friendly terms. He led Diana and myself to a small entrance at the back of the hospital. At first, there was no one there and it seemed to me we would have a short walk through a garden. No sooner inside, than from nowhere sprang a photographer who click-clicked his way in front of us. The doctor asked us to wait a minute and proceeded to deal with the photographer. Diana and I sat on a bench in the garden; a few nuns drifted by. I felt her trembling and squeezed her hand. The doctor came back for us and led us to a doorway, flanked on either side by nuns and nurses. We went into a small chamber where Henry lay. I saw at once why they had not wanted me to see him. He had not died of a heart attack as I had thought, but of a sudden massive cerebral haemorrhage, which renders the face black. Diana and I stood for a minute or two in silence, still clutching hands. I bent and kissed his brow. We turned and walked back past the silent nuns and nurses, and were driven back to the hotel unharassed, escorted by the doctor.

The same evening, as soon as the Consul had arrived, we sped off on our way to Malaga, along what seemed a steep, dangerous zig-zagging road. It must have been a very beautiful journey during the day but I did not notice much scenery. We arrived at Malaga and went to the Miramar Hotel which was almost next to the cemetery. We had dinner in a deserted restaurant. Half-way through the meal, the head waiter flung open the double doors and, walking briskly to the table, bowed and announced, 'The Lord Audley has arrived and is in the chapel.'

There seemed little else to do but say our formal 'goodnights' and retire.

The Consul's wife thoughtfully arrived the next day with a pair of shoes and gloves and handbag, for which I was most grateful as I had been travelling in a pair of blue jeans and sandals. Somehow I acquired a dress – probably Diana's. The Consul informed us that the Bishop of Gibraltar had consented to perform the ceremony and was making the one-hundred-mile journey early in the morning.

When he arrived, the Bishop came to see me in my hotel room and said briskly, 'You won't let me down will you?'

I informed him that I wouldn't and we drove to the chapel. The service was brief; barely half a dozen people were there. The British Naval Cemetery is a beautiful cemetery, up a sharp hill. I wondered how on earth they were going to get Henry up to his grave, it was very nearly at the top and the slope so steep.

The Consul's wife told me, 'We have chosen a very beautiful place where there are two slim trees, a pepper and a fir.'

Suddenly, almost from nowhere, the gardeners who had been attending the flowers and bushes dropped their equipment and, rubbing their hands down their jeans, became pallbearers. This was both moving and appropriate as Henry had been a very keen gardener. I had asked the Bishop if at a convenient moment he would place my wedding ring in the grave. Earlier there had been some confusion because they didn't like people to be buried with jewellery on. But when the server handed him the earth, I managed to slip the ring in.

After the ceremony, we had to leave him and go our different ways. Diana was to leave from Gibraltar for England and I said I would be following in two days. On the way we passed the villa in Marbella where we had lived, and made a brief stop for Diana to see it. We then went on to Gibraltar where I saw her off. Then I made the journey back to Villa Aurora. It had been a very long day.

When I returned to England and went to Chartwell for lunch, my father met me at the door. We stared silently at each other; then he took my hand and said simply, 'We must close ranks and march on.'

At that moment I was in the rawness of sensitivity. He led me into the dining room. It was a difficult lunch for everyone, but the Churchill chatter helped: it filled the room and deadened my thoughts.

I barely knew what to do. I returned to Spain with a companion, Gay Allen, to help me clear up the remnants of my brief but crowded life with Henry. It was a terrible time for me which I can hardly remember. Henry's poodle, Piecrust Hannibal, which I had given him as a Christmas present, was killed by a truck on the road near the villa. They didn't want to tell me. But I knew something had gone wrong and insisted on seeing the little body. It was better that way than fearing he had run away or been hurt.

Only a few weeks later, I was called to the phone – we didn't have a phone in Villa Aurora and I had to go along to the villa of the Swedish lady who owned the estate. She said to me it was a call from England and that I should prepare myself. I couldn't imagine what else could have happened. I went to the telephone and heard Mary's voice, 'Darling Sarah, Diana has died. There's to be an inquest.'

I was stunned. Diana's suicide was not in itself totally unexpected, but in recent years she had seemed much more stable and, working for the Samaritans, the threat of suicide had seemed to recede. She had been a tower of strength for me when Henry died. She was wonderful in other people's crises. I recalled one of the last things she had said to me, 'I am beginning to understand you. If anything awful happens to you, you go out and fight. If anything awful happens to me, I want to put my head under a pillow.'

From the earliest days of really knowing each other, I had been aware that Diana was a very different sort of person from me. Perhaps that is why she and I became in many ways so close; our differences drew us together.

Diana had made a hasty and ill-advised first marriage, which lasted only a short time, leaving her suffering serious doubts over what she regarded as her failure. Her second marriage, to Duncan Sandys, promised much better. It had been surprising to the family at first because we were all busy, led by Randolph, campaigning for Duncan's opponent in an election campaign. Duncan won the election, *and* Diana. I don't suppose it is possible for anyone to state categorically whether Diana's developing neuroses destroyed her marriage or whether marriage diffi-culties created the neuroses.

Long before the divorce, but after the birth of her children, Diana visited Antony and me in America for two separate holidays. She clearly enjoyed herself enormously, but I knew her well enough to recognize that she was unable to come to terms with the possibility that her marriage might founder. As time went on, she was increasingly to feel that she was being abandoned. The bright life had been rather successfully dimmed for her by various doctors' experiments, always wanting to help but never quite sure I believe of the effects of the new drugs and treatments they were using on certain patients. It was the day of heavy electrical shocks

which were meant to obliterate the patient's memory. Diana, ever coura-
geous, would laboriously write down on a piece of paper, the night before
an electric shock session, what it was they were trying to make her forget;
and then hide it in a suitable place.

Diana spent many sessions in hospitals and clinics, often far from home
and hard to visit. We all did what we could to help. While I was research-
ing into neuritis for my mother in 1955 in Boston, I also made inquiries
as to their treatment for nervous illnesses. They were very advanced and
moving rapidly away from shock treatment. I became convinced for a
while that no doctor had done enough to gauge Diana's glandular system.
Then I began to realize that I knew absolutely nothing about this sort
of problem. Oscar Nemon, the Jugoslav sculptor whom Diana introduced into our family and who was to do what I think were the finest
sculptures of my father, was an enormous support to Diana. His help
cannot be over-praised.

In one letter I wrote to my mother from the South of France where
I was staying with my father on holiday for a few weeks in November
1955, all the confusions we found and love we felt for Diana are
expressed, if somewhat incoherently on my part:

I arrived here fairly exhausted and of course anxious as to the developments
after I left about Diana. As far as I can gather it does not sound exactly as
if it had been smooth sailing. However, I was so relieved when Papa got your
telegram asking if Diana could come out here. He was about to write himself
and he felt this place would be good for her, so completely removed is it from
her anxieties. The only people she *could* meet would be people she had never
met before and so, perforce, conversations would have to take a different
course.

She looked incredible when she arrived, even after the journey: a little silver
and gold fairy running across the tarmac to embrace me. Physically she has
about 3 hours' stamina, and then she is really spent. She feels the heavy sedation
she still takes is a physical burden. But I pray for the moment she does not
leave it, as inside her she is still greatly troubled. She is quiet though and can
talk about it all. She has a feeling of having been greatly wronged. This is not
specific, it does not relate to any one person, or even any special time in her
life; but this feeling persists, accompanied by a feeling of unfulfilment and
lack of recognition. Again, it is not too specific – and obviously this is where
a good analyst should be able to help. She is in an accepting frame of mind and
would jump at any positive idea to help her in the future.

The trouble is that Diana really needs a philosopher! I mean that if she
has a 'thought' or an 'idea' that she can chew on, it helps her enormously.

But like one often has to put up with clergymen who are not brilliant at explaining things, or schoolmasters or psychiatrists or friends who may have dull minds, she is frequently let down and sees only the aching void ahead, and that no one can help her out of her troubles.

Well of course Papa does. A few sentences from him and she is comforted and calmed. He has been wonderful with her, and physically she is improving every day. The English papers here are full of the nun who claims she was wrongly confined to a mental home – and of course the 'Daily Express' has a series of articles called 'Are the doctors going too far?' At first I thought, oh Lord, what now? But then I realized that perhaps it was a good thing for her to read them. I pick my way through a path of eggshells. Carl Lambert says it's nonsense and you can say anything to a person in this state, and it does not matter. I disagree. You cannot lie; but I cling to silence as I have not often done before: better nothing if one cannot say something helpful.

Jean Batten, the flyer, came to dinner; she is exactly Diana's age. It was obvious she is a deeply unhappy and frustrated woman. Her nice character and self discipline keep her going, but cannot hide the fact that she feels life is over. The war stopped her flying at the peak of her career – and there is really no more personal pioneering in this field at the moment. She must wait for space ships I suppose!

She talked with a gentle resignation. It did some good to Diana, for none of us is alone; but equally that is never an answer. Papa was intrigued with Jean Batten and said she must search for new horizons – search, *not* demand – that the next part of her life might be something, *must* be something, different but not *necessarily* less great.

She laughed and went home, promising to come again and saying it had been a wonderful and inspiring evening – but we all felt sad despite Papa's words and he looked contemplative himself as he watched her drive herself away up the narrow winding drive in her small Austin, after the glories of the open sky.

Diana never led the competitive, outgoing life that I did, and sometimes her troubles became just too much to bear. She was however a tower of strength in others' troubles. For two years she worked with the Samaritans in London, regularly on call to talk to people who telephoned for a lifeline when their private seas became too rough. Down all the years she was my staunch and loving sister and friend; she always encouraged such qualities as I might have, and turned merciful eyes on my lapses which other people often could not understand. I am not convinced that Diana finally wanted to end it all; and the Reverend Chad Varah, the founder of the Samaritans and very close to Diana, has said she was found, not with her head under the pillow, but reaching towards the telephone. Diana was and remains in fond memory a gallant sister and mother. She is not forgotten.

After the funeral I was at a loss once again. Good American friends came to my rescue with the offer of a role in a play which would have a short run in Chicago. It seemed just the sort of therapy I so badly needed. Ironically, the play's title was *Glad Tidings*.

When I got to New York I called the theatre management in Chicago to say I had arrived and to ask if it would be convenient for me to get out there a week before I was due to rehearse. They readily agreed, so I booked on the first plane to Chicago next morning. The old night porter at the apartment where I was staying may not have been used to 5 a.m. calls.

When he arrived at my door, I asked, 'Could you get me a taxi, please?'

'But you're dead, I read it in the papers, you're the one that's always in trouble and you committed suicide.'

'Even if I am a ghost,' I replied, 'would you mind picking up my luggage: ghosts hardly carry this amount.'

When he had done so, I thanked him and said, 'No, it was my sister Diana who died. I am Sarah, "the one that's always in trouble".'

16

Roman Interlude

It is a distressing strain on family and friends and young children to have a grieving soul around – especially at festive seasons. What can you do? They cannot do anything – it's you and you alone who must bear it. They have got to get on with their lives. So I thought it best to stay away and I travelled home from America by sea over Christmas. The ship was almost empty and at various times of the day all classes of travellers could meet together as the different sections were opened up and merged. There were some delightful people on the ship – I won once at bingo! – and years later I discovered that the stewardess who looked after me on that trip lived next to my great friend Jewel Baxter in New York. Meeting new people was good in my frame of mind: new people may know of your grief, but they are not close enough to invite any discussion of it, so you start grafting a new skin again and building a wall around yourself once more.

The idea came to me that I would take a small flat in Rome. I had always been happy there, ever since my film-making experiences with Mario Soldati and Peter and Valerie Moore, just after the war. Rome has a curiously regenerative effect on me, as it does on so many British people, making me want to write, paint and live creatively – and seek again the riches of life. The sprawl of the city seen from the terrace above the Spanish Steps, the climate and the light which have made so many Englishmen want to live there, from Keats and the Sitwells, to sensitive loners. 'Rome lubricates the soul', as one expatriate put it – it seems to have a healing effect on people who have escaped from England's more rigidly conformist atmosphere.

For a while I lived in a little hotel, but that soon became oppressive. Much of the time I was alone. I would eat late after a few meditative drinks in perhaps the Piazza del Popolo, scratch pad at hand for poems or sketches, then go on long walks through the night streets, talking casually to the friendly Italians. Sometimes a band of ragamuffin boys would surround me, ready to quip and tease.

On one occasion I regarded them solemnly and said, 'I have lost my way. Could you direct me to ——?'

There was a short deliberation. Then the leader replied, 'Would you like us to accompany you? A lady should not really be out alone.'

'Thank you, that would be nice.'

And, linking arms, they sang me home – or nearly home, as with a conspiratorial wink I indicated that perhaps it was better if they left me before I got to my door. I realize that I can stir up anger and sometimes violent reaction; so such an occurrence showed me, comfortingly, that I can also evoke a protective quality from people.

I used to love the Roman dawns when the street lights would suddenly go out and the sky would simultaneously light up. It was an illusion of course, but there were moments when it seemed to me as if somebody upstairs was responsible for the lighting-plan over the dawn rooftops and domes and the crumbling pillars and steps of the Forum. Life seemed easier than in London. During those early days I still remained convinced that when you are in great sorrow and grief, you are better off with strangers. For one thing, you make an effort out of pride to behave in a controlled way instead of being tempted to unburden your heart or dissolve in the sympathetic atmosphere of close friends.

Then something happened: I met Lobo Nocho. A vision in Levis, a jet-age troubadour and a one-man debating society decended on me. Behaving in a controlled way after that became somewhat difficult. Many months after our first meeting, the cheaper glossies emblazoned the newsstands with such headings as 'Sarah Churchill's Affair With an American Negro', and 'Marrying Negro Singer? Sarah Churchill is Mum'. For a long time, however, we were left in peace to allow our friendship to develop, and it is the less lurid, less tabloid aspects of our relationship which I shall relate here.

Charles Hamblett, my good friend and would-be biographer, had met Lobo in Paris several years before. Remembering those days when Lobo would call on him in his small flat in Paris while he was working with *Picture Post*, Charles said he would grin with anticipation at the ring of the door-bell and the shout which would ricochet around Montmartre announcing a Nocho visitation. Lobo would give him the latest gossip from the 'Rib Joint', show Charles his saucy sketches of coupling couples,

invite him to meet a current lady-friend 'with a sister that could make
Bardot sit up and look'. Charles was in fact among the first to write about
Lobo in the London press as a painter of witty and brilliant-hued
abstracts. Lobo was also a popular jazz singer in the clubs around Montmartre and St Germain des Prés. He won the professional recognition
of Sidney Bechet, Coleman Hawkins and Louis Armstrong. Lobo had
worked with Xavier Cougat, and studied painting in Paris on a GI grant
after combat service which had begun with his enlistment in the Canadian
Army. After Pearl Harbor, he transferred to the US Army and landed
with the first troops to hit the beach on D-Day.

I once asked Charles, as we were all friends, to tell me more about
Lobo; he said he was never short of female fans. He was a man whose
existential jive-talk could catch the attentive ear of a novelist and the
discerning eye of John Huston – the director who cast him as the Devil
in his version of *The Bible* which was filmed in Rome. 'Lobo was', said
Charles, 'a natural artist-adventurer who would have flourished in
Renaissance Italy.' Apart from the non-stop dynamo which makes him
tick, Lobo has natural, built-in confidence which keeps him buoyantly
afloat in his global wanderings. He now has a permanent home in New
York, where as battle-worn friends we meet from time to time. In our
Roman days he would talk enthusiastically of 'moving in on the action
in Hong Kong', of going to paint a volcano in the Canaries before it
exploded, and of his circle of lady admirers whom he called 'Buddy Girls'.

Once, in an unusually subdued mood, Lobo said, 'Sas, someone said
to me last night – and I'm not sure whether it was complimentary or
not – "Lo, wherever you are, you look as if you come from somewhere
else."'

I laughed and said I thought that was fine and he should be very proud.
Indeed, the strange, sometimes almost mystic look of his face – the proud
look of an El Greco grandee – could well create a problem even to a
seasoned anthropologist. Lobo could look like the Devil and he very
often played on it. While he was acting the Devil for Huston, often on his
way from his dressing room to the set, extras he passed would cross
themselves.

I was first introduced to Lobo at a luncheon party in a restaurant and
then at a cocktail party in a private home. Some ten days after this second
formal introduction, I was perched on the piano in the Little Bar on the
Via Sistina, singing a song into the microphone. The Little Bar was a
good, safe place to be after midnight, and the pianist-entertainer Nicola

who performed in the back bar – there was invariably a dice game going on in the front bar – always allowed guests to join him at the mike. If you made a fool of yourself, everyone would roar with laughter in the nicest possible way. It was always friendly laughter, and that would probably encourage somebody else to get up and sing their version of 'Home on the Range' or 'I Left My Heart in San Francisco'. On that evening, Lobo walked in alone. When I stopped singing, he applauded and invited me over to his table for a drink. We stayed for several drinks and then we left together and strolled back to his flat on the Via del Corso, where he lived with his paintings, his guitar, and his standard poodle – Lady Cha-Ba-Dah. Anyone who took pains to find space for a large red poodle in a tiny one-roomed apartment crammed with paintings, *and* knew his jazz, had something.

Laughter began to come back to my life and, thereafter, my wanderings about the city were seldom solitary. Lobo introduced me to his Roman friends: painters, blues and folk musicians, beat poets. On our wanderings, Lobo would talk enthusiastically of his plans as an artist and his idea to flood homes and restaurants and bars and public buildings with the results of his revolutionary ideas on the subject of Lobo-Lite. I was fascinated by his incredible super-vitality and his completely original turn of mind. In any other person, and at any other moment, this suddenly new and wild jazzed-up talk and manic fantastication of ideas and facts might have been quite horrifying to me. But coming from Lobo it stimulated my own ideas and took me away from the loss of Henry. It was a kind of therapy – like being taken from my still-stunned self and dropped into a cold bath. It was not to be by any means a completely comfortable relationship, but it helped to bring me fully back to life again.

My period of mourning was over. The major healing of the misfortunes and mistakes in my life had, in any case, been done by Henry and, for a while, I had simply wanted to sit down and not bother about anything again. But it was impossible not to bother about living when you were with Lobo. Every day there was going to be some form of ruction, of noise, of disturbance. Well, at least an absence of silence.

With Lobo, wherever we went in Rome, there would always be great shouting and screaming and yelling across the road. You couldn't walk for more than a few minutes without someone calling, 'Hi, Lo!' They would come running across the street, beautiful black friends, beautiful brown friends, beautiful pallid hungover white friends. Nothing during

those strange days was ever done on a low decibel level, and for weeks
that became months I sat back and let Lobo's energy carry me along.
He'd lived a strange, upheaved life himself, and gradually I discovered
the deeper Lobo, below the high decibels.

April Ashley surprised me by turning up in Rome. She was looking
beautiful, if somewhat outrageous, after separating from her husband
and had rented a flat in Trastevere, a district much frequented by tourists
and where painters, poets and musicians lived their usual bohemian existence. We had joyful parties for which April did the cooking; parties which
started at noon and went on till sundown, when guests would depart
through the twilight to prepare for the long, glittering Roman nights.
You would bump into old acquaintances or make new ones. But Rome
was like that: if you wanted people, they were there; if you didn't, you
went your way and nobody minded.

The infamous *paparazzi* were much in evidence then, as the city was
choc-a-bloc with filming projects and film stars. Many stories were to
spring up about April's and my assumed frolics, not necessarily together.
Once, so the story went, she hired a *carrozza* and wheedled the driver
to let her take his place. The horse was sometimes ridden by tourists and
the tired driver thought happily of the late-night fee and handed over
the reins. The streets were deserted and, immaculately dressed, a creature
from another world, April stirred the horse into action and made him
gallop down the street like a vision of a Roman legionary from an ancient
time. The Via del Corso runs from Piazza Venezia, once Mussolini's palatial if somewhat prisonlike home, to the beautiful Piazza del Popolo.
When they arrived in the square, April dismounted gracefully, paid handsomely, patted the horse, picked up her skirts and paddled in the pool
of the fountain, leaving behind a bemused *carrozza* owner and horse who
decided wisely to make their way home.

Another horse and carriage story was my own. Leaving the Little Bar
one evening and not wishing to go straight home, I took a carriage to
take me on a tour of Rome, a tour which would end up at my own
apartment at the Via Marguta, which runs parallel to the Via del Corso
– a spitting distance from Lobo's, but far enough away to discourage
the attentions of the *paparazzi*. The driver drove me past the Capitol
and then, with brakes on but almost sliding, down to the Piazza Venezia
past the Piazza d'Espagna, towards my *pensione* in the Via Marguta.
When I had made my, I hope, equally gracious descent, I paid the driver
and then, as my friend Mario Soldati would have said, 'in the spread

of the moment' was about to tip the horse 1,000 lire when, with a scream and an agility which belied his apparent age, the driver leapt to the ground saying: 'No, no, signora!' and I replied: 'But he's the one who's done all the work.'

I think the *paparazzi* were disappointed that neither April nor I – nor indeed our other friends – quite fitted their tape measure. Weekends would include going out to places like Fregene to seaside restaurants where, attired in bathing suit, bikini or jeans according to your figure or inclination, you could eat, drink and dance to the sound of the sea gently plashing; and if you felt inclined, you could take a dip. The *paparazzi*, of course, were looking for orgies along the lines of *La Dolce Vita*. I'm sorry to say that I neither saw nor attended an orgy. Curiously, I do not remember Lobo ever accompanying us all to Fregene. A familiar phrase of his would be, 'No, Sas, I must go and check my traps.'

Another favourite haunt of mine, down Via Marguta, was the Taverna dei Artisti. It was run then by a tall, blond, northern Italian called Signor del Vecchio, shadowed by his tall and equally handsome dark son called Mauro, who had a beautiful voice, speaking and singing, and had great ambitions for the stage. The first time I wandered in alone I was immediately welcomed. It was a place where you could go and sit at a table by yourself without any ulterior motive being attached to your behaviour as a *sola signora inglese*. I was soon befriended by the family and would join them at their family table. I discovered that the bands who played in the Taverna – all highly professional musicians – were out of work 'for the moment' and sang for their supper.

After a few weeks, Mauro asked me shyly whether he could take me out to lunch one day; he wanted I'm sure to discuss his dramatic ambitions. I said I would be delighted – and so, of course, were the *paparazzi*. Mauro borrowed his father's flashy car and took me to one of the most expensive restaurants on Il Pinzio. Leaning across the table to ask in halting English what I would like to eat, he provided the long focus cameras with what appeared to be a most intimate shot in romantic, idyllic surroundings. While I was making up my mind whether to have avocado stuffed with shrimps, or just plain with vinaigrette, they were taking photographs which, I must say, when they came out the following day only too easily provoked captions of the sort favoured by the most slushy novelists. There was one headline which read: 'Will Winston Churchill Like his Future Italian Son-in-Law?' Mauro turned up the next day in deep distress. Almost classically beating his breast, he said, 'Tell

me you don't think I did it on purpose.' I assured him that of course
I did not and we continued good and firm friends. I told him there was
only one way to deal with this situation: he must carry a Shakespeare
in Italian and I would carry a Shakespeare in English, we would both
put on our walking shoes and, armed with the protection of the Bard, he
would show me most of Rome – on foot. By this ploy we finally dis-
couraged the *paparazzi*, loaded down as they were with camera
equipment. They got tired a good deal sooner than we did. Papa del
Vecchio also banned them from his restaurant and I found there a
haven of peace and good Italian friends.

But it was fun time for everyone. It was, in any case, one of the few
times in recent history when cheerfulness was breaking out all over; a
time when the Beatles had just detonated the most explosive blast of
popular sound since the birth of the blues and the dream merchants were
inventing Swinging London. New York was working its way to being
renamed for a while Fun City and Rome itself was still riding the crest
of the saccharin wave that Fellini had set rolling with his *Dolce Vita*.
The brief, pendulum years had started to swing. Infused by the daemonic
energies of Lobo, I instinctively swung along with the mood of the times.

But there was serious work to be done: an exhibition of Lobo's works.
We were lent an empty house by an American friend who had just moved
in and had no furniture yet. Why didn't we, she suggested, give the exhibition there? She would have to repaint the place anyway. So we could
stick pictures up on the wall any old way. Well, since Lobo, like so many
artists, was not endowed with the wherewithal for proper mounting or
framing, the friends gathered together and up went the pictures with tacks
or Scotch tape. Friends made sandwiches; drinks were bought or
brought; the friendly press wrote up our endeavours. The scene was
dazzling with Lobo's particular forte – colour.

Being Rome, flowers, rubber plants and decorations appeared mysteri-
ously. Helpers emerged from everywhere; at first stimulated by curiosity,
they stayed to be entranced. On the night, it seemed half Rome was there
and, being a lovely climate, people were able to spill out merrily onto
the terrace and street. The ultimate glory was when Roloff Beny, the
world famous photographer, who was engaged on one of his world-wide
camera adventures, arrived at the exhibition with a CBC film crew in
his train. We were all gloriously filmed and interviewed and televized
– even if the picture sales were less than glorious!

Later in London, my niece Edwina Sandys, at the beginning of her own painting career, just moving in to an empty house and having heard about the happy-go-lucky success in Rome, suggested her own house should be used for a similar venture. All was well again; the climate fortunately promised to equal Rome's, so people could spill out on her balcony and, as I lived in the same street, I opened my house too. Everything was going well until first-night nerves began to show as the Scotch tape ran out. There was a scream. Lobo demanded 'thumb tacks'. We looked at each other in amazement. 'Thumb tax?' I muttered. I had heard of income tax, super tax, dog tax, all kinds of tax, even death tax, but never thumb tax. A friend suggested he meant a drawing pin; whereupon Lobo took wing and flew up several storeys quite unaided muttering, 'I don't need a drawing *pen*!' Fortunately, the scene was calmed by a box of drawing pins being found and all the pictures were up by the time the first proper guests arrived.

It was as well that Lobo offered such diversity and diversions because 1964 was to be another year with its full complement of sorrows, although there were many joyous family moments as well. It was the year when I felt the call from home growing ever stronger and began to decide that my second Roman holiday was coming to an end. It was the year when Randolph began his last journey. It was the year when Christopher was badly hurt in a riding accident. It was the year, happily, when young Winston was married to Minnie D'Erlanger and it was the year of my father's ninetieth birthday. Sadly, it was also the year when Vic Oliver died. I was taking a short holiday with my friend Lorraine Merritt in Capri. One day I saw by the look on her face that something dreadful had happened, that she had heard bad news.

I said to her, 'Tell me, quickly, what's happened?'

'Vic has died in Johannesburg.'

This was indeed a body blow. Apart from anything else, Vic had invited me to go with him, to star with him, on his trip to South Africa and I had had to say no.

That April, I had been playing *Fata Morgana* at the Ashcroft in Croydon. My mother and father had come to see me; it was to be the last time my father ever saw me on stage. By an extraordinary coincidence, Vic Oliver was playing at the next-door theatre in *Music for the Millions* and it was my mother who later pointed out to me that we had finally had our names next to each other in lights.

It was a wonderful evening when my parents came to the theatre. Unfortunately, they were put in the front row; it was a kind gesture, but it was a mistake since the stage was high and my father had difficulty in holding his tired head up so that he could see me properly. But, at the end of the show, when the audience had left, he was wheeled onto a bare strip of floor which miraculously rose to stage level. It was a theatre which could be used to accommodate large audiences or orchestras. The curtains were drawn back to reveal the cast; his eyes twinkled with delight. Perhaps he was remembering the early days when he loved the music halls. Ellen Pollock, who produced and appeared in the show, caught his eye, and there was also April Ashley, who was making serious attempts at that time to take up a stage career, away from the nonsense she had been enduring in her cabaret performances. Always one to recognize a pretty face, my father smiled cherubically at her. Whisky and soda and a cigar were brought for him, and the cast drank his health in champagne.

Then my mother said, 'Winston, I think it's time we were going home to dinner.'

'What, all of them?' he asked.

'No, they have another show.'

I'm not certain he was not disappointed! I remember how amusing we all found it in that production to see David Hemmings playing an innocent virginal young man – somewhat different from his real-life experiences. As with so many of the plays I have been in, it was a most enjoyable production, and it was good to be able to slip next door for a chat with Vic. I was sure I was right to turn down his offer of a share in his South African tour, but that did not make the blow of his death any less severe.

Mary wrote to me in Rome:

17 August 1964

Darling, darling Sarah,

I know how saddened you will be by Vic's death and send all my loving thoughts to you. I know how much you loved him, and what a whole long chapter of your life he was. And I'm so glad you and he were friends always. I shall never forget his sweetness to me. I was very fond of him ....

Her letter went on to tell me of a dreadful riding accident Christopher had sustained. The children were clearly marvellous, fetching help and sustenance and at no point panicking. Apart from the severe pain Christopher had to suffer – a pain I'm sure Mary shared – the accident came just before a General Election campaign. Mary was thrown into the middle of the political maelstrom as she read all his speeches at meetings in his own Bedford constituency. He held his seat.

I went home for my father's ninetieth birthday. The room at Hyde Park Gate where we were to have dinner was so constructed as to have a gallery with a sweeping staircase. In that room, my mother had had a lift constructed, not unlike a gilded bird-cage, into which the brooding eagle would be placed to descend from the Olympian heights, and to be wheeled to his place at the table. I remember when I arrived there were big crowds gathered outside the house hoping for a glimpse of my father. There were photographers and cameramen, and even a little group of musicians serenading under the window. When he stood, unaided but obviously with help close by in case of need, to wave from an upstairs window, there was a roar of applause from outside. Then, when he made his appearance on the inside gallery, all of us inside stood and applauded. Randolph went to assist him, but he waved him away, not unkindly, and, to the amazement of all of us, he made the curving staircase all on his own.

At dinner, I sat on one side of him, and Anthony Montague-Browne sat on the other. Towards the end, he said to us both, 'I would like to make a speech,' and he started to rise to his feet. But as this would not have been a good thing for him, for had he stood, the blood would have drained from his head and it could have been damaging for him, Anthony instead suggested to my father that perhaps Randolph could say a few words. Randolph made a brief and eloquently loving filial salutation to him. We all rose and raised our glasses, and the evening, though short, ended in triumphant spirits for us all. The guests left first, as I suspect he wanted to use the gilded cage to get back up the stairs. It was barely two months later that he fell into what would prove to be the final coma.

I had returned to Rome, where I planned to spend Christmas. One dark night shortly after Christmas, Lobo appeared at my *pensione* door, and said that the police had been in touch with him. My sister Mary had asked them to find me to say that I must go home immediately. I went straight to catch the plane.

For some ten days, as I recall, my father seemed to eat nothing. We saw that his mouth was kept moist with water and with glycerine. Those of us who could be there sat around the room and tried to talk naturally. At times there would be no flicker of life at all, then sometimes his hand would begin to move in painting gestures, and we would know that he was happy. Needless to say, we wondered what particular scene was crossing his mind. At other times, he would make the gesture of smoking an invisible cigar and, again, we knew that he was happy. One wonders how deep a coma goes. Sylvia Henley once tried placing an unlighted cigar in his hand, but he waved it away. He was already beyond mortal necessities. It was strange how he seemed to come much more alive between midnight and 2 a.m. Winston and Arabella on one occasion were so excited by these signs of movement that they called the nurse.

'Did he usually work late at night?' the nurse asked them.

'Yes,' they said.

'That, then, I'm afraid, is the explanation.'

It looked as though the habits of a lifetime were as hard dying as was the man himself. But at 8 a.m. on 4 January 1965 he died peacefully and patriarchally, with the closest of his family around him. Anthony Montague-Browne was there, and so was Lord Moran, who said simply, 'He has gone.'

We went into my mother's sitting room, where no conversation was really necessary, or perhaps possible. Anthony Montague-Browne went to the office and picked up the telephone to pass on the message that 'Operation Hope Not' – the code name to the Duke of Norfolk who had to marshal the lying in state and the funeral parade – had begun. Some time after we had heard the news over the radio, Randolph came back into my mother's room with a book about Lord Randolph Churchill and said, 'Would you believe it, he has died on the same day, and at almost the same hour that his father died.'

At last there were cars to take us to our various destinations. I had been staying with Celia Sandys. A more steady and consoling companion, it would have been hard to find. Before driving away, she drew my attention to the milkman, who doffed his cap and held it across his breast. News had travelled fast. Also, she pointed to Sergeant Murry, my father's last detective, whose duty was finally over. He looked grief-stricken. I got out and embraced him, then we drove away.

17

Keep on Dancing

I find at any ending of a phase in my life, just as an actor must look for a new role, so must I find a new job. After my father's funeral and reassuring myself that my mother was in reasonable spirits, it was time to return to Rome to wind up my affairs, and, although we remained friends, it was a parting of the ways with Lobo.

During the course of my life, I had been asked many times to write my life story. My reply had always remained, 'I'm not sure I have lived it yet!' However, it eased me then to begin to write a loving tribute to my father and, in 1966, I was to write my first book, *A Thread in the Tapestry*, which started life as four articles for the *Sunday Express* and the New York *Daily Post*.

I think most people, including perhaps even his known enemies, loved my father because he had remained an oak tree: the symbol of our land. My mother, his 'Darling Clementine', always a stalwart companion by his side, was to me, if secretly, a weeping willow tree which could still silver the land. With such parents I was formidably armed as I looked for a new job, and for new 'toys'. It was to be a strange assortment of different endeavours during the next ten years which were to shape what, for ease of reference, became known as my 'one-woman show'.

What makes a 'lone show', after a varied life? You spend a lot of youth pretending to be somebody else, and the rest discovering that you are yourself. Since that day in 1935 when I entered the Palace Theatre to audition as a dancer/chorus girl, I had never been a pessimist. But now, suddenly, after my father's funeral, I was fighting against gloomy predictions of my future; I became aware of the years waiting in front of me. I plunged stubbornly on, never without the help of my faithful family and friends – when I would let them. I want to use this last chapter to describe my life in recent years: some of the adventures and travels, usually alone but never friendless and invariably with one or more fellow conspirators close at hand.

My yo-yo life, what I called my 'horizontal yo-yo' between America and England, began again and I began dabbling in new interests. Painting, which had fluttered intermittently through my life, took shape again when, at Lobo's introduction, I went to a lithographing house in New Jersey, the Graphic House run by Steve Mandarano, where some of the best painters – including Salvador Dali – send their work to be lithoed. My special teacher there was Elizabeth Schippert.

The Graphic House was to be my invaluable help and support for some two years; I have kept in regular contact with them ever since my first introduction. A few years ago, I was invited to share with the fine young Anglo-Canadian artist Curtis Hooper in preparing some special lithographs and intaglios commemorating my father's life and achievements and his continuing part in American history. My part was to prepare the intaglios – the bas reliefs at the bottom of the paper, almost invisible so as not to distract from the fine portraits done by Curtis Hooper. I also chose my father's sayings that went with the pictures.

I could understand my father's love of drawing and painting as relaxation and as concentration – the pencil certainly sharpens the eye and, as he wrote in *Painting as a Pastime*: 'Splash into the turpentine, wallop into the blue and white ... large, fierce strokes and slashes of blue on the absolutely cowering canvas. Anyone could see that it could not hit back.'

Because of my various mishaps certain professional doors were now closed to me. But here I took courage from my father's dictum: that a door should never be closed but, if it is, you should open it and find out what's going on behind it. If the majority think you're unemployable, you've got to employ yourself. Though my 'one-woman show' was not to be, and never will be, a total release, I found through it another key to my father's inner existence in the many varied hobbies he had pursued. My mainstay for the show remained my poetry, where I felt completely free to talk about myself and found the audacity to do it. I discovered that I could be a public storyteller. I built my scripts out of my poetry and prose and my letters and made the effort to translate it into theatre.

The preliminary skeleton of the show consisted of a first half where I read other people's poetry; and the second half was devoted to reminiscences of my father and my own poetry. I was encouraged by a review in the *Evening Standard* by Milton Shulman, who said that I was more moving in my own work. Although I still had all my acting training, perhaps I was becoming more convincing and confident as myself than as an actress. And so I grew, in later shows, to concentrate on my own work rather than other people's.

Lobo painted some vivid mobile panels which we intended to have printed on silk, so that we might be able to roll them up on poles and carry them with us as part of our travelling circus. But, sadly, it was an idea which was not put into effect, because, as usual, there was not enough money. In the end I went back to relying on whatever resources the various theatres could offer and used my own lighting chart, which was readily adaptable to any theatrical lighting rig.

The only props I used eventually were a piano and an elegant easel of my own. It is the essence of a one-woman or one-man show to cut to the minimum the potential strain on the resident company or theatre where you are playing. The great thing about a piano, however, is that it is the only instrument that an artist or musician is not expected to carry. But again you had to be readily adaptable, for the piano might be an upright, a mini, a boudoir grand or a Bechstein. The only thing that mattered – and it was the main proviso of all contracts – was that the piano be tuned to the required pitch. We might be thousands of feet up, as we were in Johannesburg, or performing below sea level, as we did in Holland, but the pitch and tuning must be just right. It was a detail as important for me as for my fellow conspirators.

The first of my fellow conspirators was Hugh Hastings. Hugh had had a major triumph with the show, *Seagulls over Sorrento* – a triumph followed, as so often happens in show business, by hard times which led him eventually to the piano-bar where I had the good fortune to meet him. He was later to become, as he said, 'the oldest member of the Young Vic Company'. Hugh proved to be a most delightful, talented and humorous man. He contributed some material and also appeared in *A Matter of Choice*, which was the name we gave to our first show. This title went through many changes, as did the show itself. Hugh wrote quite a few sketches for me, since he was used to being in revue. We played a considerable number of dates; it was suggested after one of our shows that we should go and join in the show at Brighouse, one of the big clubs in the north of England. I went on without any prior publicity and made quite a success of it. This had such strong echoes of my life with Vic Oliver in vaudeville that it gave me the confidence to believe that there might be a worthwhile future career ahead.

The range of the show developed. When Hugh and I played in Holland, just outside Amsterdam, we began to add some comic turns. Hugh wrote a very funny sketch about a prison visitor in a top-security jail. We didn't use a name, but the description of the escape in the plot obviously referred to the spy George Blake, who had just escaped and happened to have been born in Amsterdam. The audience howled with laughter and we had a hard time keeping straight faces. In the plot, the woman prison visitor brought the convict a present, a flower pot with some geraniums. The prisoner explained that he was not allowed to have flowers, and asked if they could not be put on top of the wall in the prison grounds where he could see them by standing on his bed in his cell. The flower pot was placed so as to reveal to the prisoner the exact block outside which rescue awaited.

I love playing comedy, and Hugh was a fine comedian and a straight back-up man as well. The show deepened and broadened with every performance, and we received some encouraging reviews. I made one brief appearance with the Irish poet Ulick O'Connor in Cork. Many of the audience arrived from outside places by coach and we were forty minutes late starting; but they were enthusiastic and a joy to play to. I was speaking the famous poem of Rupert Brooke, 'If I should die, think only this of me/There is some corner of a foreign field . . .' And I paused, realizing I was in the very heart of Ireland. Ulick quickly picked it up and finished: 'that is forever England'. The reviews and sales of *A Thread in the Tapestry* made me sure I was right to be striking out as an author.

On the morning of 6 June 1968, my nephew Winston called me to say that his father, Randolph, had died peacefully in his sleep during the night; he had been found by his devoted secretary, Andrew Kerr. Randolph's health had visibly deteriorated during the previous two years, although he had been seriously ill for about four years. During those years he had become close friends with his immediate neighbours in East Bergholt in Suffolk. The couple had accompanied him once or twice on trips to Marrakech for his health and the wife had taught Randolph to be an enthusiastic gardener. She was extremely kind to him in his declining years and reversed the belief he once confided in me that: 'I have not yet seen beauty other than through a woman's face.'

The sun shone on the day of his funeral and after the service we all had lunch on the terrace at Stour. Randolph was loved by his children and would fill his house as often as possible with young people. He used to say to me: 'I do not wish to die a lonely old man.' That afternoon in Suffolk showed that he died with the love of his family and of his two wives – Pamela, Winston's mother, and June, Arabella's mother. Some people have said he died a bitter man, but in my opinion that is far from the truth: disappointed in his early dreams he may have been, but whatever his character, Randolph did not die a bitter man. I shall not forget that sunny day in June.

My next major co-conspirator was the distinguished and sophisticated jazz pianist Dennis Wiley, whom, like so many of my close friends, I had met while I was in Rome. Dennis was then and remains a much sought-after accompanist. He seems to 'feel' along with you. Our most important tour together was in South Africa. We were to play Johannesburg, Cape Town and Port Elizabeth, and then go on to Salisbury, Rhodesia, now Zimbabwe. Although the beginnings of unrest were to be seen everywhere there, we had no unfortunate or disagreeable instances which affected us personally. I took Katie Jones along with me for company and to help me with the many quick changes of costume required by my show. Katie couldn't understand that ladies weren't allowed to drink in most of the bars. I explained to her that if she felt like a drink it would be better to have one in the hotel. She also found it difficult to grasp the rules of apartheid which required blacks to sit in different parts of buses from whites and shop in different places. On several occasions she almost got us into trouble by being in the wrong place; but no one seemed to mind when they heard her Welsh accent. When we were in Cape Town, we did get away to a fairly disreputable and enjoyable bar. In the docks area there was a dive, we were told, much frequented by visiting ships' crews where rules about colour or sex were virtually ignored. When we found it, we discovered it was lit entirely with yellow lights, insofar as it was lit at all. There was practically no chance of being able to identify what colour any of the customers were. It was quite hard to identify people's sex there as well.

In Johannesburg my dressing room was down many stairs and Katie and I observed an interesting notice that said if the height was proving too much for us and we were over sixty-five, we were entitled to our own private oxygen supply! This made me want to smile, but when I remembered that five years before Vic had died of his heart attack in that same theatre, I moved up from the dressing room and dressed off stage, behind some hastily erected screens.

While I was in South Africa with Dennis Wiley, three young Italians congratulated me on being engaged, so they insisted, to one of their relations. I was walking through the hotel lobby on my way to the theatre when they came up and told me that they were so happy that I was to marry their cousin. I asked politely what his name was. They told me the name of a man whom I, of course, had never heard of. When I told them this, they protested that I had met him in Rimini. They told me that they had read the story in the South African newspapers. They were nice young people, and eager to congratulate me. I said I was on my way to the theatre and would they bring me the newspaper.

They said, 'You *are* Miss Sarah Churchill?'

'Yes. So how can I be in Rimini?'

The next morning, I received the newspaper cutting of the story from Rimini. My informants must have realized it was all wrong because I never saw them again. The story as it appeared in an American magazine a few days later is worth quoting in full:

In Italy these days, one of the leading conversational topics involves Sarah Churchill, 54-year-old daughter of the late Winston Churchill.

Although she is twice his age, Sarah Churchill plans to marry a 27-year-old ex-waiter, Renzo Renzi of Pesaro. For Sarah Churchill, it is an expensive love.

To date she has bought her fiancé an $11,000 Maserati, 54 custom-tailored suits, and given him a money allowance large enough for him to use part of it to support his mother.

In the restaurants of Rimini where Sarah and Renzo have become celebrities of a sort, the waiters know that the English lady cannot tolerate Italian wines, and prefers to drink vodka or whisky, un-iced, with her meals.

The odd couple first met at an art exhibition; subsequently they moved into the Grand Hotel in Rimini.

Miss Churchill says that after their marriage they will live in Paris. Renzo, who doesn't particularly like to discuss his marital future, is most enthusiastic about his bride-to-be's latest gift to him: a tailored mink coat.

There then appeared a fuzzy picture of two people getting into a sports car. The lady wore a white scarf and dark glasses, an easy disguise, and she might have managed to pass herself off as me, although she was clearly a good deal larger and heavier. In the follow-ups, some papers still persisted with the story, although by this time the picture used was one of me having dinner in South Africa with Dennis Wiley, who was described as the wretched Renzo.

It was fortunate that I was sufficiently busy with my South African tour not to have too much time to wonder what was going on in Rimini.

I did, however, contact my mother who wrote to the newspapers concerned: 'I am not aware of my daughter marrying anybody, and I am sure I would be the first to know.' Taking legal action proved, in the end, quite useless. But I was able to take some practical action: at the end of our tour in South Africa, Dennis and I flew straight to Rome where, thanks to arrangements made by good friends, we were able to put on the show for four nights at the Teatro dei Satiri. The reviews of the show and feature articles about me all described how I had come straight to Rome from my South African tour. Rumours of Rimini were effectively scotched.

I was obviously in for some entertainment from the press. Later that year, the *Daily Mail* printed one of my favourite portraits, with my hair very long, taken by Vivienne, Antony Beauchamp's mother. On the other side of the page they printed a newsphoto of me – wearing a grey short-cut wig and accompanied by a tall, dark, handsome man. The story insisted that I wanted short hair without cutting my own and that here I was on holiday with Arwin McKelly. Now there may well be an Arwin McKelly somewhere in the world but, if so, I haven't met him. The man I was pictured with was my friend Michael Harvey, a well-known Western cowboy actor. How far can you go?

My looks have frequently led to cases of mistaken identity, but with a voice like mine I never lasted very long in the celebrity spot on *What's My Line?* However thick the blindfolds, the panel always seemed to guess me immediately. I'm told by my friend Ellen Pollock that I can do a reasonable cockney accent, but as for other accents, as with my father, it's hard to disguise my voice. So I was rather optimistic, as well as excited, when I was invited to appear on the Japanese television version of the programme.

I felt quite bleak when we got to Tokyo and discovered that not only did I not have the right inoculations, nor was there anyone from Japanese television to meet me, but that my 'papers were not in order' – that dreadful phrase which haunts so many refugees but which you don't expect when you arrive to take part in a television show. Apparently, the Japanese customs and immigration officials were not prepared to believe that a passport issued in Gibraltar was an authentic British passport. I called for an atlas, found Gibraltar and pointed out that it was marked as strictly British. They still were not satisfied, and the British Consulate was apparently closed. The main question was 'Who asked her?' There came a moment when I had to reply, 'You, the Japanese, asked me, and if you don't want me, I'll wait for the next plane home.' I even went so far as to say that I had always heard about Japanese politeness and good manners but that I had not seen much of them so far. That seemed to do the trick. Soon people from the television station were on the scene. I was finally rescued and rushed to the studios late for the show.

My instructions were to disguise my voice, but because I was angry at being made late, I went straight on to the set, where the panellists had their blindfolds on, and, determined to make the best of it, I announced my name. Frankly, I was furious; but I apologized for being late and said I had no control over Japanese airlines.

My agent's representative said afterwards she hadn't known whether or not to let me go on. Things did not change after that fiasco. I realized that I had been asked on to the show as something of a gimmick. But I pointed out that my contract did say that I was to perform some of my own work after the panel show. And so it was arranged that I should have a show of my own the next week to read my poems, and a new interpreter was assigned to me.

From then on, my Japanese hosts did everything possible for me. I was shown the sights and they all lived up to the brochures. I was shown gardens and palaces and I learnt where you are supposed to take your shoes off. Finally, the true test of finding yourself in another country, I was invited by my new interpreter to meet her family. They owned and ran a small bar in Tokyo. I was welcomed there and made to feel at home. Since they seem to expect Europeans to be physically bigger, some bars arrange their seats so that you sink very low. I almost vanished without trace: at chin level with my saki, I had hysterics. So did they. The hardest thing about international relationships is to understand another country's sense of humour. We share the tears. At last, I felt I was in the real Japan. They even asked me whether I should like to go to a nightclub. I agreed. When we were there, somewhat to my dismay, the nightclub owner came to speak to me and through the interpreter said, 'We understand you are a singer, please come and sing a song for us.' It was flattering and my companion from the agency urged me on. But I said to her, 'It's no good. The only song I can think of at the moment is "Show Me The Way To Go Home", and I don't somehow think that's quite appropriate!'

After I had recorded my show for Japanese television, somewhat to the astonishment of my hosts I announced that I would prefer to go home via Australia. Not understanding their blank response and faces, I said that naturally I would pay the difference on my round trip ticket. I had with regret to say goodbye to my English companion as she was to continue on her own round-the-world trip. Recalling maps from childhood days, I was convinced that Australia was only a short hop, say from England to the Channel Islands. I sent a telegram to my Australian friend, Delphine Clues, who happened to be in Sydney. On receiving it, though she has kindly never told me so, she must have felt like jumping off the Sydney Harbour Bridge. I was on the plane before she could think up a reply, but gallantly she was waiting for me at the airport to inform me that it was Easter weekend. When I had awoken on the plane, I had found to my astonishment that Neptune had become god of the air as well as the sea: on crossing the equator, I had been presented in my sleep with a certificate welcoming me to the southern hemisphere.

As a reasonably seasoned traveller, I have always kept to one useful rule: when you arrive in a strange place, ask for a local newspaper. The first thing I looked for was the racing page. There was some amazement on the part of the airline staff at the possibility that I had flown all the way from Tokyo to put money on a horse. I let the illusion remain and tried to think of a suitable horse to back. Since I had flown on Qantas airline, I decided on a horse called Quanto. It promptly proceeded to win the Sydney Easter Cup.

Finally, I had run out of my winnings from the excellent Quanto and it was time to say goodbye and go home. For once, I was conscious of which hemisphere I was in and knew it would be a long journey. I did not know, however, that political requirements were such that we had to go – as it seemed to me – twice as far as anyone would choose who was interested in getting home in good order. We seemed to pass some of the most romantic names in the world – Java, Singapore, Calcutta, Karachi, Tel Aviv, and we also seemed to have to stop in many of them. What is called in the brochure 'non-stop' proved to be a series of short hops. I began to feel I was flying with a kangaroo. I chose an inner circle ride, acknowledging I had to cross the equator but wishing to avoid the Arctic. In Amsterdam, I had to change for the last hop and the plane politely waited for me. I finally landed at Heathrow, found a taxi, stacked it high with my luggage and, feeling very queasy, headed for home.

In the mid-1970s, the bicentenary of the United States almost coincided with the centenary of my father's birth. It was a time for joyous happenings for both countries – and for us in our family, the remembering was enhanced by the fact that Winston Churchill was half American. My first cousin, John Spencer Churchill, the painter and sculptor, was engaged to design a series of plates for Silver Creations, an American firm. The intention was to feature five scenes where my father's life related to America; the plates were to be produced one each year for five years and they were intended to be hung on the wall as medallions. My part was to design a different presentation box for each of the plates. One side of the plates was to be prepared by English silversmiths and the other by Silver Creations in the USA. The two sides were then bonded together, the whole symbolizing the unity of the two countries. A whole pound weight of silver was to be used in each.

In order to launch the series I had to pack my bags and set off again on my travels. This time through many cities of the United States, accompanied by my friend and press agent, Jewel Baxter. Jewel, who remains one of my closest friends in America, had jumped to fame with her identical twin sister Ann when they featured all over America in the famous hair preparation advert: 'Which Twin Has The Toni?' I had first met them when I had been playing in *Grammercy Ghost* before its run on Broadway. We had all become firm friends and when Jewel went full time into the public relations business, it was a delight to have her look after my interests. Part of my job was to promote the sales of the commemorative plates – a sort of up-market sales-lady. Many of my American friends bought the plates and when we got to Hollywood there was particular excitement because John Wayne, whom I had never met before, threw a party for me and – oh glory! – bought four plates.

The tour gave me an unusual opportunity to see the 'other side' of American law enforcement. There was a scare in a store I was visiting.

A man approached me and said, 'I know you see the Queen every day.'

I looked at him more closely; the poor man looked somewhat deranged, and I smiled rather vaguely.

Handing me a grubby piece of paper, he said, 'Can you give her this message?'

It seemed to me that the only proper answer was, 'I shall give it to her the next time I see her.'

I said this as politely as I could and, since he clearly wasn't going to buy a plate, moved on to another customer.

As I was leaving the store, two large gentlemen stopped me and asked to read the piece of paper for the Queen. They said they were FBI agents and after checking the paper said they had decided to give me full protection just to be on the safe side. When they asked me to step into their large black car, I must admit my thoughts went back to past adventures in Malibu. I had a flash of apprehension which faded as soon as it arrived, and I got into their car. I am lucky enough never to have had a gun pointed directly at me, but early training with my father made me feel reasonably at ease under the protection of the police and security men. My two new acquaintances drove me swiftly to the hotel where one of them took up his position inside my suite. Being equally well-trained about drinking on duty, I didn't invite the G-man to drink, but asked him if he could order something for me to eat and drink. He did all the ordering and made sure that it was he who opened the door to the waiter.

The next day, we were taken with great efficiency to the airport for our outward flight. Unfortunately, once security is put on it is very difficult to modify it. I felt quite trapped by the care they were taking of me. So much so that I said to Jewel that the agents were making me conspicuous. We contrived a plan which would allow me to go the ladies' room while Jewel went to the bar. I was able to breeze out of the ladies' like any other traveller and join her there. We had given them the slip and I'm afraid to say a few anxious moments. But they were very good and once the plane – and everyone else – had been triple checked, we were allowed on board and reunited with my company. We were only a few hours late in taking off for our next destination.

But I must tell you now about the last of my principal co-conspirators. The first time I met Idris Evans was when he was the piano-entertainer at the famous New York restaurant, the Camelot. It became a very popular artists' rendezvous, for such is the persuasiveness of his Welsh charm that people feel relaxed and in good humour in his presence. He is well known as an excellent pianist and his adaptability to situations and personalities has carried him far. He was to prove not only a friend but an astute and shrewd businessman who guided my steps towards something that frequently escapes my attention – safeguarding myself. For instance, he made me become a member of the Performing Rights Society (PRS) and has regularly and devotedly continued to play the few ballads I have written.

One of the most interesting occurrences after I began working with Idris was when we went to Utrecht in 1973 for the Phillips Awards. Among the recipients were Leopold Stokowski who made a fuss of me – we had met briefly at one of his concerts in New York – Claudio Arrau, the pianist, and Isaac Stern, the violinist. The festival itself was divided into two parts – classical and pop. For some unknown reason, Idris and I found ourselves doing a thirty-minute spot in a beautiful church, no longer consecrated for religious observance, but frequently used for concerts, at 10.30 on a chilly morning. On this occasion, with Idris accompanying me, I used the spoken word. To this day, we have never quite discovered why we were there – we were not even Phillips recording artists – but we were content to ask no questions and it remained for us both a memorable and proud occasion. It might have been nice to know whether we were thought of as classical or pop but perhaps we were simply guests of honour. There was certainly a good lunch afterwards.

Quite soon after the Utrecht performance, I was approached in London by a young Norwegian freelance journalist who wanted to interview me. I did not really feel like being interviewed just then and asked Audrey Willis to deal with him. Audrey, who after years of working for my father was very familiar with Churchill approaches to things, explained to this young man, Bjorn Granvolden, that I was prepared to do interviews about specific events such as my performances but was not prepared to undertake general interviews. To his great credit, Bjorn admitted that he had once before been sent by a German magazine to construct a damaging article about me without even meeting me. Now, having met me, he said he would prefer to be a friend than an interviewer. I was impressed with his openness and even recommended that he might do an interview with my niece Edwina Sandys about her painting. Bjorn became something of an unpaid public relations man for me and it was his suggestion that Idris and I undertook a very special engagement in Norway. Of the many dates we have played together, Oslo was an obvious highlight. It reunited for me the world I had been born into with the world of my choice.

It was a matter of great pride to me that I was invited to take part in the Norwegian National Day television programme. I have enormous admiration for the Norwegians and I recalled my father's funeral when resistance fighters from all over Europe had attended with their flags. A journalist who spotted the Norwegian flag asked the flag-bearer for his name; the friendly but firm response was: 'We were unknown then, and we shall remain unknown now.' The programme was introduced and compered by the well-known Norwegian personality, Erich Buy, who is bilingual: he would ask me questions in Norwegian and English and then translate my answers for the viewers. It was a two-hour recording and I understand that extracts are still used from time to time on Norwegian television. Erich is well known as a performer as well as for commentating and announcing, so I felt very much at ease performing some of my songs accompanied by Idris who was also made to feel completely at home.

The next day, Erich told us that we were about to embark on a mystery tour. The reason for his secretiveness became clear when we discovered that we were to take the trip in an army helicopter. Every year, near national day, Norwegian television and show business stars would go into the mountains to remote settlements to bring entertainment and to take part in simple services of commemoration. The only way to get to many such places was by helicopter and Erich was determined we should accompany him. We piled into the helicopter – quite a multinational group, including a visiting American cellist and Erich and his wife as well as Idris and me.

It was carefully pointed out that, whatever our thoughts about helicopters – and mine were not entirely favourable, despite not normally being scared of flying – Dutch courage was strictly not in order. The distant stop was a revelation: the beautiful, remote sanatorium where survivors of World War II were looked after in peaceful isolation.

Just as we were ready to leave, we saw a small girl running through the snow towards us clutching a bottle. She said breathlessly that her father had sent her and that he was sure we would like something to see us on our way home. Now we were off duty and so the bottle was handed round. I think it may have put me off sherry for life. It was a good deal sweeter than I should normally have preferred, but it was the combination of the sherry and the motion of the helicopter which very nearly made me disgrace the RAF. As we were nearing Oslo, I saw an extraordinary scar shape in the mountain. I asked Erich what on earth it could be since it was clearly man-made.

'That,' he declared, 'is something you've often seen on TV; it's our famous ski-jump.'

Emboldened at this stage by the sherry, I replied, 'In that case, we should go down it.'

Somewhat to my astonishment, the helicopter pilot immediately agreed, turned the machine until we were positioned above the start, then swooped down with the skids seeming to touch the snow but at a safe distance. It was as near as possible, I believe, to the extraordinary sensation of ski-jumping and was a magnificent piece of flying.

In the year which would have seen my father's hundredth birthday, on 4 December 1974, Idris and I were invited to do a concert by the Churchill Centenary Trust and by the Biker-Cholem Hospital for children of all races and creeds who had been caught in the crossfire of the Arab–Israeli war. The Churchill association with Israel has been there almost from that country's beginning. We naturally agreed, and with the backing of the Gwent Choir from Wales with whom we had performed before, we gave a concert at the Royal Court Theatre in London. We had hoped my mother would arrive, but at this late date all her public appearances were day-to-day decisions. There was, however, a full complement of family as well as many other friends, and the young Duke of Marlborough opened the show. It was simply a happy and glorious evening and funds were raised for both charities.

Three years later, Idris and I were to travel to Israel under the auspices of the Variety Club whose famous 'tents' and international charity work are well known in almost all the corners of the world. It was an official occasion and although we were asked as performers, the crowning glory was to be invited to be part of the foundation-stone laying ceremony for a new wing for the children at the Biker-Cholem Hospital.

Now I live in Eaton Square, where the fallen blossom makes a pink carpet on the pavement. I look out of my window and marvel at the stalwart courage of the Londoners passing by on their daily rounds while hostages are taken and bombs explode. In the course of a long, full life, people have often come to me for advice. I am flattered that they should find me sympathetic and I always try to give them my undivided attention. I generally realize fairly quickly that there is little I can say or do to solve a particular problem beyond offering a friendly ear. However, for those who still look to me after my tumultuous life, I offer the only advice I can give myself, which is, of course, 'Keep on dancing!'

Index